dangerous
GAMES

dangerous

GAMES

FACES, INCIDENTS, AND CASUALTIES OF THE COLD WAR

★ ★ ★

James E. Wise Jr. and Scott Baron

NAVAL INSTITUTE PRESS
Annapolis, Maryland

Naval Institute Press
291 Wood Road
Annapolis, MD 21402

Library of Congress Cataloging-in-Publication Data

Wise, James E., 1930-
  Dangerous games : faces, incidents, and casualties of the Cold War / James E. Wise, Jr. and Scott Baron.
    p. cm.
  Includes bibliographical references and index.
  ISBN 978-1-59114-968-2 (alk. paper)
  1. Cold War–Biography–Anecdotes. 2. Cold War–Anecdotes. I. Baron, Scott, 1954- II. Title.
  D839.5.W57 2010
  909.82'5–dc22

                                                                            2009051806

Printed in the United States of America on acid-free paper ∞

14 13 12 11 10   9 8 7 6 5 4 3 2
First printing

*Dedicated to Natalie Hall, our personal editor,
whose superb talents have guided us through the
rocks and shoals of our literary endeavors.*

*May her life be filled with fair winds
and following seas!*

CONTENTS

PREFACE

The United States emerged as the wealthiest, most powerful nation in the world at the end of World War II. Although the United States and the Soviet Union had been allies during the war, there was always a lurking mutual mistrust between the countries. When the Soviets expanded their sphere of influence in Eastern Europe and proceeded to build a huge nuclear arsenal, the United States found that it was no longer the dominant power in the world: thus began the era of what became known as "The Cold War," which lasted several decades.

In light of the recent Russian resurgence and its aggressive handling of the Georgian situation and limitations of energy exports, Eastern European countries have become increasingly alarmed that Russia is attempting to re-create a sphere of influence over satellite states of the former Soviet Union. In 2008, President Dmitry Medvedev of Russia stated the Kremlin would move short-range missiles into Kaliningrad, a Russian landmass on the Baltic Sea, if the United States proceeded with a missile-shield program, parts of which would be positioned in Poland and the Czech Republic. The Russian missiles would be capable of striking NATO territory.

To add to the mounting tension with the West, Russia, in its attempt to become a world power once again, has begun to show its flag in the Western Hemisphere. In December 2008, two Russian navy nuclear-powered warships conducted exercises with Venezuelan naval forces in the Caribbean Sea. Upon completion of the exercises, one of the Russian warships, *Admiral Chabanenko*, passed through the Panama Canal, the first such happening since World War II. (The Canal had been closed to the Soviets during the Cold War.) Prior to the naval exercises, two Russian Air Force Tu-160 Blackjack strategic bombers visited Venezuela to conduct flight-training maneuvers. Since 2004, Venezuela has purchased more than $4 billion of weapons from Russian suppliers. Additionally, Russian oil companies have approached Venezuela about building storage tanks for crude oil and assisting the country in refurbishing a Soviet-era refinery in the port city of Cienfuegos, on the southern coast of Cuba. There are also reports that Russia intends to drill for oil in deep Gulf of Mexico Cuban waters.

For the past few years, Russian air reconnaissance long-range aircraft have renewed their snooping operations off the coasts of Western nations. In February 2009, on the eve of President Barack Obama's visit to Canada—his first trip abroad as president—a Russian Bear bomber probed the Canadian Arctic airspace, only to be turned away by Canadian CF-18s (supersonic Hornet fighters). In July 2009, the British Defence Committee announced that Russian Bear aircraft had approached British airspace on eighteen occasions since 2007 (ten flights in 2007, six in 2008, and two in 2009). The aircraft were intercepted by quick-reaction Tornado F3 or Eurofighter/Typhoon fighters. And, in early August 2009, two nuclear-powered Akula-class Russian attack submarines patrolled off the coast of Maine in international waters.

The Cold War was only cold in that the major powers, the United States and the Soviet Union, did not engage in a nuclear war. But during the period there were wars, spying, shootdowns of numerous aircraft, captures of military and civilian personnel, murders, defections, a space race with men put into orbit, and an eventual moon landing. *Dangerous Games: Faces, Incidents, and Casualties of the Cold War* is a return to that era. The book includes a compilation of little-known or long-since-forgotten stories that will capture the interest of readers and remind them of the cost in human life when two major powers place the world in jeopardy.

Do the aforementioned aggressive Russian activities portend a second cold war between the United States and Russia? Perhaps. Only time will tell.

ACKNOWLEDGMENTS

Readers will note that we've dedicated this book to a member of our team, Natalie Hall. As we've mentioned before, Natalie is our personal editor. Her skill in blending author and coauthor inputs into a seamless, error-free manuscript requires exceptional professionalism. Natalie has met this unique challenge and continues to produce superb work.

WE OWE SPECIAL GRATITUDE TO Natalie Hall, Hannah Cunliffe, Nicholas Dujmovic, Dale J. Gordon, Jack Green, Glenn E. Helm, Lena Kaljot, Bert K. Mizusawa, Timothy T. Pettit, Paul Revai, Chris Robinson, Doug Sterner, Dianne Dellatorre Stevens, Brent Stolle, Rob Taglianetti, and Robert J. Tolle.

Additionally, we would like to thank James M. Caiella, Thomas Cutler, Janice Jorgensen, Rick Russell, and their colleagues at the U.S. Naval Institute.

INTRODUCTION

The term "Cold War" is most commonly used to describe a period of conflict and competition that existed between the United States and the Soviet Union (USSR) and their allies and satellite states between 1945 and 1991. That term is also used to describe the tension that existed between Communist and capitalist countries to exert influence on the post–World War II political landscape.

THE FIRST USE OF THE TERM "COLD WAR" is attributed to Bernard Baruch, an American financier and adviser to President Truman, who stated in a speech in April 1946, "Let us not be deceived: we are today in the midst of a cold war."[1]

There is no consensus among historians as to its beginning. Some date it back to the effect on U.S.-Russian relations following the triumph of Communism at the end of the Russian Revolution in 1917. The United States had supported the White Russians against the Communists, and refused to recognize the new Soviet government until 1933. The rise of fascist states in the 1930s created an uneasy alliance between the Soviet Union and the West that ended with the defeat of the Axis powers at the end of the World War II in 1945.

Nor is there agreement on when—or even whether—the Cold War ended. Some date the end to the thawing of relations through glasnost and détente, a thawing brought about by the election of Mikhail Gorbachev as Communist Party general secretary in March 1985. Others ascribe the lessening of tensions to the fall of the Berlin Wall in November 1989, or the end of the Warsaw Pact and the fall of the Soviet Union itself in 1991.

Whatever its origins or the causes of its demise, the term "Cold War" is a misnomer: it often was not "cold." Several conflicts brought both sides to the brink of nuclear war. Neither was it a "war" in the classical sense, with limited wars of containment in Korea and Vietnam.

In one sense, the Cold War could be considered World War III, with confrontations occurring across the globe in locales as diverse as Czechoslovakia, the Congo, Cambodia, and Canada. Its battles occurred on land, at sea, in the skies, and in outer

President Ronald Reagan standing with President Richard von Weizsacker of the Federal Republic of Germany on his right and Helmut Schmidt, Chancellor of the Federal Republic of Germany, on his left at Checkpoint Charlie in West Berlin, 11 June 1982. (National Archives and Records Administration)

space. It was fought by diplomats, soldiers, and spies, and its motivations were both patriotic and pragmatic.

The Cold War was the Space Race and the Arms Race. It was the Marshall Plan and the Truman Doctrine. It was the North Atlantic Treaty Organization (NATO), the Southeast Asia Treaty Organization (SEATO), and the Warsaw Pact. It was the Iron Curtain and the Berlin Wall. It was the Domino Theory, the Missile Crisis, and the Hungarian Revolution. It was Sputnik and Gemini, Yuri Gagarin and John Glenn. It was fallout shelters, the H-bomb, and Mutual Assured Destruction (MAD). It was the demilitarized zone (DMZ), the Bay of Pigs, and McCarthyism. It was Soviet tanks in Prague, and Special Forces teams in El Salvador.

This book is not a history of the Cold War. Rather, it is the story of the men and women, both heralded and unknown, who fought in it, and whose valor often went unappreciated and unrecognized. Many, including the authors, matured in a world where the Cold War was an everyday presence. Although raised in the belief that freedom and democracy would leave Communism on "the ash heap of history" and with faith in liberty's inevitable triumph, most doubted they would see that triumph in their lifetime.

Now, as historians grapple with the Cold War's place in history, there is an increasing awareness of and appreciation for the service and sacrifice of those who stood on the ramparts during a conflict whose events continue to exert influence in today's world.

chapter one

FIRST BLOOD
The USMC in China, 1945–49

Following the end of World War II, the alliance of convenience that had existed between the Communists and the Western democracies, as both united to battle the Axis powers, came to an end. Cooperation was replaced by competition for power and influence in the vacuum of power in many regions, a vacuum created by the defeat of Germany, Japan, and Italy. It was in China, long occupied by the Japanese, where the first—albeit limited—confrontation between Communist and American forces took place.

On 30 September 1945, elements of Maj. Gen. Keller E. Rockey's Third Amphibious Corps (IIIAC) came ashore at Taku Bay, at the mouth of the Hai River. In the vanguard were the 7th Marines whose landing craft (LCTs) were greeted by cheering, enthusiastic Chinese who sailed out in small craft to escort and welcome the Marines. The greeting was in sharp contrast to the Marines' first intervention in China more than a century earlier during the Opium Wars.

On 19 June 1844, Acting Lt. George Henry Preble led an armed landing party of Marines and sailors from the USS *St. Louis* ashore at Whampoa Island, off Canton, to rescue American merchants from rioting Chinese. The Marines secured the traders' compound, dispersed the rioting Chinese, and remained in place until the Treaty of Whampoa was signed on 22 October that same year, guaranteeing Americans free trade in China. It was the first of a series of deployments of Marines into China.[1]

A decade later, on 4 April 1854, U.S. Marines and sailors from the sloop-of-war USS *Plymouth* landed at Shanghai when Imperial Army soldiers, engaged in fighting insurgents led by T'ien Wang, occupied the foreign trading settlement, including the American Consulate. Captain Kelly of the *Plymouth* landed a force of seventy

Marines of the 1st Marine Regiment marching through Tangku to board trains to Tientsin. They had followed the 7th Regiment ashore during the initial landings. (U.S. Marine Corps)

Marines and sailors and one field howitzer. They were joined by thirty American volunteers with two additional howitzers. Along with British Marines, they attacked Chinese forts menacing English and American interests.[2]

Marines would return to China periodically for the rest of the century. The Boxer Rebellion in 1900 resulted in a quasi-permanent Marine presence in China that lasted until 1941, continuing even during the Japanese occupation of Manchuria that started in September 1931.

The IIIAC had received orders to prepare for operations in China within forty-eight hours following the end of World War II. Originally slated for Shanghai, the decision was made to redirect the deployment of Marines to North China instead.

A force of fifty thousand Marines would be divided between the Hopeh and Shantung Provinces with the First Marine Division (made up of the 1st, 5th, and 7th Marine regiments and 11th Artillery) deployed to Tangku, Tientsin, Peking, and Chinwangtao; and the Sixth Marine Division (made up of the 22nd, 29th, and 4th Marine regiments and the 15th Artillery) deployed to Tsingtao in the Shantung Province (although the 4th Marines would remain behind in Japan).[3]

The First Marine Air Wing (1MAW)—comprising the 12th, 24th, 25th, and 32nd Marine Air Groups (MAGs), including three VMF fighter squadrons (F4U

Corsairs) and two VMO "grasshopper" observation squadrons—would be positioned at airfields in Tsingtao, Tientsin, and Peking. Corps headquarters would remain with the 1st Marine Division.[4]

A tumultuous welcome greeted the arriving Marines. One officer of the 7th Service Regiment reported the "Chinese military and civilian authorities were cooperative in the extreme" and the Japanese garrison offered no resistance, and happy, flag-waving celebrants were everywhere. Soon, though, the Marines found themselves thrust into the middle of a civil war between Chinese Nationalists and Communist factions, a struggle that had been ongoing since 1927, and that had continued even during the Japanese occupation (1931–45). With no national government in place and both parties vying for control, economic chaos and collapse with resulting starvation seemed a likely scenario.

The initial mission of the Marines was to support a major postwar foreign policy objective of creating a strong, unified, and democratic China that would be strong enough to restrain the Soviet Union from seizing control of mineral-rich Manchuria. The publicly stated mission was to facilitate the surrender of 630,000 Japanese troops and civilians in China and see to their repatriation to Japan. Additionally, the Marines were tasked to ensure order and economic stability, all the while remaining neutral between the two warring factions.[5]

Army Lt. Gen. Albert Wedemeyer, Commander of U.S. Forces in China, was more specific in his Directive No. 25 to Marine Major General Rockey. Besides receiving the enemy surrender, he was tasked with locating and liberating Allied POWs and in assisting the Nationalist government in occupying key areas. At the same time, he was ordered to stay out of Chinese civil affairs.[6]

The Soviet forces already in Manchuria had refused to allow the Nationalist forces of Chiang Kai-shek to land and had turned control of the ports over to the Communists, as well as substantial stores of captured Japanese ordnance and munitions. Against American advice to first consolidate his hold on North China, Chiang Kai-shek resolved to enter Manchuria overland through the Chinwangtao region. He committed his best troops to attack north into Manchuria, beginning on 14 November 1945, leaving mostly ill-trained militia troops south of Manchuria and placing a disproportionate amount of responsibility on the Marines for maintaining order in south China.[7]

Besides garrisons in the major cities, Marines of the 1st Division's 7th Regiment found themselves in small detachments guarding the rail and bridges between Chinwangtao and Tangku to ensure the delivery of coal to Shanghai and Peking, essential to avoid economic collapse. Mao Tse-tung, the leader of the Communists, was not fooled by American claims of neutrality. The 1st MAG under Maj. Gen. Claude Larkin was transporting the 92nd and 94th Nationalist armies to Peking; their presence freed up Nationalist soldiers to fight the Communists. Unwilling to

U.S. Marines are standing guard at the railroad station in Peitaho, China. (U.S. Marine Corps)

take on the Marines directly, Mao ordered a campaign of low-intensity harassment against the Marines.

On 6 October, a reconnaissance patrol of the 1st Marines guarding engineers working to clear the road between Tientsin and Peking was fired on by a force of 40–50 Chinese Communist soldiers twenty-two miles northwest of Tientsin, wounding three Marines. On 8 October, Marines returned in force with tanks and air cover and cleared the road. Two weeks later, on 19 October, snipers fired on a jeep patrol of the 7th Marines near Tangshan, wounding two. A week later, on 26 October, the target was a 5th Marine jeep patrol outside Peking, wounding one. The battle was not one-sided. On 18 October, six Communist soldiers were killed when they fired on a Marine-guarded train between Peking and Langfang. Clearly, the welcome mat was no longer out to the Marines in China.[8]

Norman Osborn Sr., a sergeant with Company C, 1/5 Marines recalled, "The reason we were in China at that time was to help get the Japanese out . . . but they [the Communists] saw us as a threat. We Marines were frequently under fire from Communist Chinese and many Marines were killed or wounded."[9]

The first Marine fatality occurred on 4 December 1945, when two Marines of 1/29 were hunting near the 7th Marine outpost guarding the rail lines through the village of Bob Ban Jon, west of Anshan. They were fired on by two Chinese. One of the Marines, Pfc. James M. Gilbert of Company B, was killed. The other Marine feigned death, and watched the two men withdraw to a nearby village. Enraged by this attack, the battalion executive officer (XO) set up a 60-mm mortar outside the village and issued an ultimatum to surrender the two men or be shelled. When the thirty-minute deadline expired, twenty-four rounds of white phosphorous were fired outside the walls. Although no one was hurt, news of Marines firing on an unarmed village was not received favorably in the United States, and calls increased to bring the Marines home.[10]

Even as Gen. George C. Marshall, President Truman's special emissary to China, arrived in Chungking on 20 December 1945 to try to negotiate a cease-fire and truce, both sides maneuvered to gain the advantage. A top-level Committee of Three was formed with Chiang Kai-shek appointing Gen. Chang Chun as his representative and Chou En-lai representing Chairman Mao. A cease-fire took effect at midnight, 13 January. An executive headquarters was established in Peking with operational teams of one American, one Nationalist, and one Communist to monitor the cease-fire. Both sides violated the provisions of the cease-fire, and the Communists strengthened their military position as Soviet occupation forces withdrew from positions in Manchuria, turning over stockpiles of Japanese weapons and munitions to the Communists.[11]

Throughout the first half of 1946, infrequent attacks on Marines continued. Bridge and rail sentries were sniped at, and low-flying observation airplanes were fired on. On 16 January 1946, Communist guerillas attacked a 7th Marine supply convoy near Tangshan, wounding two. GySgt. Andrew Bobbish, a member of Company A, 1/5 died of wounds sustained on 7 April when his hunting party was fired on near or in the vicinity of Lutai. On 5 May, a sentry of the 5th Marines was wounded when the bridge he was guarding near Tangku was attacked by mortars. Two days later, Communists again attacked the 7th Marines at Lutai, wounding one. On 21 May, a Headquarters Company Marine, Pfc. James D. Eborn Jr., died from wounds sustained when a reconnaissance patrol of the 1st Marines was attacked by fifty to seventy-five Communists in a village ten miles south of Tientsin. A second Marine was wounded.

To make matters worse, during this period Marine forces in China were being reduced, beginning with orders to disband the 6th Marine Division on 13 December 1945, to become the 3rd Marine Brigade. As trained combat veterans with enough points rotated home for demobilization, they were replaced by young, inexperienced, and poorly trained Marines who would receive on-the-job training in the most basic of military subjects. "I think the closest thing to my 'post boot camp training' was going to China since we did not have Infantry Training Regiment (ITR) that comes after boot camp today."[12]

By June 1946, IIIAC headquarters was deactivated, and the 24,252 Marines remaining were designated Marine Forces, China. It became apparent that further reductions were probable, which encouraged the Communists to issue a manifesto attacking U.S. policy in China.

On 13 July, seven Marines guarding a bridge near the village of Peiteiho were ambushed and captured while seeking ice for the detachment mess. They were not released until 24 July, after the Communists demanded the Marines apologize for their unlawful entry into a "liberated area." Five days later, in what was the largest direct assault on American Marines in China to date, a force of three hundred uniformed Chinese Communists ambushed a supply convoy near Anping.

At about 9:15 AM on 29 July, a convoy of nine supply trucks with Marine drivers and a United Nations Relief and Rehabilitation Administration (UNRRA) truck with a Chinese driver, accompanied by two Army staff cars and three jeeps of Marines bound for Peking, departed Tientsin. They were escorted by thirty-one Marines of 1/11 Marines and a ten-man 60-mm mortar section from the 1st Marines in two one-ton reconnaissance trucks, three "deuce and a half" two-ton trucks, and four jeeps, two of them equipped with Telecommunications System (TCS) radios. The escort commander, 2nd Lt. Douglas Cowin, a twenty-two-year-old from Ann Arbor, Michigan, placed himself and two jeeps and two trucks at the point of the column, and the remaining vehicles in the rear.[13]

At about 11:05 AM, the convoy lost contact with the 11th Marines. At noon, as the convoy approached the village of Ta Hsiao San Ho, approximately thirty-five miles southeast of Peking, the Communists executed a well-planned ambush. The site selected was a stretch of raised roadway bordered on both sides by ditches, with high cornfields extending to the edge of the ditch. The village was set off five hundred yards from the road. A copse of trees extended to a small walled compound on the east (right) side where a machine gun had been positioned to cover the road.[14]

The lead vehicles were slowed by large rocks in the road, then stopped by two oxcarts without wheels that obstructed the road. As Cowin, in the lead jeep, dismounted to evaluate the situation, a grenade exploded at his feet, killing him instantly. Eleven other grenades detonated along the convoy, and heavy rifle fire erupted from the trees to the east. Most of the Marines on point were killed or wounded.

The mostly unarmed Marine drivers and passengers managed to scramble into a ditch for cover, however. The rear guard was stalled and blocked by the convoy and began taking fire from the right side and left rear. Platoon Sgt. Cecil J. Flanagan moved up the line on foot, directing return fire as the rear section's mortars and heavy machine guns, directed by an Army officer, kept the Communists from advancing.

At 1:15 PM, during a lull in the firefight, three Marines in one of the rear jeeps raced back toward Tientsin for help. Between 3:30 PM and 4:00 PM, Communist fire intensified, then ceased as bugle calls signaled a withdrawal. After nearly four hours, the fighting ended, and transitioned into an eerie quiet.

An Army major with the executive headquarters took command, had the wounded quickly loaded into the vehicles, and ordered the column forward toward Peking with Flanagan's Marines providing a rear guard. Three damaged trucks were left behind; the column reached Peking at 5:45 PM.[15]

Meanwhile, the jeep racing at breakneck speed to Tientsin had overturned, injuring one officer and one enlisted Marine. They were able to commandeer a Chinese car and arrive in Tientsin and report to the regimental commander, Col. Wilburt S. Brown.

At 4:30 PM, a heavily armed combat patrol departed Tientsin while the regimental XO went aloft in an OY-1 "grasshopper" of VMO-6, which flew over the area at 5:30 PM and counted fifteen enemy dead. When five Corsair fighters of MAG-24 reached the area at 7:17 PM, there was no sign of the enemy or of any bodies.

When the four hundred–man rescue force, accompanied by two 105-mm self-propelled howitzers, arrived on scene, there was little to do except collect the Marine dead, tow the damaged trucks, and proceed to Peking. Losses from the action, besides Lieutenant Cowin, were Pvt. Lawrence Punch and Pvt. Gilbert Tate, both killed by grenades in the initial attack, and Pfc. John Lopez, who later died from his wounds. Ten other Marines were wounded. All the casualties were from the 1/11.

Gen. Marshal ordered an investigation into the unprovoked attack, but the Communists obstructed the effort. Commanders ordered increased aerial surveillance, radios that were more powerful, and larger and stronger patrols. To Marshall, the attack was an indication of the hardening of attitudes by the Communists toward the Marines. The Marines began to pull back and concentrate their positions in the major cities. Marines no longer guarded the rails or bridges, or rode the coal trains.[16]

On 18 September, General Rockey was replaced by Maj. Gen. Samuel L. Howard as commander of the 1st Marine Division. Reorganizations decreased troop levels further. The diminishing number of Marines, rather than assuaging the Communists, spurred them to bolder action.

The Marines maintained a large ammunition supply point (ASP) at Hsin Ho, a village located on the rail line between Peking and Mukden, about twenty-five miles southeast of Tientsin near the Gulf of Chihli. The ASP was commonly guarded by a detail of about fifty Marines of the 1/5. The location was so remote and the terrain so difficult that Marines patrolled on horseback.

On the night of 3–4 October, a sentry discovered Communist troops, estimated at company strength, breaking into the depot to steal ammunition. The sentry exchanged fire with the intruders. Alerted, the main guard force rushed to the area in trucks, only to be forced to dismount under intense enemy small-arms fire, which wounded a driver. The Marines held off the attack. As additional reinforcements responded from Tangku, the Communists hastily withdrew into the darkness, leaving behind one dead and one wounded.[17]

In the fall of 1946, the Communists were losing the struggle, yet neither side was inclined to cooperate with Marshall's peace proposals. Chiang felt no need to negotiate from a position of strength following his temporary victories in Manchuria, and Mao feared negotiating from a position of weakness. Despite warning from his American advisers, Chiang's overextended military and economy would soon collapse, critically reversing the situation in China.

Marshall, realizing civil war was inevitable, ordered American participation in the executive headquarters ended. He was recalled by President Truman on 6 January 1947. The following day, he was named Truman's new secretary of state. Plans were made to withdraw the remainder of Marines from China, with the exception of a small detachment that would remain to guard the U.S. naval training facility at Tsingtao. On 1 April, operational plans were issued for the withdrawal and redeployment of the 1st Marine Division.

The last major clash—and the deadliest—between the Communists and the Marines took place on the night of 4–5 April, when the ASP at Hsin Ho was again attacked. Marines of Charlie Company, 1st Battalion, 5th Marines had the duty that night. Sergeant Osborn recalled, "We were located between Tientsin and the Port of Tangku. About ninety-five percent of the Marines on duty there were 17–18 year olds and right out of boot camp. Most of the combat Marines were back in the United States. . . . [We] didn't expect the Chinese to try anything like this since we had just spent World War II as allies."[18]

The ASP was located just south of Manchuria and north of the village of Hsin Ho. It was in the shape of a triangle with the apex to the north and sentry posts located along its three-mile perimeter. The Marine sentries tried to stay warm in night time temperatures of 40° Fahrenheit. The surrounding desolate terrain was made up of unending marsh, with only grasses growing.

At about 1:00 AM, Pfc. Jacob Jereb had just returned to Post No. 3 after walking the length of his post, where he'd chatted briefly with Pfc. Peter Stankiewicz at Post No. 2. Since he believed the area to be secure, he stepped behind an ammo shack and was enjoying a forbidden cigarette when he heard a noise. He looked out to see Chinese soldiers cutting the concertina wire that surrounded the perimeter. He shouted out, "Bay a dung!" (stand where you are). When the Chinese failed to comply with his order, he opened fire with his M-1 rifle. At 1:15 AM, bugles blared as 350 Chinese Communists of the 8th Route Army simultaneously attacked the perimeter at several widely separated locations.[19]

One group attacked the northernmost position, between Posts No. 2 and 3. As small-arms fire and grenade fragments peppered his position, Stankiewicz, although wounded, returned accurate fire, stalling the Communists' advance. Nearby, Jereb had also come under intense fire from multiple directions. Wounded, he'd fallen back into a field behind the shed. Jereb lay still as the Communists searched for him. He was saved by the expeditious arrival of the jeep patrol.

Behind the wheel of the jeep was Pfc. Anthol Clark, with Pfc. John Pelaro beside him. Pelaro was armed with a Browning automatic rifle (BAR). Manning a .30-caliber air-cooled machine gun mounted in the back was Pfc. Salvatore DiNenna and the assistant gunner, Pvt. Joseph Powroznyk. They had been checking on Pfc. David Sellers at Post No. 7 when they'd heard shots and rushed toward the sound of the guns. As Jereb later recalled, "As they came around the corner, they ran right into the Communists who were already on the road. They bailed out of the jeep and started returning fire, but there were just too many of them. They were all around them and were throwing grenades. I thought they were all killed." In that, Jereb was mistaken: Clark, although wounded, survived by playing dead.[20]

At the ASP guardhouse, the officer of the day, 2nd Lt. William R. Medlock, contacted Tangku by radio to report shots fired near Post No. 3. He then dispatched Platoon Sgt. Norris Cole with a 60-mm mortar team and a rifle squad in a jeep and 6x6 truck to respond, but they were attacked with grenades and small-arms fire as they passed Post No. 1. Dismounting, Cole, one of the few World War II vets in Charlie Company, deployed his Marines into a horseshoe-shaped defensive line, and they began to return fire.

Ignoring intense fire despite his wound, Pfc. Alfred E. Perkey stood exposed at the back of the truck as he unloaded two 60-mm mortars. He continued to unload a machine gun and small-arms ammunition before being wounded a second time. Setting up his mortar in an exposed position under fire, he managed to fire off several illumination and fragmentation rounds before receiving a third, mortal wound. He collapsed and died at his mortar tube. Pfc. Dale Whiteis, Cpl. Fred Harrington, and Pvt. Frank C. Spencer Jr. were also among the wounded, Spencer mortally. Outmanned and outgunned, Cole had his Marines secure the wounded who could walk, and withdrew to the guardhouse.[21]

Two other groups attacked farther south, but these were only diversions for the real target: the heavy artillery and mortar ammunition located along the eastern perimeter.

"When the attack took place, I had just been relieved from my guard post at midnight and was in the Quonset hut where we were billeted while on guard. . . . I was armed with an M1 Garand .30-caliber rifle, three clips of ammunition, and a bayonet. As the Communists attacked, we ran to the road that ran though the ASP and was close by. The roads were elevated and we laid down behind the berm. We were surrounded by rice paddies, and there was no cover."[22] The Communists set fire to two ammo sheds, causing explosions and confusion, and fires lit the clear night sky.

Back at Tangku, the radio watch, Cpl. James Erwin, woke the company commander, Capt. Henry V. Joslin. Joslin, accompanied by 1st Lt. Mildredge

Shown are some of the tanks of the 5th Marines as they pass along the streets in convoy on their way to Tangku. (U.S. Marine Corps)

Manguman, the company XO, led an armored column to relieve the besieged Marines. An M7 B1 fully tracked self-propelled 105-mm Howitzer led the relief force, followed by a jeep and two 6x6 trucks. The Communists had anticipated this and had mined the roadway from Tangku.

The Communists initiated the ambush by detonating the mine under the howitzer as the column approached the ASP, blowing up the tracks and disabling it, thus blocking the roadway as well as wounding several Marines. The remaining Marines dismounted, and, using the vehicle as cover, fought off the Communists for several hours in the darkness. They used only small arms (BARs, M-1 rifles, and .45-caliber pistols) because they were unable to set up a machine gun or mortars under the heavy enemy fire.

Pfc. John Peterkin was wounded by grenade shrapnel and Lieutenant Mangum by machine-gun fire. Only fifteen yards separated the two forces. Chief Hospital Corpsman Audrey Scandett remained with the wounded with several Marines for security as Joslin led the rest on foot north to the guardhouse.

Exploding ammunition lit up the sky as Joslin arrived at the guardhouse after 2:00 AM. After receiving a report from Cole, Captain Joslin led Sgt. Herb Newman, Cpl. James Erwin, and Pfc. Charles Fuller forward to look for the missing. They first located the body of a Marine, later identified as Private Spencer, then found Clark, Jereb, and Stankiewicz, all wounded. Nearby lay DiNenna, Pelaro, and Powroznik, all killed in the initial attack. Arrangements were made to evacuate the wounded: F4U Corsair aircraft were to be on station at first light.

The Communists withdrew at dawn, using horses to pack out the stolen munitions. The Marines pursued them for eight miles, but were never able to reestablish contact. The Communists disappeared into the countryside. They left six uniformed dead behind, and took an estimated twenty wounded with them. Marine casualties were five killed (Pfc. Salvatore DiNenna, Pfc. John T. Peloro, Pfc. Alfred E. Perkey, Pfc. Joseph Powroznik, and Pvt. Frank C. Spencer Jr.) and eighteen wounded.[23]

Three Marines, Pfc. Jacob Jereb, Pfc. Peter Stankiewicz, and Pfc. Alfred Perkey (posthumously) were awarded the Silver Star for gallantry in action. Jereb's citation states, "[When] a large number of dissident forces penetrated his sentinel post," Jereb "unhesitatingly opened fire and although exposed to an intense volley of automatic weapons and grenade fire at close range, continued to direct an accurate stream of small arms fire until he fell wounded."[24]

Stankiewicz's citation states, "[He] proceeded forward and engaged in a firefight with an overwhelming number of dissident forces. Although pinned down by hostile fire and seriously wounded by an enemy grenade . . . [he] delivered accurate and concentrated rifle fire . . . diverting the advance until reinforcements arrived."[25]

As part of the relief force, Perkey disregarded "the barrage of close range fire to climb back on the truck" where he "unloaded two mortars, a machine gun and ammunition . . . successfully placed one of the mortars in action, and after firing several rounds was mortally wounded by an enemy hand grenade and fell at his post."[26] Six Bronze Stars and twenty-three Purple Hearts were awarded, in addition to an unknown number of Silver Stars.

Two weeks later, on 21 April, the Marines turned over the ASP to Nationalist forces. During the next few months, the Marines continued to downsize their presence in China. In April–May, the 5th Marines and the 1st MAG deployed to Guam. By September, when the 1st Division cleared Tientsin and left for the States, the only Marines left in China were at Tsingtao.

On 25 December 1947, Communists ambushed a Marine hunting party of five Marines outside Tientsin, killing one Marine, Pfc. Charles J. Brayton, a nineteen-year-old from New York. The Marines had allegedly crossed into Communist territory at Wang Tan Yeun, after which no word was heard. No information as to their whereabouts or condition was received until mid-February 1948, when the U.S. government was notified that four Marines had survived and were being held captive by the Communists. Cpl. William Pollard, Pfcs. Thomas Kapodistria and Carroll W. Dickerson, and Pvt. Robert Hart were not released until 1 April 1948. Private First Class Brayton was the last Marine killed in China.[27]

The 6th Marine Division participates in the celebration in Tsingtao, China, 1945. (U.S. Marine Corps)

In the fall of 1948, the long-predicted military and economic collapse of the Nationalists in Manchuria came to pass, and the ultimate defeat of Chiang's Nationalists became inevitable. At the end of May the following year, as Mao was poised for final victory over the Nationalists, Marines safely evacuated the last Americans dependents from Tsingtao. Among the Marines that departed Tsingtao that spring was Pfc. Eugene Alden Hackman, who would become famous to future movie viewers as Gene Hackman.

During four years of occupation duty in North China, the Marines had never unleashed their full fighting power against the Chinese, but they would get their chance two years later in North Korea.

chapter two

ELIZABETH BENTLEY
Red Spy Queen, 1945

On 23 August 1945, Elizabeth Bentley made her way by train from New York City to New Haven, Connecticut. The matronly, plainly dressed, 37-year-old woman walked into the New Haven FBI field office and asked to speak with an agent. Agent Edward J. Coady met with her, and listened carefully as Bentley asserted that an associate of hers, Peter Heller, claimed he was a U.S. government investigator. Bentley said that Heller had asked her to spy on the activities of a company she worked for, United States Service & Shipping Corporation (USS&S), which was actively doing business with the Soviet Union. Heller had told her she might find some interesting information about the Russians, which she could pass along to him. Heller assured her the information would be delivered to U.S. government security agencies. Bentley asked Coady if Heller was in fact an agent, and Coady replied that he was not. In fact, Heller worked for the New York State Division of Parole in the Executive Clemency subdivision. That office reviewed records of prisoners the governor was considering for parole. Heller was not associated with any U.S. government counterintelligence agency: he was merely a man involved in an extramarital affair with Bentley, an unstable woman, and had used his cover story to keep her interested and wary of him so she would not make any demands. As it turned out, Bentley had another agenda in seeking an answer to Heller's identity. She wanted to find out if the FBI knew anything about her.

D uring their two-hour discussion Agent Coady began to wonder why an intelligent, articulate woman like Bentley would associate with a man such as Heller, and why she would board a train in New York and travel to New Haven to report her suspicions about another New Yorker. When he attempted to solicit information about her own activities, he was stonewalled. He

Elizabeth Turrill Bentley. (National Archives and Records Administration)

finally concluded the woman was on a "fishing expedition" and they parted, neither one satisfied with the meeting.

Coady had no idea that the woman sitting across from him was an American-born Soviet spy. She had made the decision to defect to the American side. Because of her fear that the KGB, American Communist Party members, and the FBI were closing in on her, she hid in the shadows as she sought to connect with the Bureau.

During the next two weeks, the New Haven office did not contact her regarding Heller. Then in mid-September a story broke in the *New York Times* that a Soviet agent, Igor Gouzenko, a code clerk working at the Soviet Embassy in Ottawa, had defected and that Canadian and American agencies were on the verge of discovering the details about a North American spy network focusing on atomic espionage. Though Bentley knew nothing of this operation, exposure of it might reveal information about the two networks she operated in the United States. To make matters worse, Louis Budenz, a longtime party member, defected the following October. She had met him several times when she collected mail from Canada for delivery to her KGB handler in New York. This link would lead directly to her if revealed, and the FBI would be on the hunt for her. So the threat of arrest and perhaps death became real as her enemies began to close in. Arrest by the FBI or death by the

KGB, or perhaps by American party members who wished to keep their identities unknown, became real possibilities.

Elizabeth Bentley decided to "come in from the cold." She believed her best option was to surrender to the FBI and become an informer. Because she ran two spy networks, she had solid cards to play. She had names of hundreds of American Communist Party members, including high-ranking officials actively serving in the U.S. government, corporation executives, covert Soviet business fronts, and KGB operatives actively committing espionage in the United States.

★ ★ ★

Elizabeth Turrill Bentley was born in New Milford, Connecticut, on 1 January 1908, to Charles and Mary Bentley. Elizabeth's ancestors had lived in New Milford since 1632. Her father managed a number of dry-goods stores and her mother was a schoolteacher. Charles and Mary were die-hard New Englanders whose roots went back to shortly after the arrival of the Mayflower. Her father was not a successful businessman, so the family was constantly on the move as he sought new employment. From an early age, Elizabeth was a lonely, withdrawn child with few friends. The Bentleys finally settled in Rochester, New York, where Charles ran a temperance newspaper and Mary provided food for the poor and homeless. Following her graduation from high school, Elizabeth attended Vassar College in Poughkeepsie, New York, on a scholarship. During her four years at Vassar (1926–30) she kept to her books. She was hardly noticed, and did not socialize. She was described by her classmates as a plain, lonely girl—a "sad sack." However, her experience at Vassar did expose her to "radical thinkers" such as Hallie Flangan, who was a one-woman political movement at the college.

During the 1920s, Vassar was noted for its progressive ideas. Bentley was exposed to campus lectures given by speakers such as social critic Lewis Mumford, historian Will Durant, Socialist Party presidential candidate Norman Thomas, civil rights leader W. E. B. Du Bois, and socialist and pacifist Scott Nearing, who lectured on Soviet Russia. Bentley joined the campus chapter of the League for Industrial Democracy (LID), a left-wing, reformist group. She was not a political person, but she agreed with the League's philosophy—that greed and profit grabbing resulted in much of the suffering in the world. This just happened to be the same philosophy espoused by her mother years ago while working with the poor. Although she had a low profile among her classmates while attending Vassar, she was exposed to the radicalism sweeping over the campus.

One year before Bentley graduated from Vassar, she was devastated by the death of her mother. Emotionally exhausted, she decided to use some of her inheritance money on three excursions to Europe over the next few years. Although still shy and reluctant to socialize, she took a liking to a British engineer on her initial trip and experienced her first romance. When she returned, she took a teaching position at Foxcroft School in Middleburg, Virginia, where she taught Romance languages (she had majored in English, French, and Italian at Vassar). After two years, she spent a summer studying at the University of Perugia in Italy, and the following summer at the Middlebury College Language Program in Vermont. In 1932, she left Foxcroft to attend graduate school full time at Columbia University. By this time, she had become personally more confident and was recognized as a competent teacher. She also found associating with men enjoyable. While at Columbia, she fell in love with a student. Although they had planned to marry in 1933, she broke off their engagement when she was awarded a fellowship to the University of Florence. Before she left for Italy, her father passed away. Now alone in the world and free of all vestiges of her strict New England upbringing, she went abroad to enjoy all she had missed. She began to drink excessively and bedded down men of all ages and professions. In Florence, while in a drunken stupor at parties, she would engage in outrageous acts that mortified others. She also often borrowed money she never paid back. She eventually gained the reputation as a lush, a leech, and a slut.

While in Florence, Bentley lived under Mussolini's fascist rule. Though not a fascist, she joined a university student's fascist group in order to enjoy the many benefits offered by the regime to control young people. Bentley completed her year of study in 1934 and headed back to New York on board the SS *Vulcania*. She came back to an America in the full throes of the Great Depression. With a year left to finish her master's degree, she would need to find employment so she could live and pay tuition. There were no vacancies in teaching, so she was forced to seek secretarial work. To this end, she completed courses in typing and shorthand at Columbia.

She was aghast at the conditions around her in New York. Nationwide, millions of people were out of work. Misery and hunger were everywhere. There was a feeling in the air that the great American experiment had failed, that something was very wrong with this once-prosperous country.

While seeking employment, Bentley found living accommodations in a cheap rooming house in Morningside Heights near Columbia. There she became friendly with Lee Fuhr, a nurse attending Columbia's Teachers College, who lived down the hall in her building. Fuhr had worked in cotton mills to put herself through nursing school. She had lost her husband and was struggling to support herself and her child. Lonely for companionship, Bentley befriended Fuhr. In the course of their conversations, they agreed on the dangers of fascism. Fuhr felt so strongly about the issue that she had joined a group called the American League Against War and Fascism. She invited Bentley to come to the group's meetings. Bentley was impressed by the roster league members. Upon attending her first chapter meeting (a chapter formed by students and professors at the Teachers College), she was taken by the fervor, energy, and intelligence displayed by its members. They were passionate about politics and the future. Fuhr encouraged Bentley to get more involved by helping the league with research on Italian fascism. The work could be done at the League's Manhattan headquarters in a building on lower Fourth Avenue. When Bentley went to the building to do her work, she met a young man named Harold Patch, one of the editors of the League's publication, *Fight*. Soon thereafter, she joined the League; it was not long before she found out the League was a Communist front. Bentley had finally found a home. She enjoyed the comradeship of the party members and attended meetings frequently. She worked as the party secretary for the chapter and wrote for the newspaper. It was not long before her life revolved around her Communist activities.

In early 1938, the Columbia University Center found a full-time job for Bentley at the Italian Library of Information on Madison Avenue. With her fluency in Italian and secretarial experience it was a natural position for her. She soon discovered, however, that the library was a propaganda ministry for disseminating positive information about the Mussolini regime. At first appalled by what she read in the anti-Communist fascist documents that ran counter to her now-bedrock beliefs, she considered quitting the job. However, on reconsideration she thought perhaps the party might like to know what propaganda was being fed by the fascists to the American public. Later she discussed the matter with a party comrade who directed her to visit a high-ranking executive, identified as "F. Brown," at party headquarters. He suggested she collect copies of all such materials and deliver them to him. Without realizing it, she had put herself undercover using her position at the library to steal Italian propaganda documents.

Starting in the summer of 1938, she delivered documents and pamphlets to Brown. During the following year, she gradually noticed he did not seem to be interested in the materials. Convinced the documents were of importance, she asked for the name of a party member who was interested in the Italian labor movement in the United States. Brown gave her the name of Jacob Golos, a man who would change her life forever.

Golos was an émigré from Lithuania who was an American citizen. He was also a member of the Communist Party and head of the World Tourists Travel Agency, which was a front for Soviet industrial espionage. Initially, Bentley did not know who he was, and knew him only as "Timmy." She later learned his real name, and through him met Earl Browder, head of the Communist Party of America.

Although Golos convinced Bentley her work at the library was vital, he saw in the woman great potential for more-serious espionage work. He admired her intellect, enthusiasm, and initiative. On her own initiative, she had been spying for the party; she was worth cultivating. Golos told her to report to him when she had sensitive materials for him. At the end of their first meeting, he told her she was no longer an ordinary Communist but a member of the underground. In this capacity, she was to cut off any ties to her party friends; he would be her only point of contact with the party. Bentley was thrilled with her new status.

After working at the library for a year, Bentley was abruptly fired. The library had discovered she had written a number of anti-fascist papers while studying at Columbia. Golos immediately put her to work doing low-level espionage work. At first, Bentley found this short, rather homely man mysterious and overwhelming, but soon found his intensity and commitment to the party appealing. His belief in her perseverance and willingness to take the necessary risks to further the party cause strengthened her determination to make a difference in changing the ills of society she witnessed around her. In time, she began to think more broadly, to believe her work would play a part in changing the world.

Bentley initiated numerous meetings with Golos; eventually they became romantically involved. (Unknown to her, Golos had another mistress in New York and a wife and child in Russia.) Golos began to train her in the art of espionage. She learned how to lose a tail, use a payphone whenever possible, burn any incriminating documents, never identify herself by her real name—in others words, how to disappear as a known person. Golos became her mentor, lover, her everything. She gave up her friends, and her life revolved around one human being: Golos.

Using contacts, Golos was able to get Bentley a job as secretarial assistant to Richard Waldo, a conservative executive who was owner and president of the McClure newspaper syndicate. She kept a close eye on his movements, kept a list of the people he contacted, and scanned numerous documents in his office, reporting anything unusual to Golos. The party thought he was a German agent and Bentley was assigned to keep tabs on him. She lasted four months before Waldo fired her during one of his frequent office rages. Golos, however, had other work for her. She next operated as a mail drop and courier. She carried copies of U.S. government documents to other agents and couriers, and she entertained men, who had been singled out by Golos, in order to spy on them.

In late October 1939, U.S. government agencies served Golos with a subpoena directing him to turn over World Tourists Travel Agency records to a grand jury. The government had long suspected the company was a front for the Soviet Union, and—along with the *Daily Worker* and a publishing company—that they were agents for the Soviet Union. The grand jury indicted Golos. After ten days of testimony, however, Golos was allowed to plead guilty to a lesser charge of failing to register as an agent of a foreign power. He walked away with a suspended sentence and a $500 fine. Following the demise of the World Tourists Travel Agency, Golos inserted Bentley as a vice president at the USS&S, which replaced the World Tourists operation as a Soviet front. When Golos fell ill with heart trouble, Bentley played an increasing role in the operation of USS&S. In addition to the long hours she spent at the company office, she traveled to Washington, DC, every two weeks to meet with contacts, ferrying documents back and forth. Several of her contacts were in executive positions within the U.S. government. The documents contained sensitive political, scientific, and technical information that she turned over to Golos. Golos would pass them to his handler who forwarded them to Moscow. Her load of paperwork became so large she started carrying a large knitting bag to transport them. In time, she ran two spy networks, known as the Silvermaster and Perlo groups. Each had about thirty members. Aside from her courier duty, she kept a close comradeship with the contacts, listening to their problems, advising them, and dispelling any worries they might have—and ensuring they remained committed to the party.

In December 1940, Golos learned he was the target of another congressional committee that was investigating Soviet espionage activities in the United States. Sensing he was about to be served with a subpoena by the Dies Committee (precursor to the House Un-American Activities Committee, or HUAC), he carried whatever sensitive materials he held to Bentley's apartment on Barrow Street, where the two of them burned the documents in her fireplace. In the process, Bentley observed numerous letters and pamphlets in Russian, dozens of American passports, and a folder containing Golos's KGB credentials. This confirmed what Bentley had suspected: her mentor worked not for just the U.S. Communist Party, but also for the KGB.

In addition to his troubles in America, Golos learned that Moscow was not happy with him. He was independent minded and outspoken, often expressing dissident opinions. In fact, some suspected he was a Trotskyite. Following his conviction in the World Tourists investigation, there were those in Moscow who felt he was too visible to counterespionage agencies in America and could no longer effectively run two major spy networks in the United States. Moscow was determined to take charge of the networks using Russian-born KGB personnel. For Golos, the downturn in events proved to be too much for him. On Thanksgiving Day 1943, Golos died of a heart attack on Bentley's living-room couch. Bentley called an ambulance, but it arrived too late. Although in shock and devastated, she knew some things had to be done before the police arrived. When the medics left her alone for a few minutes, she bolted the door and rifled through Golos's pockets, retrieving papers containing coded contact telephone numbers, which she put in her purse. She told the police he was a business associate of hers who had a bad heart. The police were satisfied with her story. After they left, some undertakers from the International Workers Order, which was friendly to the party, took Golos's body away. The next morning, Bentley went to the World Tourists building and cleaned Golos's office of any incriminating documents. In addition to papers, there was $12,000 in cash: she gave the money to Earl Browder later that morning in his office. She asked for his advice regarding the handling of her two network espionage contacts. He told her to carry on as before, that he would handle the Russians who were anxious to take control of her contacts.

The day after the funeral, Bentley met the man who was to replace Golos. His name was Itzhak Akmerov (code name "Bill"). He was the leading KGB operative without diplomatic cover in the United States and was married to Browder's sister. From the start, Bentley did not like or trust him. He immediately started challenging her for control of her contacts. She adamantly resisted, and refused to pass the names of her contacts to Akmerov. However, in the summer of 1944, the KGB wrested control of the Silvermaster Group from her. Later that year, she was forced to turn over the Perlo Group, and was told to hand over six of her solo agents. Although her meetings with Akmerov were often contentious, he soon realized that Golos had underreported her contributions over the years. He realized that Bentley clearly was a totally committed agent, well trained, and highly intelligent. She was best suited to recruit new sources within U.S. government circles and the American corporate world. Although she had never received a salary before, and had only been reimbursed for traveling expenses, the Soviets began giving her a salary, along with a new fur coat and an air conditioner. They told her she was to be awarded the Soviet Order of the Red Star Medal in recognition of her valuable services to Russia. Bentley was confused by all this attention: first they took away her networks, then they rewarded her. Gradually she realized she was being forced out, and became depressed, starting to drink heavily. She moved into a hotel in Brooklyn. The game was over.

★ ★ ★

In late August 1945, after returning from her trip to the FBI in New Haven, Bentley waited in her New York hotel to hear from field agent Coady. In October 1945, she wrote a letter to the New York FBI field office in which she related the story of Peter Heller. She was contacted by the field office and given an appointment date of 16 October with field agent Frank C. Aldrich. Two months after her visit to New Haven, she found herself sitting across a desk from Aldrich. Although the conversation initially was about Heller, she went on to tell the agent she knew people that were highly suspicious, in her opinion, who were perhaps Russian espionage agents. She offered to meet with one of them so the FBI could monitor their conversation. Asked for more details, she rambled on, would give no names, and started speaking in generalities. At the end of the meeting, Aldrich did not know what to make of the woman. Either she was hiding important information and was not ready to reveal it, or she was just another mental case like those who often walked into the field office with some outlandish tale.

Before she left his office, Bentley wrote down a contact telephone number where Aldrich could reach her. In a subsequent discussion about the meeting with Special Agent Edward W. Buckley, the office's Soviet expert, Buckley encouraged Aldrich to contact her and set up another visit. She might be worth looking into. A few days later, Aldrich tried to contact Bentley, but she was out of her USS&S office. When he was able to make contact, she seemed to be struggling with herself about meeting him again, which made the situation all the more interesting. Buckley talked to her and told her that if she had any information about un-American activities, she needed to relate her information to the FBI. The Bureau would offer advice and guidance. The following day, 7 November, Bentley, dressed in a dark suit and matching hat, met with Special Agent Buckley in his office in lower Manhattan. Sitting in with Buckley was Don Jardine, the most knowledgeable agent in New York on Communist activities.

Buckley and Jardine were gentle with her because she was tense and nervous. Gradually, she began to reveal more information. Although it came out slowly, Bentley told them her story. They asked how she had become mixed up in what appeared to be a complex, dangerous operation. Bentley charted her journey into Communism, starting with her first trip to Italy, and how she returned to America wanting to help build a better world than the world under Mussolini she had witnessed in Italy, returning to her home country to find it in the middle of a depression. Jardine became fascinated with her story and saw her as an idealist—a misguided idealist who had gotten in over her head. Bentley talked about Golos, the World Tourists Travel Agency, and the USS&S, both of them Soviet front organizations. Then she began to name names, in all 150 of them. They just flowed out of her. She added extensive details.

She had lost her soulmate, Golos. After all her hard work as a Communist Party member, as a courier and spy, to be mistreated and cast off by the Soviets was traumatic. She was now alone, scared, and despondent. She needed a new noble cause that was bigger than herself. She found this cause in defecting. She had become an anti-Communist, determined to be a warrior in her new role.

Realizing they had struck gold, Aldrich and Buckley spent hours writing their report, which ran 170 pages. At 1:30 AM on 8 November 1945, they teletyped it to J. Edgar Hoover, director of the FBI. Hoover was ecstatic, as were the agents in the New York field office. There was only one problem: like a well-trained spy, she had no corroborating evidence in the way of paperwork to back up her story and names. Many of the names, however, were already on file at FBI headquarters. Two other agents took over her case, and interviewed her fourteen times during November. She kept her job at USS&S and went to work daily, since this was now her only source of income. Additionally, if she quit it might tip off the Soviets that she was up to something. During her interviews, she became more confident and her recall was amazing. At each interview, she remembered more details. By all standards, the FBI considered her to be a credible informant.

Over the next two years, Bentley was reinterviewed as agents checked out the details of her statement and follow-on remembrances. They wiretapped and tailed her Communist contacts. At one time, the FBI had two hundred agents working on her case. However, trouble arose when the Soviets discovered Bentley had defected. The British Secret Service's (SIS, or MI6) new Section IX (counterespionage against the Soviet Union), was headed by Soviet double agent Kim Philby, who would escape to the Soviet Union in 1963. Philby intercepted cables sent by the United States to the British detailing the Bentley case. He promptly notified Moscow, and the Soviets ceased their covert operations in the United States and recalled their agents.

The American Communist contacts named by Bentley were brought before a grand jury in 1947. Among them were Harry Dexter White (former assistant to the secretary of the treasury), William Remington (chairman of a commerce department that allocated exports to the Soviet Union), and Lauchin Curric (former assistant to President Franklin Roosevelt and President Truman). All vehemently denied her charges, while others took the Fifth Amendment. Thomas J. "The Hat" Donegan, special assistant to the U.S. attorney general, tried the case. When it appeared no indictments would be forthcoming, Donegan took a different tack. While keeping the grand jury in session, he prepared a new case that accused the American Communist Party of conspiring to advocate the overthrow of the government by force and called for the indictment of high-level party leaders. The Smith Act of 1940 gave Donegan and his staff the vehicle to establish this new strategy. Under the Act, it was a crime to print, publish, edit, issue, circulate, sell, distribute, or publically display any written or printed matter advocating the overthrow of the U.S. government. Donegan won the day when the grand jury handed down sealed indictments against the twelve-person national board of the American Communist Party. However, none of the other contacts Bentley named was indicted.

Hoover knew that many of the agents Bentley revealed were guilty because of an army decryption operation code-named Venona. Since 1943, Army code breakers had been examining Soviet diplomatic cables to find out if the Soviets were attempting to make a separate peace with Germany. As it turned out, the deciphered cables contained information about Soviet spying operations in the United States. In reviewing the contents of these cables in 1946, the U.S. government discovered that hundreds of citizens, immigrants, and high-ranking American officials carried on covert relationships with Soviet Intelligence agencies. Bentley (code-named "Clever Girl") was mentioned frequently in the cable traffic. But would the FBI use such information against those named in the Bentley case? Hoover decided against using the Venona intelligence, since doing so would reveal to the Soviets that the United States had broken one of their most secretive codes, and would compromise ongoing counterintelligence operations. He decided the price was too high to pay for convictions of spies that were no longer active. Although Hoover wished to continue to pursue the people Bentley had named, without Venona it would be her uncorroborated statement against some very bright, well-connected, prominent people who would no doubt hire the best lawyers in their defense. Surely, the result would be an acquittal for all of the accused.

Bentley, deeply disappointed with the outcome, decided to go public with her story. On 21 July 1948, the *New York World Telegram* printed the first in a series of articles regarding Soviet espionage activities in America. Before the first article appeared, Bentley had met with the *World Telegram* reporters for months during the spring and summer of 1948, providing them with the details of her work as a Communist covert agent. The newspaper's headline blared, RED RING BARED BY BLOND QUEEN. Though Bentley's name was not mentioned, the paper cast her as a svelte blond. However, as a result of the exposé, the newspaper got a call from the legal counsel of a Senate investigating committee eager to look into the issue of Communist spies in the federal government. Bentley had not wanted her story to end up buried in some government file safe. She got her wish and then some.

The Ferguson Committee convened its first hearing on "the Communist conspiracy" on 30 July 1948. Bentley was the key witness. The target of the committee was William Remington. Bentley made her first public appearance as she walked into the Senate hearing room. The media immediately took note that the plump brunette was neither blond nor svelte. Bentley, now in her late thirties, was plain looking and simply dressed. Her testimony during the Senate hearing was direct and riveting. She spoke without notes, was articulate, and never wavered from her story. Committee members saw before them an intelligent, confident woman, a very credible witness.

The day following her Ferguson Committee appearance, the HUAC convened to investigate further the loyalty and alleged party affiliation of those named by Bentley. The HUAC had already held hearings on suspected party members or "fellow travelers" (those who sympathized with the Communist Party, but were not members) in the motion picture industry. Ten individuals were indicted, convicted, and sent to jail. Many others were subsequently blacklisted by Hollywood. Bentley also testified during the trials of accused spies William Remington (who served with the U.S. War Production Board), Abe Brothman (chemical engineer who passed secret blueprints to her), Harry Dexter White (former assistant secretary of the treasury), and "atomic spies" Julius and Ethel Rosenberg. Remington was eventually convicted of perjury and given a three-year prison sentence. While serving his time at Lewisburg Penitentiary in Pennsylvania, he was stabbed to death. Brothman was convicted and jailed for two years. White died of a heart attack three days after his appearance before the HUAC. Bentley linked Julius Rosenberg with Golos, and the Rosenbergs were electrocuted on 19 June 1953.

In need of money, Bentley wrote her autobiography, *Out of Bondage: The Story of Elizabeth Bentley* (1951). In her book, she portrayed herself as a naïve and innocent woman, the victim of cunning associates. The book was melodramatic and

Elizabeth Bentley, Vassar College graduate and KGB agent in the United States during World War II, became a leading anti-Communist spokesperson. She appeared on *Meet the Press* and spoke frequently on national radio. (U.S. Library of Congress)

failed to detail seriously her journey into the Communist world, and the significant, dedicated role she played as an espionage agent. Although the book was successfully serialized by *McCalls* magazine, book sales were poor and Bentley was nearly broke financially. Unfortunately, she enjoyed an expensive lifestyle, and was never adept at managing money. She continually sought financial support from the FBI. Since she was still valuable to the Bureau during the 1950s and would remain so for the rest of her life, Hoover approved funds to resolve her financial problems.

During her turbulent times in the early 1950s, Bentley studied the Catholic faith with Monsignor Fulton J. Sheen, who made it a personal mission to convert former Communists. (Later, as an archbishop, he lectured on moral issues of the day on the popular television series *Life Is Worth Living*.) Bentley was an embattled woman who had lost her faith in Communism and was seeking a stabilizing force to find solace in her life. Throughout the late 1940s and 1950s, she managed to continue her education and teach at various colleges. In the fall of 1949, she was hired to teach political science at Mundelein College, a prominent Catholic school for women on Lake Shore Drive in Chicago. Because she was still called on to give depositions and act as a consultant for the FBI, she found it almost impossible to maintain a normal teaching schedule, however. She was forced to resign from Mundelein after one semester. In 1953, she was offered a teaching position at the College of the Sacred Heart in Grand Coteau, Louisiana. At the time, she was fending off libel suits filed against her by many she had named as Communist agents. In addition, the IRS was after her for not paying taxes on her book and magazine earnings, and parents of her Sacred Heart students learned of her past and many indiscretions and complained about her to the college staff. Facing such problems, she became despondent and started drinking heavily again. In 1956, she left Sacred Heart and took a job at the Cathedral School of St. Mary, an Episcopal school on Long Island. Again, her past caught up with her, especially since her autobiography was available at the school library and was read by her students and their parents. She next moved back to Connecticut and took courses to complete her master's degree at Trinity College in Hartford.

Finally, after thirteen years as an informant, she notified the FBI she would no longer be available. She wanted to make a complete break with her past life. Her last teaching job was at a penal institution for girls, Long Lane School in Middletown, Connecticut. It was during her fifth year at Long Lane that she fell ill. Doctors performed exploratory surgery and found she had terminal cancer. She never awakened from her surgery. She died on 1 December 1963. She was fifty-six years old.

For more than twenty years Elizabeth Bentley had been called many names: sinner, villain, traitor, saint, hero, and patriot. She was an intelligent woman, resourceful, at times confident, determined, and steadfast when she believed in a cause. But she was also a depressed and unstable soul who drank too much, was promiscuous, and on occasion displayed a wild streak. In the 1960s, the Venona transcripts and some Soviet archives material were made available. With these revelations, there was finally a definitive and public verification of the basics of Bentley's story, and a new appreciation of the impact her defection had on Soviet espionage operations in the United States.

chapter three

LT. GAIL HALVORSEN AND THE BERLIN AIRLIFT, 1948–49

I n July 1948, as Douglas C-47 "Gooney Bird" and Douglas C-54 "Skymaster" transport planes of the Berlin Airlift thundered overhead, a twenty-eight-year-old USAF first lieutenant stood by the perimeter fence of Tempelhof Airport in West Berlin. As he watched the planes land and take off, he saw a group of about thirty children watching the planes, too, and decided to go over and talk with them. It was a meeting that would significantly alter the Cold War and positively impact postwar relations between the United States and Germany.

★ ★ ★

Following the German surrender on 8 May 1945, Soviet and Western (U.S., U.K., and French) troops stretched across Germany, which had been divided roughly along the Elbe River into two countries: East Germany and West Germany. Earlier, in February 1945, Franklin Roosevelt, Winston Churchill, and Josef Stalin had agreed at the Yalta Conference to divide an occupied Germany into three—later four—zones of occupation. Now that the Allies were victorious, President Truman, replacing the late Roosevelt, met with Stalin and Churchill (later Clement Attlee) at Cecilienhof, the home of Crown Prince Wilhelm Hohenzollern, in Potsdam, Germany, from 17 July 1945 to 2 August 1945. The Potsdam Conference, as it came to be called, attempted to finalize plans for administering a defeated Germany.[1]

Administration of occupied Germany was to be coordinated by a four-power Allied Control Council (ACC). Germany was divided into four sectors (American, British, French, and Russian), each under the control of its respective military governor. Additionally, the German capital of Berlin was divided into four sections. In theory, its policies would center on the "five D's": demilitarization, denazification, democratization, decentralization, and deindustrialization. Each power would seize industrial resources in its own zone of occupation as reparations, with the Soviet Union trading agricultural products for additional industrial equipment.[2]

Based on the Morgenthau Plan, Joint Chiefs of Staff Directive 1067 (JCS 1067) stated the Allied powers should "take no steps looking toward the economic rehabilitation of Germany [or] designed to maintain or strengthen the German economy." The goal was to eliminate Germany's ability to wage war. The means to do this was by deindustrializing its economy to 50 percent of its 1938 capacity.[3]

Unfortunately for the plan, it soon became apparent that a weakened German economy negatively affected the economy of the whole of Europe, which was desperately trying to recover after being decimated from almost six years of war. As Lewis Douglas, chief adviser to Gen. Lucius Clay, the U.S. Commissioner, stated, "It makes no sense to forbid the most skilled workers in Europe from producing as much as they can in a continent that is desperately short of everything."[4]

Germany's deteriorating economy created conditions of near starvation in much of Europe. Combined with a growing Communist influence, it caused the United States to reconsider a clearly punitive policy in favor of one designed to create a stable and productive Germany as the economic center of Europe, and as a bulwark against encroaching Communism. On 30 July 1946, the United States and Britain merged the economies of their respective zones in Germany in an attempt to stabilize the economy. "Bizonia," as it came to be called, became operational in January 1947.

In the summer of 1947, Secretary of State Gen. George Marshall, citing "national security grounds," finally persuaded President Truman to replace JCS 1067 with JCS 1779. This directive asserted, "An orderly, prosperous Europe requires the economic contributions of a stable and productive Germany." This policy was in conflict with the Soviet interest in a weakened Germany: the Soviets wanted Gemany reduced to an agricultural nation without an industrial base with which to wage war. There were also many who hoped that economic instability would lead to civil unrest and perhaps a Communist uprising in Germany.[5]

Other pressures at the time influenced Western–Soviet relations, as attempted Communist rebellions in Greece and Turkey prompted President Truman to announce to Congress on 12 March details of a plan that came to be known as the Truman Doctrine. Pledging American assistance to all "free peoples who are resisting attempted subjugation by armed minorities or by outside pressures," he asked Congress for $400 million in military and economic aid for both Greece and Turkey. It was the beginning of the policy of "containment" designed to limit Communist expansion.

To help implement this doctrine, the Marshall Plan—officially known as the European Recovery Plan (ERP)—was put into effect three months later on 12 July 1947. It provided for the economic reconstruction of Europe. Both sides understood, however, that the heart of the battle would take place in Berlin. As Soviet

Foreign Minister Vyacheslav Molotov noted at the time, "What happens to Berlin, happens to Germany; what happens to Germany, happens to Europe."[6]

It was inevitable that, as the two competing economic structures worked toward opposing goals, tensions would increase and cooperation would decrease. It became apparent through the later months of 1947 that there would be no agreement on the issues of reparations, currency reform, or joint control of the industrial Ruhr region, so the Western allies proceeded with plans to unify the western regions of Germany.

On 23 February 1948, representatives of the United States, Great Britain, and France, joined by Belgium, the Netherlands, and Luxembourg, met in London to plan for Germany's participation in the Marshall Plan and the creation of a West German government. The Soviet foreign minister, Molotov, protested these meetings as a violation of the Potsdam Agreement. It was as effective as Western protests over the Communist takeover in Czechoslovakia—that is to say, not effective at all.

At a meeting of the ACC on 20 March, Marshal Vassily Sokolovsky, the Soviet military governor in Germany, directly asked Gen. Lucius D. Clay and Gen. Sir Brian Robertson, the U.S. and British military governors, about the London conferences. Sokolovsky was told the subject was not up for discussion. Sokolovsky and the entire Soviet delegation rose as one and walked out, effectively ending the ACC.

In mid-March, representatives of Britain, France, Belgium, the Netherlands, and Luxembourg signed an agreement to come to each other's defense; this agreement is known as the Brussels Defense Pact, and was the beginning of NATO.

On 31 March, the Soviets announced that all Western military trains going into and out of Berlin would be stopped and inspected, the purpose of which was primarily to inconvenience and harass the Western forces. The following day, 1 April, General Clay ordered all train traffic stopped, and initiated an airlift, code-named "Operation Little Lift," to supply the six thousand Western troops in Berlin. Five days into that airlift, on 5 April, a Vickers Viking of British European Airways took off on a flight to Royal Air Force (RAF) Gatow in West Berlin.

Although the plane was within one of the three air corridors agreed to by treaty, it was buzzed by a Soviet Yak-3 fighter plane. As the British pilot took evasive action, he collided with the fighter, and both planes crashed, killing the Soviet pilot and ten others on board the British European Airways plane. Both sides blamed the other, but the Soviets dropped their demands for inspection five days later on 10 April, the tenth day of the airlift. They continued, however, to harass road and rail traffic periodically.[7]

Other factors contributed to the tension between the Soviets and the West. The Western Allies wanted to combine their sectors into a single political and economic unit and establish a uniform currency for West Germany. On 18 June 1948, they announced the introduction of the new German Mark (Deutschmark) to replace the almost worthless Realm Mark. Four days later, on 22 June, the Soviets introduced their own currency for East Germany.[8]

During this time, the Soviets began efforts to isolate Berlin, which lay deep in Soviet territory. On 12 June, the autobahn into Berlin from West Germany was "closed for repairs," and on 15 June, road traffic between the sectors was stopped. All barge traffic was halted on 21 June. On 23 June, the Western Deutschmark appeared in Berlin, further angering the Soviets.

At midnight on 23–24 June 1948, the Soviets began to cut electric power to the Western sectors of Berlin, and Soviet troops encircled the city, beginning the Berlin Blockade. At 6:00 AM on 24 June, due to "technical difficulties," all rail access into the city was halted, with the exception of some "essential" military traffic. The West was limited to a single military train once a night. For all intents, Berlin was now a city under siege.[9]

The following day, 25 June, the Soviets announced they would no longer supply food to those parts of Berlin under Western administration. Clearly, the Soviet intent was to force a withdrawal of the Western powers from Berlin. The city had only thirty-six days of food and forty-five days of coal on hand. The options appeared to be either withdrawing or forcing the blockade—which would risk war.

General Clay understood the importance of staying in Berlin when he cabled his superiors on 13 June: "There is no practicability of maintaining our position in Berlin, and it must not be evaluated on that basis. . . . We are convinced that our remaining in Berlin is essential to our prestige in Germany and in Europe. Whether for good or bad, [Berlin] has become a symbol of American intent."[10]

Clay wanted to send a large armored column "peacefully" down the autobahn to Berlin with orders to use force only if attacked, but President Truman, with concurrence of a majority of Congress, believed the risk of war was too great. Additionally, the Soviet Army greatly outnumbered U.S. and U.K. forces, both of which had demobilized following the end of World War II.[11]

Although the West argued the treaty granting them the right to be in Berlin carried with it the right of access to Berlin, the Soviets disagreed. The argument could not be resolved, since the ground routes had never been finalized in an agreement. The same could not be said for the air corridors into Berlin. On 30 November 1945, a written agreement with the Soviets provided for three twenty-mile-wide air corridors into the city. An airlift would either break the blockade or force the Soviets into shooting down unarmed cargo planes in violation of the treaty.

Thus began a monumental airlift that would last 324 days. Its 277,685 flights carried 2,326,406 tons of cargo into Berlin. Originally referred to as the "LeMay Coal and Feed Delivery" in honor of Air Force Lt. Gen. Curtis LeMay, commander of the USAF in Europe, it was later nicknamed "Operation Vittles" by Brig. Gen. Joseph Smith, the initial U.S. commander of the airlift, and "Operation Plainfare"

Lt. Gail Halvorsen, USAF, meets with the children of postwar Berlin. Assigned to transport food and supplies into a blockaded West Berlin, he pioneered Operation Little Vittles, airdropping candy to German children and becoming known as the Candy Bomber. (National Archives and Records Administration)

by the British. By any name, it clearly displayed the Western Allies' resolve to remain in Berlin.[12]

For the airlift to work, though, it would need to bring in government supplies sufficient to support not just the garrisoned troops, but also the Western sectors of Berlin. Additionally, it would need to move rapidly to prevent starvation during the approaching winter. When asked by Clay if the airlift was feasible, LeMay replied, "We can haul anything."[13]

Berlin needed a minimum of two thousand tons a day to subsist at a minimum level, but the Air Force had only 102 Douglas C-47 Skytrain ("Gooney Bird") and two C-54 Skymaster transport aircraft available in Europe, with the capacity to airlift barely enough resources to supply the Berlin garrison. A test run delivered twice the needed payload, however.

The key to supplying Berlin would be in the planning and organization. To that end, on 27 July Maj. Gen. William "Willie the Whip" Tunner was brought in to take command of the airlift. Tunner, a veteran of flying the "Hump" over the Himalayas to supply China during World War II, standardized operations so efficiently that at its height planes kept intervals for the entire 177 miles (274 kilometers) flight, and landed every three minutes around the clock. It was so tightly scheduled that if a pilot missed his landing, he was required to return to the starting point to reenter the airlift.[14]

General Clay requested all available C-54s from the Pentagon, and whatever other air resources were available. By early July, Skymasters had arrived from the Canal Zone, Hawaii, Alabama, and Texas. The Navy sent two squadrons of R5Ds, the Navy version of the C-54. The British contributed Dakota, Avo York, and Handley Page Hasting aircraft. Commercial transport planes arrived from Australia, New Zealand, and South Africa.

Even the K-9 corps contributed. An American pilot, 1st Lt. Russ Steber, took his dog "Vittles" along on 131 missions. The boxer logged over two thousand miles and had his own, custom-made, parachute by order of General LeMay himself. Fortunately, he never had to use it. The same cannot be said for Steber, who was forced to parachute into Soviet territory when his plane lost its engines. He was captured, interrogated for several days, and then returned to the West. Stebner had several other close calls, and received the Distinguished Flying Cross for flying a record 415 missions.[15]

Transports flew into Berlin in the northern and southern corridors, and departed via the center corridor. They carried a variety of cargos, including salt, dehydrated food, medical supplies, equipment, machinery, soap, newsprint, petrol, and coal (which was essential for Berlin's survival in the winter and comprised 65 percent of the payloads), and more than twenty tons of candy![16]

★ ★ ★

On 17 July 1948, 1st Lt. Gail Halvorsen was at Tempelhof Airport in Berlin with his movie camera, hoping to take some film of the conquered city. Halvorsen, an airlift pilot, was supposed to be resting, but instead had "hitchhiked" a ride into Berlin to go sightseeing. Normally assigned to fly transport missions to Central and South America with the 17th Military Air Transport Squadron stationed at Brookley Field, Alabama, Halvorsen volunteered for the airlift to take a buddy's place. As he said, "Stalin was threatening world peace and they needed pilots in Germany. My buddy, with a set of twins, was on the list, and didn't want to go. I was single, so I volunteered to take his place."[17]

Halvorsen, a devout Mormon, was born in Salt Lake City on 10 October 1920, the second of three children. He grew up on small farms in Utah and Idaho during the Great Depression. He graduated from Bear River High School in Garland, Utah, and earned his pilot's license through the Non-College Civilian Pilot Training Program before joining the Civil Air Patrol in September 1941.

Forty high-intensity lights placed in two parallel rows of twenty lights illuminated a 3,000-foot approach to the main runway at Tempelhof airfield in Berlin. The 200,000-watt system was designed to assist the landing of Operation Vittles USAF and USN planes during periods of poor visibility. The lights were placed in straight rows, marking the extensions of the width of the runway. The left row of lights, as seen by the pilot on the landing glide, was red, and the right row yellow. (National Archives and Records Administration)

On 6 June 1942, Halvorsen joined the U.S. Army Air Force (USAAF). "The war was on, and I wanted to get in it. I wanted to fly, wanted to be a pilot." He was sent to San Antonio, Texas, for preflight training, after which he volunteered for fighter pilot training with the RAF at Miami, Oklahoma. (Since the skies over England were unsafe for training, many RAF pilots trained as pilots in the United States.) After earning his RAF wings, he returned to the USAAF and was assigned to fly transports in the South Atlantic Theater. "They didn't need fighter pilots, so they put me in transports. I flew C-47s from Natal, Brazil, to Africa, and ferried aircraft from the Ascension Islands to Europe."[18]

Now, at around 2:00 PM on that afternoon in July, Halvorsen saw a group of twenty to thirty German children watching the landings, and went over to talk with them. "I was surprised. They didn't ask for gum or candy. Instead they said, 'We don't have enough to eat. Just give us a little. . . . Someday we'll have enough to eat. But if we lose our freedom, we'll never get it back.' You see, the American style of government was their dream. Hitler's past, and Stalin's future was their nightmare."[19]

With only two sticks of gum in his pocket, Halvorsen gave it to them, promising that if they would share and not fight, he would return the next day and drop more candy from his plane. When they asked how they would know which plane was his, he promised to wiggle his wings. This led to his nickname of "Uncle Wiggly Wings."

True to his word, Halvorsen collected all the candy he could from his fellow pilots, and attached miniature parachutes to it. The next day he, his copilot 2nd Lt. John Pickering, and engineer Sergeant Elkins "bombed" the children of Berlin with candy on their approach to the airport. It was a significantly different payload from the payloads American pilots had dropped on Berlin only three years earlier.

His initial efforts were not greeted with enthusiasm by his commander. "When my superiors found out about what I was doing, my colonel chewed me out because I didn't have permission, and the general found out about it before the colonel, my commander. And that's bad news . . . but the general said it was a great idea, keep doing it. That's when it really took off."[20]

Supported by the media, this miniairlift became known as "Operation Little Vittles," and Halvorsen gained the nickname "Candy Bomber," a title he shared with the twenty-five other crews that became involved in the effort. They were supported by the American Confectioner's Association, who donated tons of chewing gum, Hersheys, Mounds, and Baby Ruth candy bars. They were also supported by twenty-two schools in Chicopee, Massachusetts, who attached little parachutes to the candy. Halvorsen and the others were able to distribute more than twenty tons of candy to children all over Berlin. This candy drop served to raise morale of both the pilots and civilians in the besieged city. Halvorsen received the Cheney Award in 1949, awarded for "an act of valor, extreme fortitude, or self-sacrifice in a humanitarian interest."[21]

"There was never an average day," Halvorsen recalled. "We flew in rain, ice, snow and fog, during the day, and in the dark. In the beginning, we flew three trips a day because there weren't enough planes, but that was reduced to two trips as more planes arrived."[22]

With continuous operations in inclement weather and minimum maintenance, accidents were inevitable. "The accident rate was remarkable for the volume of traffic. We had one hundred twenty serious accidents . . . sometimes we flew with what were considered minor problems [that] would have grounded the airplane in normal operations . . . [and] several airplanes crashed and burned in the Soviet controlled East Germany."[23]

In August 1948, a new airport, Tegel, opened in the French sector of Berlin. By September, the daily total of supplies into Berlin rose to seven thousand tons, due in part by the replacement of C-47s with larger capacity C-54s. In October, the American and British airlifts were combined and the United States recalled ten thousand pilots, flight engineers, and radio operators to active duty. In the interim, diplomatic efforts to end the blockade were unsuccessful.[24]

Unloading the cargo at Tempelhof Airport. Navy Airman Robert H. Davidson, Aviation Machinist's Mate (Airman Apprentice), of Meridian, Texas, directs the unloading crew at the Berlin terminus of the airlift, 9 January 1949. (U.S. Navy)

The airlift continued to deliver increasing volumes of goods as time passed. During the first week, the airlift average was ninety tons a day. By 16 April 1949, a day remembered as the "Easter Parade," the airlift delivered thirteen thousand tons, with planes landing on the average of every 61.8 seconds, a record. Additionally, unloading was made more efficient by having the crews remain on board the plane. "Weathermen" would come out to the planes in jeeps with weather updates, and a snack bar on a wagon would provide food and drinks, while workers unloaded the supplies. Halvorsen remembered "[Tunner] put some beautiful German Frauleins in that snack bar. They knew we couldn't date them, we had no time. So they were very friendly."[25]

That December, "Operation Santa Claus" delivered gifts to ten thousand Berlin children and Bob Hope visited airlift bases to perform for American troops. In January 1949, with their six-month tour of duty complete, the first Americans began to rotate back to the United States. Among them was Lieutenant Halvorsen. By 18 February 1949, more than 1 million tons of goods had been airlifted to Berlin.

On 21 April 1949, the airlift's 300th day, the amount of supplies going into the city by airlift equaled the amount of supplies going in by rail before the airlift. It had become clear that the Western Allies could continue the airlift indefinitely. The Soviet blockade had failed. Worse, it had been a diplomatic disaster. Five days later, on 25 April, the Soviet news agency TASS (Telegraph Agency of the Soviet Union) reported a willingness by the Soviets to end the blockade. At 12:01 AM on 12 May 1949, the Soviets lifted their barricades and restored access from West Germany to Berlin. The airlift was over, at a cost of seventeen American and seven British planes, resulting in the loss of thirty-one American and thirty-eight British pilots and air and ground crews. (See sidebar.)

On 23 May 1949, the Federal Republic of Germany (FRG) was established in West Germany, followed by the creation of a Communist German Democratic Republic (GDR) in East Germany on 7 October. The airlift continued through 30 September to rebuild a strategic reserve in the city. The lessons learned during the Berlin Airlift would serve the United States military in future airlifts.

Lieutenant Halvorsen returned to the United States on 24 January 1949. The Air Force sent him to the University of Florida as part of the Air Force Institute of Technology. "I didn't have much school, so the Air Force sent me to Florida where I earned a Bachelor's and Master's Degree in Aeronautical Engineering."[26]

His later assignments included research and development at the Wright Air Center in Ohio, attendance at the Air Command and Staff College in Alabama, the Pentagon, and the Air Force Space Systems Division at Vandenberg Air Force Base where he helped develop the Titan III launch vehicle and the manned orbital laboratory. His final assignment was as commander of Tempelhof Air Force Base and Air Force representative in Berlin.[27]

Halvorsen retired from the Air Force as a full colonel on 31 August 1974, with the award of the Legion of Merit and the Meritorious Service Medal. Since then, he has participated in another airlift, Operation Provide Promise in Bosnia-Herzegovina, and has attended Berlin Airlift anniversaries and reenactments. He wrote about his experiences in a memoir, *The Berlin Candy Bomber* (2002).

The Berlin Blockade failed and the Berlin Airlift succeeded, in large part due to the support of the German people of Berlin whose morale was lifted by Operation Little Vittles. As Halvorsen recalled, "What [the candy airdrop] meant was not chocolate, but hope, which is the most important thing you can have in a crisis. The Berliners were the heroes. They lived for freedom when they had no food."[28]

Fatalities of the Berlin Airlift

★ ★ ★

With 277,685 flights flown during the Berlin Airlift, it is not surprising that accidents occurred, and that some of those accidents resulted in fatalities. What is surprising is that the number was so low, considering the frequency of flights (one takeoff every three minutes at its height), fatigued pilots flying several flights daily, severe weather conditions in the winter months, and constant harassment from Soviet aircraft and ground installations.

During the course of the operation, thirty-one American and thirty-eight British pilots, aircrew, and ground support personnel, as well as eight German civilians, died in airplane crashes and accidents.[1]

For the United States, this broke down to twenty-eight Air Force personnel, one each from the Army and Navy, and one civilian, involving three C-47 crashes, eight C-54 crashes, and one R5D crash.[2]

The first crash of an airlift aircraft occurred around midnight on 6 July 1948, when an empty C-47 crashed after striking a clump of trees three-fourths of a mile from Wiesbaden. The weather was described as very bad, with a low ceiling and poor visibility. There were only minor injuries to the two crew members, but flights were suspended for seven hours.[3]

8 July 1948

Mr. Karl V. Hagen (Department of the Army)
1st Lt. George B. Smith
1st Lt. Leland V. Williams

Two days later, on 8 July, the aircrew of another C-47 was not as fortunate, resulting in the first fatalities of the airlift. At 10:28 PM on that day, the pilot, Lieutenant Williams, took off from Wiesbaden, cleared for Tempelhof airport. There was a light rain and a low ceiling. Seven minutes later, the C-47 crashed near Königstein, ten miles to the northeast. The cause of the crash was never determined. Karl Hagen, a German-born American, was working for the military government, and traveling as a passenger.

25 July 1948

1st Lt. Charles H. King
1st Lt. Robert W. Stuber

On 25 July, a C-47 crashed into an apartment building in Berlin after striking a tree while approaching Tempelhof airport, killing both crew members aboard. In a spontaneous demonstration of gratitude, the Berliners built a memorial at the site with flowers, candles, and a plaque that read, "Two American fliers here became sacrifices of the blockade of Berlin. . . . Once we were enemies, yet you now gave your lives for us."[4]

24 August 1948

Capt. Joel M. DeVolentine
Maj. Edwin C. Diltz
Capt. William R. Howard
1st Lt. William T. Lucas

Early on the morning of 24 August, a C-47 piloted by Major Diltz, with Captain Howard as copilot, departed Tempelhof after unloading its cargo. Twenty-seven minutes later, a second C-47 took off, piloted by Captain DeVolentine with Lieutenant Lucas in the second seat. The two planes, flying in almost zero visibility, collided at 8:30 AM over Ravolzhausen. It was the only crash involving two aircraft. With four killed, it was the second-worst loss of life during the operation.[5]

2 October 1948

Pfc. Johnny T. Orms

On 2 October, a fire truck driven by Private First Class Orms collided with a C-54 Skymaster that was taxiing onto an active runway prior to taking off at the Rhein-Main Air Force Base. Orms was killed instantly by the plane's propellers. Assigned to the 61st Installation Squadron at Rhein-Main, he was the first enlisted man and only member of the Army to be killed. This was the first of two ground accidents.[6]

18 October 1948

1st Lt. Eugene E. Erickson
Capt. James A. Vaughan
Sgt. Richard Winter

Rhein-Main was the site of another accident sixteen days later. A C-54 Skymaster, returning empty from Berlin, was descending on approach when it struck a tree with its right wing at 5:45 AM. All three crew members on board were killed.

5 December 1948

1st Lt. Willis F. Hargis
Capt. Billy E. Phelps
TSgt. Lloyd C. Wells

On 30 November 1948, the fog over Berlin was so thick that only ten flights were able to land at Tempelhof in a twenty-four-hour period. From late November through early December, the whole of Europe was enveloped in dense fog. The operation rotated between canceled flights and mad activity when the weather temporarily cleared.

On 5 December, a C-54 piloted by Captain Phelps took off from Fassberg late in the evening for the Gatow airfield in Berlin. Loaded to maximum weight with coal, an essential cargo for wintertime Berlin, the transport lifted off into marginal weather of a light drizzle and fog with a two hundred–foot ceiling and one-mile visibility. It crashed shortly after takeoff within two and a half miles of the airfield, killing all three crew members instantly. Although an official cause of the crash was never determined, it is believed that crew fatigue and a sense of urgency to keep flying were contributing factors.

Captain Phelps, as the pilot of a B-17 during World War II, had been awarded the Distinguished Flying Cross for flying bombing missions over Berlin. On his last wartime mission, he had been forced to bail out after his plane was destroyed by flak, and he had spent the last year of the war as a P.O.W. At the time of his death, he was flying his 167th mission over Berlin.[7]

11 December 1948

AMM3 Harry R. Crites

The only Navy fatality, Airman Machinist Mate 3rd Class (AMM3) Harry R. Crites, occurred when an R5D aircraft (a Navy version of the C-54) crashed near Koenigsberg, Germany. Crites, the flight engineer, was the only one on board killed.

7 January 1949

Capt. William A. Rathgeber
Pvt. Ronald E. Stone
Cpl. Norbert H. Theis
Sgt. Bernard J. Watkins
1st Lt. Lowell A. Wheaton
1st Lt. Richard M. Wurgel

On 7 January, a C-54 took off from Rhein-Main on a routine 2.75-hour flight to the maintenance facility at RAF Burtonwood in England, when it crashed thirty miles out. On board was the pilot, Wurgel, the copilot, Wheaton, the flight engineer, Watkins, the radio operator, Theis, and two passengers, Rathgeber and Stone.

The weather was good, only a light rain, and there was a six-mile visibility. They had already made contact with the tower at Burtonwood when the plane inexplicably crashed killing all on board. It was the only Operation Vittles crash in England, and the worst loss of life during the operation. A cause for the crash was never officially established.

12 January 1949

1st Lt. Craig B. Ladd
TSgt. Charles L. Putnam

Shortly after midnight on 12 January 1949, a C-54 crashed and burned four miles east of Rhein-Main. It was snowing, with a 1,500-foot ceiling, poor visibility, and strong winds. Two crew members were killed.

18 January 1949

1st Lt. Robert P. Weaver

Lt. Weaver was killed and two others injured when the C-54 he was piloting crashed and burned six miles east of the Fassburg RAF station. The C-54 was empty, returning from Berlin, and was on its final approach at 1:30 PM. Weaver initially survived the crash, only to die later from his burns.[8]

4 March 1949

1st Lt. Royce C. Stephens

On 4 March, 101 miles northeast of Frankfurt near the Soviet-zone village of Heroldishausen, a C-54 piloted by Stephens crashed after an oil leak in an engine resulted in the engine catching fire. Stephens remained at the controls to allow the crew and passengers to bail out, then placed the craft on autopilot. The plane struck the ground before he could exit the aircraft.[9]

12 July 1949

2nd Lt. Donald J. Leemon
TSgt. Herbert F. Heinig
1st Lt. Robert C. Von Luehrte

The only crash to occur after the lifting of the blockade occurred on 12 July, when a C-54 hauling ten tons of coal to Berlin crashed twelve miles west of Rathenow, in the Soviet zone. When both the Number 3 and Number 4 engines malfunctioned, Von Luehrte, the pilot, Leemon, the copilot, and Heinig, the flight engineer, all remained on board attempting to stabilize the aircraft as it rapidly lost altitude. All three were killed when the aircraft struck the ground. They were the last fatalities of Operation Vittles.[10]

Additionally, forty-three British and Commonwealth fliers and twenty ground personnel lost their lives in ten crashes with fatalities during the operation.[11]

[chapter four]

THE FIRST COLD WAR SHOOTDOWN, 1950

In the seaside city of Liepaja, along the Latvian coast, there is a monument dedicated "to the sailors and fisherman who perished in the sea." Atop a thirty-six-foot-high limestone pedestal, the bronze figure of a woman gazes out on the Baltic Sea, awaiting the return of her sailor. Unveiled in 1977, it is a popular meeting place for locals, and a frequent background for tourist photographs.

On 8 April 2000, with Latvian officials and the U.S. ambassador in attendance, a plaque was added to the pedestal to commemorate an event that had occurred fifty years earlier. The plaque reads, "In Memorial of the missing crew on the U.S. Navy PB4Y-2 aircraft BUNO#59645 shot down at sea off Liepāja on 8 April 1950."[1]

It then lists the crew's names:

> *Lt. Jack Fette, USNR*
> *Lt. Howard Seeschaf, USNR*
> *Lt. (j.g.) Robert D. Reynolds*
> *Ens. Tommy L. Burgess*
> *AT1 Frank L. Beckman*
> *AD1 Joe H. Danens*
> *AD1 Jack W. Thomas*
> *AL3 Joseph J. Bourassa*
> *CT3 Edward J. Purcell*
> *AT3 Joseph Rinnier*

U.S. Navy PB4Y-2 Privateer bomber (U.S. Naval Institute Photo Archive)

On that sunny afternoon of 8 April 1950, a U.S. Navy Consolidated PB4Y-2 "Privateer," designated "HB-7" of VP-26 (Patrol Squadron 26), took off on an electronic surveillance flight from Wiesbaden Air Force Base in West Germany with a crew of ten Navy men (four officers, six enlisted) on board. It was shot down by a flight of Soviet Lovochkin La-11 "Fang" fighters, the first "shootdown" of the Cold War. Although wreckage was recovered, no remains or survivors of the crew were located. In total, ninety servicemen would be lost in ten shootdowns off the coasts of Communist countries. However, high-altitude U.S. Air Force U-2 spy aircraft were shot down as they flew over the Soviet Union and Cuba during the Cold War.[2]

In 1950, VP-26 was home based at Port Lyautey, French Morocco. VP-26 was made up primarily of PB4Y-2 Privateers, with three of the craft assigned to Detachment A, at Wiesbaden. It was one of the first Navy units to fly hurricane reconnaissance missions; it also had participated in the Berlin Airlift. Later, it would support the "quarantine" during the Cuban Missile Crisis and fly missions in Vietnam. The three Privateers at Wiesbaden were specially configured for electronic reconnaissance and gathered intelligence on Soviet naval activity. They also tested the air defense response along the coasts of Eastern bloc countries.

The PB4Y-2 was the Navy single vertical tail version of the B-24 "Liberator" (the Navy had previously used unmodified B-24s, designated PB4Y-1), with four Pratt & Whitney R-1830-94 radial engines (1,350 horsepower each). It was designed as a long-range patrol bomber, and saw service in World War II. All armament had been removed from the Wiesbaden PB4Ys in August 1949 to make room for surveillance equipment. The PB4Y had a maximum speed of 237 miles per hour (382 kilometers per hour), a range of 2,820 miles (4,540 kilometers), and a service ceiling of 20,000 feet (7,000 meters).

On 8 April 1950, Lieutenant Fette's PB4Y, nicknamed "Turbulent Turtle," took off and headed north from Wiesbaden toward Copenhagen and the Baltic Sea on a "Ferret" flight. Ferret was a code name for aerial reconnaissance flights begun in 1949 to record and analyze Soviet radar and electronic equipment.[3]

Because of the lack of human intelligence coming out of the Soviet Union following the start of the Cold War, the United States and Great Britain attempted to fill intelligence gaps regarding Soviet industrial and military capacity through aerial reconnaissance. There were no satellites or high-altitude jets yet, and the vast territory of the Soviet Union made peripheral reconnaissance inadequate. Overflights became the only viable alternative, with a resulting improvement in air defense and interception by the Soviets.[4]

At 6:24 AM on 8 April, at the Soviet airfield at Kaliningrad (formerly Königsberg), a flight of four Soviet fighters scrambled on alert as yet another American "intruder" threatened to invade Soviet airspace. Sr. Lt. Boris Pavlovich Dokin took off with his wingman, Lt. Ivan Ivanovich Tezyaev, followed by Sr. Lt. Anatolij Stepanovich Gerasimov and his wingman, Lt. Yevgraf Satacv. They climbed to 13,000 feet and headed north to intercept the plane.[5]

At 4:39 PM, the "Turbulent Turtle" was flying at an altitude of 12,139 feet, five miles southwest of the Latvian coast, when it was intercepted by the flight of four Soviet "Fang" fighters piloted by Senior Lieutenant Dokin and his squadron. As part of the Soviet Air Defense Force, the National Air Defense Forces (Voiska Protivovozdushnoi Oborony Strany) were likely to be especially motivated because it was Soviet Air Defense Day.[6]

The La-11s were single-seat, piston-engine, long-range Soviet fighters with a maximum speed of 420 miles per hour (674 kilometers per hour), a range of 1,393 miles (2,235 kilometers), and a service ceiling of 33,620 feet (11,000 meters). They were armed with three 23-mm cannons, each with seventy-five rounds of ammunition.

The Soviet fighters took positions to the front and rear of the Privateer and both of the lead fighters rocked their wings and turned to the left, signaling the aircraft to follow. Rather than following, Fette turned to the right and made a sharp descent toward cloud cover below in an attempt to evade the fighters. The Soviets fired a warning burst, then targeted the PB4Y after claiming that the American aircraft returned fire, an impossibility considering its unarmed condition.[7]

The Soviets insisted the PB4Y had penetrated thirteen miles into Soviet territory, over Libau, Latvia, initially identifying it as a B-29, and maintained the aircraft had opened fire on the Soviet fighters. The Americans claimed the unarmed Privateer was on a navigation training flight to Copenhagen, Denmark.[8]

Later, Soviet pilot Gerasimov, in an on-camera interview with filmmaker Dirk Pohlmann for the Zweites Deutsches Fernsehen documentary "Shot Down Over the Soviet Union," stated, "[E]verything was known in advance about the Privateer

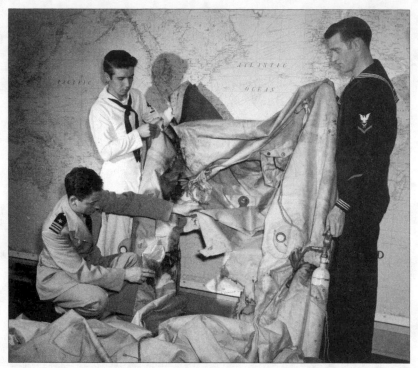

Lt. Cdr. M. W. Cagle, Wade E. Myers, YN3, and David M. Fentamaker, YN3, all assigned to the office of the Chief of Naval Operations (CNO), inspect two life rafts from the Privateer shot down by the Soviets on 8 April 1950. (U.S. Naval Institute Photo Archive)

flight," even the takeoff time. Gerasimov also stated the attack took place "approximately forty kilometers [twenty-five miles] off the coast." He reported seeing parachutes and receiving orders not to fire on the parachutists. They circled above during a rescue operation. Upon their return, they signed reports dictated to them by a senior officer.[9] Two Swedish fishing trawlers recovered two damaged life rafts and a nose wheel with a bullet hole in it among the debris.

An eight-day U.S. search and rescue effort was mounted. Although some wreckage was recovered, no survivors or remains of the crew were located, and the search was abandoned on 16 April. A day earlier, the commander of the U.S. Air Rescue Mission, Capt. D. J. Klinger, stated an inflated life raft had been spotted by a search plane, and that all of the supply pockets had been manually opened, suggesting at least some of the crew had survived the crash.[10]

Rumors circulated that members of the crew had survived, had been interrogated, then tried for espionage, and were sentenced to twenty-five-year terms of imprisonment in Soviet forced-labor camps. Some returning Americans reported rumors of one crew member in a prison camp near Taishet, Soviet Union. Other reports indicated as many as eight crew members survived the crash. To this date, Russian authorities maintain there are no Americans being held against their will in the former Soviet Union.[11]

Following the attack, the bomber was last seen by the Soviet pilots descending steeply into a cloud bank. Later, an inspection of the scarred pieces of wreckage fished from Baltic waters indicated that the aircraft had been on fire when it crashed into the sea.[12]

On 9 April 1950, the ten crew members were declared "presumed dead" and were posthumously awarded the Distinguished Flying Cross.

chapter five

ACTOR JAMES GARNER IN THE KOREAN WAR, 1950

Army Pvt. James Scott Bumgarner, later to be known as Hollywood actor James Garner, was the first draftee from the state of Oklahoma during the Korean War. His war story is unique but relatively unknown to the public.

Born 7 April 1928 in Norman, Oklahoma, to Weldon and Mildred Bumgarner, he is part Native American (on his mother's side). His heritage also includes early white settlers of the Oklahoma territory. His brother, Jack, became a professional baseball player, and at one time pitched for the Pittsburgh Pirates. Another brother, Charles, was a schoolteacher in Norman. Mildred Bumgarner died when James was six, from which time he was raised by grandparents, aunts, and uncles. Much of Garner's youth was spent around ranch hands, and he often rode horses to school. At Norman High School, he was an outstanding athlete in football, basketball, and track.

Garner suffered from wanderlust, and interrupted his schooling to spend a year as a merchant seaman on board a seagoing tug out of New Orleans. He then moved with his father to Los Angeles, where Weldon started a carpet contracting business. Garner attended Hollywood High School briefly before returning to Norman to finish his high school education, where he also joined the Oklahoma National Guard. Following graduation, he returned to Los Angeles to work with his father, but the Korean War broke out and he became the first draftee in Oklahoma to be called for duty.

After basic training, Private Bumgarner was assigned to the 5th Regimental Combat Team of the 24th Division (the Victory Division) and sent to Korea. He spent fourteen months in Korea, and was awarded two Purple Hearts, one of them for wounds received from friendly fire.

Actor James Garner. (Photofest)

Although he did not trade fire with the enemy for the first six or seven days he was in Korea, they were, he recalled, "long, bad" days. On his second day in Korea, he was wounded while on patrol. Hit in the hand and face with enemy shrapnel, he went back to an aid station and started picking bits of metal from his face using a jeep mirror. An officer came up and ordered him to go inside the aid station and have his wounds recorded and attended to. As a result, Garner was awarded his first Purple Heart. His second medal was conferred during a much more precarious situation.

One night Garner's combat team was overrun on a ridgeline by waves of Chinese ground forces. By morning, only about 40 of his group of 130 were still alive. After retreating all night, they joined with another unit early the next morning and watched as Navy F-9 Panther jets began air strikes against the Chinese positions. The American soldiers were elated and cheered the Navy fliers on until an AT-6 spotter plane flew over and misidentified Garner and his compatriots as another concentration of enemy troops.

They soon were under attack by Navy jets firing 20-mm rockets. Garner was hit in the back and his rifle was shattered. Spraying phosphorus from the rockets fired at the troops by the Navy planes hit Garner and others, burning them. Rather than remain a sitting target in his foxhole, he scurried out of his position and jumped off the side of a cliff. After suffering phosphorous burns on his neck and tearing up his shoulder and both knees, he finally came to a halt one hundred feet down the hill. A South Korean soldier who had also jumped down the cliff was in worse shape, suffering extensive burn wounds.

Garner, with no weapon but still wearing his helmet, and the South Korean, armed with a rifle, climbed back up to the ridgeline, and found they were alone. They saw no one along the ridge. Garner spoke no Korean, and the Korean soldier spoke no English, but both sensed they should move south along the ridgeline in order to catch up with their unit.

The two eventually reached the valley they had occupied the day before, only to come across a group of soldiers who were neither American nor South Korean. The large group of idle Communist Chinese soldiers paid little attention to the two men as they passed, probably thinking the Korean, who held the rifle behind Garner, was one of them and the American was his prisoner. Six hours later, still on the move, they heard the familiar sounds of Sherman tanks approaching. The Korean soldier immediately gave his rifle to Garner and took Garner's helmet, placing it on his head. He positioned himself ahead of Garner, giving the appearance to the American troops that he was Garner's prisoner and thus ensuring his own safety.

After recuperating from the minor phosphorous burns and his shoulder and knee injuries, Garner was transferred to Japan, where he worked in a base post office. During his nine months there, he made some major modifications to the postal facility, which was located in a bombed-out shoe factory. At one point, he needed materials to build a bar. When he did not get what he wanted, he simply did not deliver the mail to those who ignored his requests. It was not long before he had a bar stocked with the best whiskey, and regularly was receiving ice from a Graves Registration outfit. Garner built a theater in the largest part of the factory, and laid out a baseball diamond. He also had hot showers installed and provided the base with a swimming pool: he cleaned out the basement, cemented the floor, whitewashed the walls, and installed a ladder on the side of the "pool." Before leaving Japan, he received his second Purple Heart.

Garner was honorably discharged from the Army in June 1952. Upon being discharged, he wore the Combat Infantry Badge (CIB), the Purple Heart with Oak Leaf Cluster, the Korean Service Medal, the United Nations Service Medal, and the National Defense Service Medal.

Returning to his hometown, Garner began to study business administration at the University of Oklahoma. He left after completing one semester and headed west to Hollywood, where a chance encounter with an old friend marked the beginning of his theatrical career.

Garner is an actor who makes his work look easy. On both screen and stage, he displays exceptional versatility, and over the years he has matured into one of America's most admired stars.[1]

chapter six

CAPT. EUGENE S. KARPE, USN
Death on the Orient Express, 1950

On 23 February 1950, a railroad signal worker making a routine check of tunnel tele-graph lines found the badly mangled body of a man in the railroad tunnel south of Salzburg, Austria. Austrian police were contacted. In attempting to identify the dead man, they found U.S. Navy Capt. Eugene S. Karpe's diplomatic passport and service identification card among the torn clothes on the body. Since Captain Karpe had served for the past three years as naval attaché in Rumania, American officials in Washington said they were not eliminating the possibility that Karpe had been slain. Military attachés assigned to embassies around the world were trained in the gathering of foreign intel-ligence information and thus were closely watched by their counterparts at each station.[1]

Austrian police reported Captain Karpe had been en route to the United States for reassignment after serving as a U.S. naval attaché in Rumania. They surmised he had fallen from a door of the Arlberg-Orient Express as the train, traveling from Vienna to Paris, sped around a curve in the dark of night. The forty-five-year-old officer was the second-highest ranking American mysteri-ously killed in Austria since the end of World War II. The first, Irving Ross, an offi-cial of the Economic Cooperation Administration (a U.S. government agency set up in 1948 to administer the Marshall Plan), was found stabbed and beaten to death after having been seen in the company of four men wearing Russian uniforms.[2]

Captain Karpe was a close friend of Robert A. Vogeler, who earlier that week had been convicted as a spy and saboteur in Bucharest, Hungary, and sentenced by a People's court to five years in prison. Although Vogeler had attended the U.S. Naval Academy for two and a half years in the late 1920s (he resigned in 1931), it was not until March 1947 that he first met Karpe. After his Navy stint, Vogeler completed his college education at the Massachusetts Institute of Technology, earning a degree in

Capt. Eugene S. Karpe, USN. (U.S. Navy)

engineering. As an engineer turned businessman, he was a roving Eastern European representative of the International Telephone and Telegraph Company (ITT). The friendship deepened the mystery of Karpe's demise: the Austrian police later contended Karpe's death was not a suicide and did not seem to be an accident. U.S. Army authorities who entered the case said it looked like a planned job. Railroad men said all doors were locked automatically before the train entered the tunnel near Salzburg. A railroad employee expressed the conviction that Karpe had been murdered, since the train had doors that opened inward. Additionally, investigators found no blood around the body when it was found.[3]

The sleeping car from which Karpe fell or was thrown to his death was returned to Vienna for a thorough examination after being placed under guard. The car was made available to American investigators who checked and photographed its interior, windows, and doors. Austrian officials said that they had never heard of a person falling from such a car, which had very small windows. They added that it would be impossible for a large man like Karpe to go through the doors without turning sideward. Maximilian Pammer, Public Safety Director for the Austrian Interior Ministry, ruled out suicide or robbery concerning the incident. As to the question of whether it was an accident or a political murder, the case was kept open. He added there were no clues to substantiate either alternative. Passengers on the train were questioned by Austrian police. They reported that all of the passengers appeared to be legitimate travelers and that there was no reason to suspect them of having any part in Captain Karpe's death. One of the key passengers whom the Army questioned was Milburn R. McKitchum, of Forest Grove, Oregon, a student, who may have been the last person to see Karpe alive on board the train. In a ship-to-shore telephone interview, McKitchum, heading for New York on board the RMS *Queen Mary*, said he had breakfast and lunch with Karpe on the day he was killed. McKitchum said Karpe had had an ordinary breakfast, then a bottle of mineral water for lunch. He declared nothing had occurred that raised any suspicion the naval attaché was in danger. McKitchum declined to answer certain other questions, pending his interrogation in New York by U.S. Army agents.

Captain Karpe had visited the Vogeler home in Vienna the day following Robert Vogeler's sentencing. The Belgium-born Mrs. Vogeler and her two sons lived in the city where Mr. Vogeler operated his ITT branch office. She told investigators that Captain Karpe was one of her husband's very dearest friends. His death was a terrible shock to Lucile Vogeler. The authorities concluded there was no proof one way or the other as to whether Karpe's death was linked with the spy conviction of Vogeler.

Captain Karpe's brother-in-law told the United Press in Delhi, Louisiana, that during Karpe's last visit home he mentioned that he dreaded returning to Europe, where, he said, he was stalked by Communists who watched his every move.

An autopsy performed on Karpe's body in the U.S. Army hospital in Munich on 25 February ended inconclusively. At this point, the U.S. Army announced that a joint Army–Navy commission would be established to investigate the case further. The subsequent commission finding was inconclusive.[4]

Memorial services were held at the U.S. Naval Advanced Base in Bremerhaven, Germany, on 4 March. Two weeks later, Captain Karpe was buried with full military honors at Arlington National Cemetery.[5]

Robert Vogeler was released from prison after serving seventeen months of his sentence. In his book, *I Was Stalin's Prisoner* (1951), he wrote the following about his good friend Captain Karpe:

> *The rumor that Karpe was drunk and had fallen out of his compartment as the Arlberg Express went through the tunnel was a libel. He was not drinking at the time, because of gout, and he was completely sober in the dining car before his death. The CIC [Counter-Intelligence Corps, Vienna] experimented*

with sandbags of the same weight as Karpe (200 pounds) and thus confirmed, beyond any possibility of doubt, that he had been thrown from his compartment. His body caromed off the side of the tunnel and fell beneath the wheels of the train. In order to achieve the same result with a sandbag, it was necessary for two CIC agents to hurl it out of a similar compartment with all the force at their command.

Fish Karpe was a fun-loving bachelor who had enjoyed considerable success as a ladies' man. He had often traveled between Bucharest and Vienna on the Orient section of the Arlberg Express and he told Lucile Vogeler that on several trips he had met the same Hungarian blonde. He had met her again on his last trip to Vienna, and as usual she was on her way to Paris. Fish had made a date to meet her there on his way through to Washington. It was impossible, given the AVH's [Hungarian State Defense Authority] passport regulations, for anyone, even an attractive blonde, to travel repeatedly between Paris and Budapest except on official business. Fish had evidently been hoping to learn what her official business was.

Later, when Lucile herself became involved with the Vienna underworld, she learned of Matyas Rakosi's mistress. Old "Potato Head" [nickname for Matyas Rakosi who was the Vice Minister and Secretary General of the Hungarian Communist Party] was officially married to a Soviet "citizenness" of Mongolian origin. His unofficial wife, however, conformed exactly to the description of the blonde whom Fish had intended to meet in Paris. Even their Budapest addresses were the same. Lucile concluded, therefore, that Rakosi's mistress had something to do with Karpe's assassination. A young Rumanian, Rian Tarescu, later confessed to the Swiss police that he and two other Communist students, on orders received from a "foreign organization," overpowered Karpe and pushed him to his death. [The confession was never corroborated or taken seriously.] [6]

Eugene Simon Karpe was born in Delhi, Louisiana, on 21 August 1904. He attended Delhi High School, and entered the U.S. Naval Academy, Annapolis, Maryland, on appointment from the Fifth District of Louisiana in 1922. While there, he played class and varsity baseball for four years. Graduated and commissioned ensign on 3 June 1926, he subsequently advanced in rank, attaining that of captain in 1944. Captain Karpe (nicknamed "Fish" by his shipmates) commanded destroyers in both the Atlantic and Pacific theaters during World War II. On 20 August 1946, he was detached from the Chief of Naval Operations, Navy Department, Washington, DC, and assigned as a U.S. Naval Member of Allied Control Commission, U.S. Army Forces, Bucharest, Romania, for duty as naval attaché.[7]

The mysterious death of Capt. Eugene Simon Karpe, USN, remains unsolved to this day.

[chapter seven]

CIA OFFICERS JOHN T. DOWNEY AND RICHARD G. FECTEAU
Prisoners in China for Two Decades, 1952–73

On 25 June 1998, Director of Intelligence George Tenet presented the Director's Medal to Judge John T. "Jack" Downey and Richard G. Fecteau. Downey and Fecteau had been captured by the Chinese in 1952 while conducting agent resupply and pickup operations as part of the nation's war effort in Korea. This was their first overseas assignment. In 1954, China sentenced Fecteau to twenty years and Downey to life imprisonment. Late in 1971, nearly twenty years later, China released Fecteau; in March 1973, China released Downey. Following their release, they returned to work for the Central Intelligence Agency (CIA) and eventually retired.

The following are excerpts from the remarks made by Director Tenet at the awards ceremony:

I know that I speak for everyone in this room, and everyone in this Agency, when I say, welcome home, Jack Downey and Dick Fecteau—two great heroes of the CIA! Welcome back to the CIA!

You have never left our thoughts—not during your long years of imprisonment, and not during the decades following your retirement from the Agency. We are forever proud that you are our colleagues. You have been an inspiration to the intelligence officers who served with you, and to the generations who followed you.

Your story, simply put, is one of the most remarkable in the fifty-year history of the Central Intelligence Agency.

Director of Intelligence George Tenet standing between CIA officers Richard G. Fecteau (to his right) and John T. "Jack" Downey, taken at a ceremony where both officers were awarded the Director's Medal, 25 June 1998. (Photograph provided by the CIA History Staff)

It is the story of a daring flight over Manchuria during the Korean War. The mission: to swoop down and snatch out our imperiled agent. It is the story of an ambush—of a crash landing—and of capture. Of being declared missing and presumed dead, only to reappear very much alive two years later for a Red Chinese "show trial," where Dick was sentenced to twenty years and Jack received a life sentence.

Even more remarkable is the story of how these brave men endured decades of imprisonment, regained their freedom, and went on to live full and active lives, marked by service to their communities and their country.

Shortly after his return to the United States, Jack told his debriefer: "You come out of captivity basically about the same as you go in." Jack Downey and Dick Fecteau went in as young men—Jack was all of 22; Dick was 25. What they took in with them was the character and the values that they learned from their parents: integrity and honor and commitment to country. . . .

Phil and Jessie Fecteau, decent, down-to-earth people with an abiding devotion to this country, believed deeply that what their boy was doing was important to U.S. security and that they must do nothing to jeopardize that. Throughout nineteen cruel years of waiting, they put unquestioning faith in their government, in this Agency in particular. I pray that they never felt that their faith was misplaced.

There is no adequate way to describe the uncommon grace and fortitude with which the Downey and Fecteau families bore their burdens of grief. And to that awful weight of worry was added the burden of silence. . . .

Just imagine what it was like to hear that your son was missing and presumed dead, only to learn years later that he is imprisoned in Red China. . . .

I know that Dick and Jack feel deeply to have had such wonderful parents, and to have such wonderful families. Dick's wife Peg regrettably couldn't be with us today, due to a very sore back. And Dick's mother, Jessie, also is unable to be with us to share today's honor with her son, but we send them both warmest good wishes and know they are with us in spirit. Twin daughters Sidnice and Suzon are here. The girls were three-years old when their father was captured.

Jack's wife Audrey is here. Audrey's and Jack's marriage is a wonderful, life-affirming story in itself. Jack met Audrey Lee when he went back to New Haven after his release to visit Yale, his alma mater. Audrey is a naturalized American citizen who was born in China, coincidentally ten miles from the place where Jack was shot down. Their son, John Lee Downey, starts Wesleyan University this Fall. We also welcome Jack's brother Bill, who worked tirelessly for his release, together with Bill's wife Jean.

It is wonderful to have multiple generations of the Fecteau and Downey families here today. I'm sure that there isn't a day that goes by that Dick and Jack aren't grateful to be surrounded by your love. I salute you all.

But beyond your immediate families, we would like to think that you also feel that you have another family—your extended Agency family. There are folks here today who kept in touch with your loved ones and managed your personal affairs all these years. I know that they saw it not as a duty, but as a sacred trust. . . .

Shortly after Dick and Jack were captured, they were separated, and spent two years in solitary confinement, much of the time under interrogation and in chains. But Dick's sense of humor never left him.

On the day of their "show trial" in 1954—remember Dick and Jack had not seen one another for two years—Dick was marched into the courtroom through a battery of lights and cameras. Jack is already standing in the dock. For propaganda effect, Jack has been outfitted in a new, black padded suit, clothes, shoes, and a beanie hat. Dick sees that Jack is looking rather down and figures he needs cheering up. They order Dick to go stand next to Jack. He walks over to Jack and whispers: "Who's your tailor?"

Until Dick's release in 1971, and Jack's in 1973, the two men were listed in our personnel files as serving on "Special Detail Foreign" at "Official Station Undetermined." And serve they did. Not in the ordinary way, of course—but in a most extraordinary way. How did they serve? By keeping their faith in our country, and by being faithful to it no matter what. . . .

One of the many things we all admire about you is that neither of you have let your experiences make you bitter. When a reporter asked Jack how he'd describe the twenty years he spent in prison, he answered, "They were a crashing bore! I won't dwell upon the past because I'm too preoccupied with the present and the future." Since their release, both Dick and Jack have made every day count. . . .

Dick elected to retire from the CIA in the mid-1970s, after over twenty-five years of service. He had to be convinced to stay that long. In Dick's words: "I did not want them to make work for me. It would embarrass the life out of me." As if he hadn't done enough for this Agency and this country already! Dick later joined the staff of his alma mater, Brown University, and became Assistant Director of Athletics. He retired from the university in 1989.

Jack also opted for retirement. When he was offered the opportunity to stay, he quipped: "You know I just don't think I am cut out for that kind of work!" After leaving the Agency, at age 43, Jack enrolled in Harvard Law School. He practiced law privately for a number of years, was appointed by the Governor of Connecticut to a number of public service positions, and even started a run for Senator of Connecticut (Jack calls it his other crash!) In 1987, Jack became a Judge, like his father before him. . . .

Dick and Jack, you can be as modest as you like. But we cannot see it that way. What you did—the way you did it—is a proud part of our history that we will never forget.

You demonstrated one kind of heroism when you signed on to that perilous mission in wartime and crash-landed and survived and endured those early interrogations.

You demonstrated heroism of a whole other magnitude during those dark days of captivity that followed. In those endless years, heroism meant getting through another day, and then another, and then another, with your dignity, and your humanity, and your will, and your wit, and your honor, and your hope intact. . . .

When they came in 1971 to tell Dick he was being freed, his first question was: "What about Jack Downey?" And after his return home, when Dick was offered piles of money to tell his story, he refused the offers—despite his family's modest means—for fear that publicity would harm Jack's chances of freedom.

Two years after Dick's release, Jack's day of freedom finally arrived. Jack has described his reaction as thinking to himself: "Well, Christ, it's about time."

In this—our fiftieth anniversary year—it is also about time that you and Dick received the small tribute we confer today by presenting you with the Director's Medal. I do this on behalf of my predecessors because all of us know that at the end of the day men like the two of you—with wonderful families behind them—have sacrificed everything with grace and courage and in absolute anonymity to serve this Agency and our country. We have been truly blessed to call you our colleagues and friends.

The words inscribed on the back of the medal are simple, yet direct— Extraordinary Fidelity and Essential Service. Better words were never written to describe Jack Downey and Dick Fecteau.

We will always be grateful to you and to your extraordinary families for all that you did for our country.[1]

★ ★ ★

John Downey, a native of Wallingford, Connecticut, joined the Central Intelligence Agency in June 1951. Fecteau joined the Agency a few months later in October. Downey was a Yale graduate. Fecteau, after attending the Merchant Marine Academy for two years, transferred to Boston University and was recruited after graduation by the CIA. They were outgoing, intelligent young men. Both had played varsity football. Because of their athletic abilities, they were trained as paramilitary officers. When they joined the Agency, the Korean War was in its second year and America and its United Nations' Allies were engaged in fierce air and ground warfare with Chinese and North Korean forces. The Chinese had committed more than 150,000 soldiers to support a faltering North Korean army; MiG-15 jet aircraft piloted by Chinese, North Korean, and Soviet pilots flew into battle from Manchurian air bases.

Following their training, Downey and Fecteau were assigned to a CIA facility in East Asia and joined an ongoing operation (Operation Tropic) which involved the exploitation of a potential mainland Chinese "Third Force." CIA-trained anti-Communist Chinese agents were to be air-dropped into specific areas in China where they would link up with antigovernment guerillas to form resistance networks. The agents were to engage in intelligence collection primarily, but also in sabotage and psychological warfare, and to report their progress by radio. The operation was modeled after the successful experiences enjoyed by the OSS in the European Theater during World War II. The European operation readily received the cooperation of occupied citizens, while in China no such support was realized.

Due to a lack of resources, it was not until April 1952 that Chinese agents were trained and dropped into Southern China. The initial team of four agents was either captured or killed: they were never heard from again. The next team, trained by Downey, was dropped into the Kirin province of Manchuria in mid-July 1952. The five Chinese agents made radio contact with the CIA facility in South Korea and they were resupplied by airdrops in August and October. Another agent was dropped into the area to act as a courier between the operatives on the ground and a CIA facility not in Korea. In November, the operatives reported they had made

U.S. Air Force rending of the Fulton aerial retrieval system, or Skyhook. Aircraft shown is similar to the Civil Air Transport (CAT/CIA contract airline) plane Downey and Fecteau were in when the craft was shot down over Manchuria, China, in 1952. (USAF)

contact with Chinese dissidents and obtained important documents. They asked that the courier be picked up as soon as possible.[2]

During World War II, extraction of personnel behind enemy lines was accomplished by hazardous land routes and by light aircraft such as the British Lysander, which flew agents both in and out of enemy-held territory. However, an American, Lytle S. Brown, invented a mail pickup system in the 1920s that All American Aviation perfected. The system used two steel poles, placed fifty-four feet apart, with a transfer line strung between them. An approaching aircraft would glide over the ground station at ninety miles per hour as a flight mechanic paid out a fifty-foot steel cable. As the pilot nosed the aircraft skyward, a four-finger grapple at the end of the cable engaged the transfer rope. The flight mechanic then would winch the mail pouch on board.

By 1943, the Army Air Force began to suffer heavy losses in bomber aircraft during raids over enemy targets in Europe. The loss of aircraft and crew members led to tests of the All American extraction system for pilots downed in enemy territory. Early test results were not encouraging. Recording instruments displayed accelerations of seventeen G's and higher following a pickup, a force the human body would not tolerate. Subsequent modifications of the system lowered the acceleration rate to seven G's, acceptable for live testing. Sheep were used as test animals during early live testing.

While in captivity, Downey and Fecteau were used as props in a Chinese Communist propaganda photograph, one of many taken of the men along with a B-29 crew. Downey is at center in glasses, with his head higher than anyone else's. Fecteau is center right, standing at the table in left profile. (Photograph provided by the CIA History Staff)

A paratrooper, Lt. Alex Doster, volunteered to be the first human to test the system. On 5 September 1943, Doster was successfully extracted from his ground position by a Stinson aircraft and was retrieved in less than three minutes.

As previously mentioned, the CIA was endeavoring to establish a resistance network in Manchuria during the Korean War. The Civil Air Transport (CAT), the CIA contract airline, tested the All American extraction system as a means of bringing agents out of Manchuria. Static pickup tests were conducted in Japan in the fall of 1952. Following the successful retrieval of mechanic Ronald E. Lewis, the Agency was satisfied it had found the answer to recovering their agents safely from the Chinese mainland.[3]

On 20 November, the agent team in Manchuria was contacted by radio and told the courier would be air snatched at midnight on 29 November. CAT pilots Norman Schwartz and Robert Snoddy, both trained in aerial pickups, were charged with the mission. Initially, Chinese crew members were selected to operate the winch but it was decided that they lacked the training to ensure a successful air snatch. Two CAT personnel were selected to replace them but were pulled off the mission because they lacked the necessary clearances. Downey and Fecteau were ordered to fill the breach. They were given intensive training the week of 24 November and were ready to go the evening of 29 November.

As Schwartz and Snoddy started the engines of an unmarked C-47 Skytrain transport on a South Korean airfield near Seoul, Downey and Fecteau climbed on board. Their route to the pickup point in Manchuria was four hundred miles away, about three hours of flight time. The flight was uneventful, and Downey and Fecteau enjoyed the smooth ride. It was a cold evening, and the skies were clear; a full moon illuminated the snow-blanketed landscape below. But there was trouble ahead. Unbeknownst to the pilots and agents, the team on the ground had been captured by Communist Chinese security forces and forced to reveal the details of the pickup. The radio request for a courier pickup was a ruse and they were flying into a trap.

The C-47 flew over the designated area around midnight and saw the proper light signal blinking in the darkness below. Downey and Fecteau pushed out equipment necessary for the air snatch to the agents on the ground. Up in the cockpit, Schwartz flew the aircraft away from the area to allow time for the ground personnel to set up the poles and line for the pickup. After about forty-five minutes, Schwartz flew back into the area and made a practice run. This notified those on the ground that the next pass would be for the pickup of the courier. Several people were sighted, including a man in a harness ready for the air snatch.

Schwartz slowed the aircraft to sixty knots and started to make his run. What no one noticed was the sudden appearance of two .50-caliber antiaircraft guns that had been camouflaged under white sheets matching the snowbound terrain. Just as the C-47 passed over the pickup site, a thunderous fire erupted from the guns, sending a hail of shells into the low-flying transport. As Communist security troops emerged from the woods, the aircraft lost power, crashed into a bank of trees, and caught fire as tracer shells continued to rake the downed aircraft. Both Schwartz and Snoddy were killed. Downey and Fecteau were thrown from the wreckage. Miraculously, they survived, suffering only some cuts and bruises. The two stunned agents were quickly captured by the surrounding Chinese. One of their captors who spoke English said to them, "You are very lucky to survive a crash like this, but your future is dark!" Following the shootdown and loss of the two agents, no CIA officer would fly over mainland China again.

After questioning by Chinese security agents at a nearby police station, Downey and Fecteau were taken by truck and train to a prison in Shenyang (also known as Mukden), the largest city in Manchuria. They were put in heavy leg irons and held in solitary confinement for five months.

Although a radio message was received by the agent team that the pickup had been successful (no doubt sent by the defecting team to the CIA field team in Korea), CIA feared the worst when the plane failed to return the next morning. A CIA cover story was immediately put together that declared a CAT aircraft en route from Korea to Japan on 3 December was lost at sea. Downey and Fecteau were identified as Army civilian employees. A search of the flight route was conducted by the U.S.

military with negative results. Had the Chinese captured any of the crew, they would no doubt have made propaganda use of the incident. Since the Chinese made no mention of the incursion in the days that followed, CIA determined the men were dead. Letters of condolence were sent to the Downey and Fecteau families. On 4 December 1953, CIA declared both agents "presumed dead."

From Shenyang, the two agents were transferred to Peking's infamous Green Basket Prison built during the Ching Dynasty. Interrogation of the agents began in earnest when the two were imprisoned in the Green Basket "hellhole." The Chinese used many of the same techniques used on captured American military personnel in the Korean ground war. Interrogations could last from four to twenty-four hours. The agents were not allowed to sleep during the day, then would be awakened in the middle of the night for more interrogation after very little sleep. The Chinese emphasized they were the only ones who knew the two men were alive, and perhaps no one would ever know until the Chinese decided their fate. They were told the U.S. government did not care about them and to forget their families. Downey said after his release, "I was extremely scared. . . . We were isolated and had no idea of what was going to happen to us and had no idea of what was going on in the world."

Fecteau recalled that though he was never beaten, the mental pressure was enormous. He was placed in a five by eight–foot cell with one heavy door, no windows, and a fifteen-watt lightbulb in the ceiling. He could not hear anything and began to have mental aberrations. The Chinese interrogators pressed the two agents to admit they were CIA spies and reveal all they knew about Agency operations in China, CIA bases in countries bordering China, and the names of personnel. They both kept to their cover story that they worked for CAT. That story was blown, however, when American wire releases identified them as Army civilians. Interrogations became more intense and each had to improvise when confronted by harsh questioning. Neither had been trained in "interrogation resistance." Since both (especially Downey) knew much about Third Force operations, they found themselves in a precarious situation. They had been told during their training that if they were captured by the Communists, they might just as well tell them what they wanted to know because the Chinese would get it out of them eventually.

In time, the men began to break down psychologically. Threatened with death, the battered agents began to reveal partial truths. Downey was particularly vulnerable, since the team of agents he trained had turned on him and revealed the details of the Third Force operation. Finally, sixteen days after their capture, Downey admitted his CIA affiliation. Fecteau, on the other hand, was relatively unknown to the Chinese agents trained by Downey since he had spent such a short time in East Asia before being assigned to the pickup mission. He decided to use a simple cover story that his interrogators could not check. His story would be that he had only been with the Agency for five months and was told only what he "needed to

know." As for the names of people, he would give only first names. When the interrogators asked for physical descriptions, he would give the physical characteristics
of his fellow teammates on the Boston University football team. On the thirteenth
day after their capture, Fecteau, using his concocted cover story, confessed. His story
held up and he was able to withhold additional information safely throughout his
imprisonment.[4]

The two captives were eventually moved to Beijing where they were put on trial
as spies by a military court. They were informed that they could be shot for any of
the charges against them. Their Chinese lawyer did not argue the court's charges,
and merely pleaded for mercy. It had been two years since their capture and the
first time they were together again. The tribunal convicted Downey as the "chief
culprit" and Fecteau as the "assistant chief culprit." Downey was given a life sentence
and Fecteau a sentence of twenty years. The Chinese publically announced the
capture, conviction, and sentencing of the two agents on 23 November 1954. CIA
quickly changed the men's status from "presumed dead" to "missing in action." The
two agents were put back on the active payroll. From that point on, CIA assigned
administrative personnel to handle all aspects of their situation. Their efforts were
focused on pay and allotments, promotions, and maintenance of accrued funds.
When Downey and Fecteau were released, they were informed that they had been
promoted on a regular basis over the years, which included step increases. At the
time of their capture, their government pay grade level was GS-7, which equated
to an annual salary of $4,000. When they were released, they were startled to learn
their grade level was now GS-14 and their annual salary $22,000. Downey's accrued
funds were more than $170,000, and Fecteau's were about $140,000.

CIA also worked closely with the men's families to meet their needs. The prisoners were allowed to receive monthly packages and their families made several trips
to China to visit them. Though their CIA affiliation had to remain secret to the
American public, the Agency did disburse funds through various intermediary agencies to cover travel expenses.

While in captivity, the Agency worked tirelessly for their release. It argued
for official U.S. efforts to induce the Chinese to free them. It monitored State
Department efforts and those of other government agencies regarding the matter. All
came to naught, since U.S. policy at the time was no recognition of the Communist
Chinese government. By the early 1970s, relations between the two countries began
to thaw. That year—the year of "ping-pong diplomacy," the lifting of U.S. trade
restrictions, National Security Adviser Henry Kissinger's secret mission to China,
and the seating of the People's Republic of China at the United Nations—led to the
release of American prisoners, including Downey and Fecteau.

Nineteen years after his capture, Fecteau was released in December 1971. He
was taken by train to Shumchun, the border town between China and Hong Kong.
He was turned over to two armed guards who led him to a wooden footbridge. He

Downey is shown after his release at Shumchun, China, on 12 December 1973. Fecteau had been released in December 1971. Fecteau and Downey each had been held in captivity by the Communist Chinese for about twenty years. (Photograph provided by the CIA History Staff)

was told to cross to the other side and he would be free. A lone Hong Kong police officer met him on the other side, and took him to a military post. The American consul was contacted. After a brief stay in Hong Kong, Fecteau was flown to the United States and taken to the Valley Forge Army Hospital in Pennsylvania. During the next two months, he was given a battery of medical and psychological tests that he passed with flying colors. Amazingly, he suffered no traumatic effects.

Downey was returned to U.S. control on 12 December 1973, walking across the same footbridge as Fecteau had crossed two years earlier. He was one of 591 American military and civilian prisoners of war who were released during Operation Homecoming in 1973. Downey and Fecteau were returned to the CIA's East Asia Division as operations officers and underwent a series of debriefings. Both were in good physical and mental condition, although they both found their readjustment difficult since they had stepped into a completely changed world.[5]

Both agents later retired from the Agency, Downey in 1976 and Fecteau a year later. Both have led full productive lives since retirement. Jack Downey went to Harvard Law School, practiced law, and became a judge in Connecticut specializing in juvenile court cases. Now semiretired, he continues to practice law. In September 2002, he was honored during a ceremony to name the New Haven Juvenile Matters Courthouse and Detention Center after him. Dick Fecteau returned to his alma mater, Boston University, where he was appointed assistant athletic director. He retired from that position in 1989.[6]

In July 2002, Downey returned to China as part of a joint search team under the auspices of the Joint Task Force for Full Accounting. The team traveled to the Skytrain crash site in Northern China to search for the remains of Schwartz and Snoddy. Though they located the site and recovered remnants of the aircraft wreckage, they were unable to find crew-related items or signs of graves. The team had been told by the Chinese government the charred remains of the pilots had been found and buried at the snow-covered crash site.[7]

[chapter eight]

NO KUM-SOK
Operation Moolah, 1953

North Korea invaded South Korea during the morning hours of 25 June 1950. Staggered by the sudden intrusion, South Korean forces were forced to make a hasty retreat toward the southernmost Korean port of Pusan. President Harry S. Truman decided to commit U.S. armed forces to the defense of the beleaguered nation. The U.S. Chiefs of Staff appointed Gen. Douglas MacArthur Commander-in-Chief Far East, and placed the Seventh Fleet under his command. The United Nations called on its member nations to take equal action: sixteen countries committed combat forces while five sent medical units. The first American support elements to arrive in country from Japan were two battalions of the 24th Infantry Division that disembarked at Pusan. A bitter battle ensued as the Americans and South Koreans fought to slow the enemy advance. Within a matter of days, a Pusan perimeter was established, which allowed additional American troops and equipment to land. With a reconstituted South Korean army, the retreat was halted.[1]

While the ground fighting continued, Seventh Fleet aircraft from the carriers *Valley Forge* and the British light carrier *Triumph* together with land-based fighters and bombers destroyed bridges, oil refineries, and supply lines, and flew close ground support for the growing army of UN ground troops fighting their way out of the perimeter. Although the North Korean air force was destroyed, a new Soviet-designed jet fighter, the MiG-15, soon appeared in the skies and initially dominated the air war. American P-51 Mustangs, F-80 Shooting Stars, and F-84 Thunder jets were no match for the high-altitude interceptor. The MiG-15 armed with cannons could reach Mach 1, was highly maneuverable, and could remain in the air for more than an hour. It was not until December 1950 that a comparable American jet fighter, the F-86 Sabre-jet, arrived to take on and match the capability of the MiG fighter.[2]

North Korean Air Force pilot Sr. Lt. No Kum-Sok. (National Museum of the United States Air Force, Research Division)

Enter Operation Moolah . . . the extraordinary attempt by the United States to procure a combat-ready Soviet MiG-15 fighter. Operation Moolah made this offer: if a North Korean, Chinese, or Soviet MiG pilot defected and flew a MiG aircraft to a USAF airfield in South Korea, the reward would be $100,000. Offering money rewards for weapons and defections was nothing new. History records many such campaigns during wartime. The "MiG for money" idea surfaced in 1952 by a war correspondent who wrote about a fictional interview with a USAF general about enticing a Communist pilot to fly a MiG-15 to an Allied airfield. The USAF staff in Japan liked the idea and forwarded a revised version of the story to Washington. The concept was approved at the highest level and Gen. Mark Clark, U.S. Army Commander-in-Chief Far East Command, was authorized to offer such a reward to a defecting pilot. Revisions to the plan offered political asylum and, in the way of reward, an initial $50,000 to the enemy pilot and an additional $50,000 to the first MiG pilot to defect. The plan was ready to be put in to operation on 20 April 1953.[3]

The campaign was kicked off on that date by radio announcements and the mass dropping of leaflets by B-29 aircraft. The leaflets were printed in three languages: Korean, Chinese, and Russian. They read as follows:

> *Subject: A Road to Freedom*
> *Pilots! The Far East Command offers its help to all brave pilots who wish to free themselves from the vicious whip of the Communist regime and start a new and better life, with proper honor in the Free World.*
>
> *The Far East Command offers you refuge, protection, human care and attention. You are given full guarantee that your names will remain secret if you so desire. Pilots! Your brave move will bring you to freedom and will give you opportunity to live in the future without fear for your well-being. Besides that, your heroism and decision will help others by pointing to them the road to freedom.*
>
> *The Far East Command will reward $50,000 United States dollars to any pilot who delivers a modern, operational, combat jet aircraft in flyable condition to South Korea. The first pilot who delivers such a jet aircraft to the Free World will receive a bonus of an additional 50,000 U.S. dollars for his bravery.*
>
> *Following is a list of instructions to all pilots who desire to free themselves from the Communist yoke. Escapee pilots will fly to Paengyong-do Island, fifty (50) kilometers [thirty-one miles] south of Chodo Island. From Paengyong-do escapee pilots will proceed to Kimpo Air Base at 6100 meters [twenty thousand feet] altitude, descend over Kimpo Air Base, and proceed to make an immediate landing. UN Aircraft will accompany escapee remaining always above and behind, unless low clouds or visibility prevent escapee from locating Kimpo Air Base. If escapee is unable to make a visual let-down, he will proceed to the Seoul area at 6100 meters [twenty thousand feet] and circle with his gear down. A United States aircraft will then fly close abreast and lead the way to the landing field. Upon initial contact with UN Aircraft, or if at any time UN Aircraft attempts attack, escapee will immediately lower landing gear and rock wings violently.*
>
> *The Free World shall welcome you as an old friend as well as a hero.*
> *Mark Clark*
> *General, United States Army Commander-in-Chief*
> *Far East Command*[4]

B-29 Super-Fortresses dropped more than 1 million of the leaflets along the Yalu River on 26 April 1953 and another five hundred thousand over Siniju and

Uiju airfields in mid-May. Radio broadcasts beamed the reward offer continuously along the "Bamboo Curtain." There were no takers before the Armistice was signed on 27 July 1953.

However, Operation Moolah appeared to have an effect on the Soviets in particular. There had been rumors of dissatisfaction among Soviet air personnel. Allied broadcasts were immediately jammed by the Russians, and all Soviet pilots were grounded for several days. Perhaps there was some real fear of defections. When the Russians did take to the air again, it was as if a different cadre of pilots appeared. Though aggressive, the Russians were noticeably lacking in flying skills. During the last ninety days of the war, MiG losses were astronomical. During that period, Allied air forces shot down 165 MiGs at the cost of three planes lost. Some World War II–experienced pilots compared it to the famous "Mariana's Turkey Shoot," when the Japanese air fleet was practically destroyed. It is the opinion of some historians that the Russians, fearful of defections, only committed young politically correct pilots to engage in combat. These pilots were eager but were no match for the combat-hardened and highly skilled Allied fliers.

Shortly after the armistice was signed, a MiG-15bis suddenly flew into the air space north of Kimpo Air Base. No one on the ground sighted the southbound aircraft, since it approached the duty runway against the flight pattern. The MiG-15bis was the latest version of the jet fighter. It had a VK-1 engine that produced six thousand pounds of thrust, enabling the aircraft to fly at 669 miles per hour.[5]

The pilot flying the MiG was Sr. Lt. No Kum-Sok, a twenty-one-year-old North Korean Air Force Officer. In his later published book, *A MiG-15 to Freedom*, he described his approach and landing at Kimpo.

> *Flying at full throttle, I banked my jet fighter sharply to the right and leveled off on a 170-degree compass heading for the Americans at Kimpo Air Base. I could hear the sound of my heart pumping blood. Fifty heartbeats later I reached the border.*
>
> *Speeding southward at 7,000 meters (23,000 feet) in the cramped and cold cockpit of the Soviet built MiG-15, I watched wisps of clouds pass by below and looked down for the truce line and into the sky for enemy jets. Straining my dark-green oxygen hose and the wire to the two microphones strapped to each side of my throat, I twisted my neck left and right and looked high and low. The sky seemed safe for the time being from American Sabres and from Communist MiGs.*
>
> *My commitment to land at an American air base was now unalterable: I had come too far to return. The pilot who had taken off a few minutes before me had already landed his MiG alone at the Communist airfield. I was especially concerned with landing safely so that I could prove that I was trying to escape and not attacking the American base. If I were shot down by a Sabre and survived, I knew I would be captured and imprisoned as a prisoner of war and*

would be unable to show that I was trying to escape. This fear had restrained me from defecting months earlier.

I saw no puffs of smoke that would be a sign of gunfire from the ground at the truce line that twisted east-west among the jagged hills and mountains from coast to coast. I still faced the danger of antiaircraft fire and patrolling American Sabres. My silver craft skipped along on its swept-back wings that glistened in the sunlight. Far ahead, among ragged mountains flanked on the right by the Yellow Sea and to the southeast by the great, scarred city of Seoul, I could see the strangely dark runway at Kimpo. Although tense, I was pleased that I had reached my destination. Specks of a few Sabres were taking off and landing in a northerly direction, revealing another problem, the wind was out of the north. I would have to land with the wind at my back, for I dared not circle the field and risk being shot down by ground fire or giving American pilots a longer look at me.

I would ride the tailwind down, just as I and many other North Korean, Russian, and Chinese pilots had often done at the Dandong airfield to escape attacking American jet fighters. Peering into the sky ahead, I pulled back on the throttle and began to descend as the radio squawked into my helmet, "Eighty-seven, letter?" meaning, "Number eighty-seven, where the hell are you?" I did not answer. Up to the last moment, my North Korean commanders did not suspect that their "ever faithful Red pilot," No Kum-Sok, was escaping.

I descended directly to the runway in the wrong direction. Remarkably, none of the American pilots recognized my aircraft for what it was, a fully armed Red air force jet fighter heading directly for their home field. In fact, I do not think any American pilot or anyone else saw me coming at all. Straight into the armed American lair, against the landing pattern, I directed my MiG-15bis, a jet fighter that some F-86 Sabre pilots considered superior to their own. At that time Americans had no intimate knowledge of the MiG-15, a fighter as mysterious in 1950–53 as the Japanese Zero had been in 1941–42.

I prayed for a safe landing as I continued to descend. My left hand pulled the throttle back farther, and I pressed down on the switch that extended the air brakes from the side of the rear fuselage. Eager to signal that I was not a threat, I reached to the left and pulled the lever that lowered the wing flaps, and then I pressed down on the lever on the instrument panel to lower the landing gear. I began pushing the control stick left and right to rock my wings as a friendly sign to the treacherous gun batteries below. As I approached the gray runway, I pressed the colored buttons on the other side of the throttle to fire colored flares from the right side at the rear of the fuselage. The glowing rockets-red, yellow, green and white-seemed to hang in the air, and I hoped they would be understood as a distress signal, not mistaken for a rocket attack. I meant to show that I intended to land. . . .

Lt. No Kum-Sok is shown wearing flight gear after he defected to the West in a MiG-15bis jet fighter, flying from North Korea to Kimpo Air Base in South Korea on 21 September 1953. (National Museum of the United States Air Force, Research Division)

Heading toward me from the other end of the runway, an F-86 Sabre was descending for a landing, so I decided to touch down on the dirt strip to avoid a collision. Before I crossed the perimeter of the base, however, the other jet fighter had landed and turned off the runway, so I aimed for the runway as I pulled the throttle all the way back. But then a second Sabre appeared , obviously the wingman on its final approach to the runway. Maybe I thought, I could land before he did and the American pilot would see me and execute a "go around."

I directed my deadly fighter down at an excessive speed onto the pierced steel planked (PSP) runway and was dismayed that my sink-rate was too slow. I was in danger of overshooting the runway. Fortunately, my fighter did slow enough to land halfway down the runway, and as soon as my wheels touched down, I shouted to myself, "I made it, I'm safe, I'm free!" The strange surface of the runway, however, created a "scratchy" feeling, like a model plane landing on sandpaper. I had never felt anything like it. And as I was in my landing roll, straining the brakes, more trouble loomed, for I could tell that the other pilot did not see my aircraft. He touched down opposite me at the same time that I landed, and our fighters raced toward each other. Desperately I steered as far to the right of the runway as I could and squeezed my eyelids tight. He finally steered away just enough that our fighters passed unscathed. I opened my eyes when I realized we had avoided a head-on collision.[6]

Kum-Sok taxied his aircraft in front of F-86s that were on alert on the alert pad. One of the American pilots recalled he nearly opened up with his machine guns to destroy the MiG that suddenly parked in front of his aircraft. When the MiG canopy opened, Kum-Sok stepped out of his airplane dressed in a blue flight suit. Since he could not speak English, he simply shook hands with one of the approaching pilots (Capt. Cipriano Guerra), who in turn welcomed him. After handing his pistol to another pilot, he was taken by jeep to the 4th Fighter Interceptor Wing headquarters. Air Force intelligence learned he had been planning to defect from the first day he had been accepted into the North Korean Naval Academy at the age of 17. Kum-Sok had been brought up in a Christian environment, had attended a Catholic Mission School, and had harbored pro-Western thoughts and ideals. Trapped in a Communist society, he shouted state-sponsored slogans and proclaimed his loyalty to the party, all the while hoping someday to escape to the West and live in a free world. He considered the Russians to be illiterate peasants who often looted Korean homes.[7]

Kum-Sok landed at Kimpo a little before 10:00 on 21 September 1953. He was quickly taken to meet General Anderson in the headquarters building. The meeting lasted only several minutes, since neither could speak the other's language. Kum-Sok was then given a physical and flown a short distance to Oryudong (near Seoul) where the Fifth Air Force Intelligence Officers were located. He was to wait

Operation Moolah was an extraordinary attempt by the United States to procure a combat-ready Soviet MiG-15 fighter such as No Kum-Sok's aircraft shown here. Since no MiG-15s had fallen into the hands of the Allies, the project was basically a "MiG for money" offer to North Korean or Soviet pilots in North Korea and Manchuria. Though No Kum-Sok defected for other reasons, the USAF ended up with the latest version of the jet fighter. Early in the war, MiGs were superior to Allied fighters. It was not until the USAF F-86 Sabre jets entered the war that MiGs would encounter a fighter that matched their capability. (National Museum of the United States Air Force, Research Division)

Cockpit display of Sr. Lt. No Kum-Sok's MiG-15bis jet fighter. (USAF)

three hours under guard until an intelligence team of officers arrived from Tokyo. Many pictures were taken of him while he was in his flight gear. After changing to American fatigues, his interrogation began mid-afternoon of the same day he had landed at Kimpo: 21 September. He was questioned about North Korean air force bases, support equipment, matériel, and personnel. The next morning, he woke up and, much to his surprise, read about Operation Moolah in a South Korean newspaper. Regarding the leaflet content and escapee instructions, Kum-Sok had the following comments:

> *Since we were not in the era of the American Wild West, a bounty would not have attracted a MiG-15 pilot to deliver a plane. The offer was made in April 1953 by means of leaflets dropped over air bases in North Korea, but all the MiGs were stationed in Manchuria at the time. The leaflets written in Chinese, Korean and Russian offered $100,000 to any pilot who delivered an undamaged MiG-15 to the allies. But no Chinese or Russian pilots were stationed then on the devastated North Korean soil where the leaflets were air-dropped. I am absolutely certain that no MiG pilot ever saw one of the leaflets, or even heard of the offer. Bundles of leaflets should have been dropped in Manchuria over a MiG base in the daylight for a MiG pilot to have a chance of finding one. Before the cease-fire, an American fighter-bomber could have completed such a daylight mission, but none was undertaken.*
>
> *During the last ninety days of the war, MiGs seldom flew to North Korea. Chodo is 100km (62 miles) southwest of Paengyong-do in the Yellow Sea. To fly to Chodo would be all but fatal at that time. Moreover, flying from Chodo to Paengyong-do, 50km (31 miles) over the sea does not make any sense. Nobody had ever heard of Paengyong-do in the Yellow Sea. Finally, proceed from Paengyong-do to Kimpo, 200km (124 miles) at 6,100 meters (20,000 feet) altitude. Any MiG following such a flight path for defection would have been easy prey for the Sabre jets. The USAF had not instructed F-86 pilots with escorting procedures for defecting MiGs. They were unaware of Operation Moolah. Might I have defected then if I had seen the leaflet? Absolutely not. Flying safely to reach Pyongyang from China in 1953 was impossible. To reach Chodo out in the Yellow Sea without being shot down in 1953 was unthinkable. I would have never followed the leaflet's instructions. I would have done exactly what I did, disregarding the escape flight route in the leaflet. I waited until after the armistice and took off from a North Korean airbase close to the DMZ. It was the wisest decision in my life. As it turned out, my escape plan, including the timing, was carried out perfectly.[8]*

Kum-Sok realized that his only chance to realize his dream of freedom in the West was through defection to South Korea. Following the truce, the bombed-out airfield at Pyongyang was reopened by the Communists. His unit was ordered to the airbase; it was from here that he decided to make his escape. It would not be easy, even though he was that much closer to Kimpo airfield.

> *The Korean War Armistice went into effect at 2200 hours on 27 July 1953. My squadron was at Antung Air Base on that morning. We knew the day would be the last day of the shooting war. At late morning, two F-86 Sabres appeared above the base looking for a dogfight but there were no MiGs in the air. The planes dived down and buzzed a few feet above the runway at sonic velocity. It was quite menacing with the sonic boom and the pilots doing continuous roll-overs down the flight line.*
>
> *Most North Korean MiG pilots departed for North Korea by truck that evening. About six pilots missed the departing truck. I was one of them. We got on an old barge at the Manchurian side of the Yalu River and started to cross at night. It was very unpleasant, cool and misty. About the middle of the river, the ship got stuck on a shallow sandbar at low tide, so we spent the night on the roofless barge in a constant cold drizzle. I was tired and very uncomfortable. The pilots on the barge were jolly and jubilant for surviving the war. Was I happy too? The answer is "yes" and "no." Yes, I was happy for surviving the war. But, no, because I had an unfinished personal mission to accomplish; escaping to South Korea.*[9]

After landing his MiG, the plane was loaded onto a flatbed trailer and taken to a heavily guarded hangar. The aircraft was disassembled that same day and crated for shipping. The task of disassembling the aircraft was accomplished by the 6401st Field Maintenance Squadron. Although they had no maintenance manuals or blueprints to go by, the mechanics, using their skill and expertise, dismantled the MiG and crated the parts. They were amazed that the craft was flyable and that Kum-Sok had been able to stay in the air and escape. They found that the plane had previously been reassembled and that many of the systems were on the verge of being nonfunctional. The aircraft parts were secured in the cargo hold of a C-124, and the MiG was flown to Kadena Air Base in Okinawa the following day.

Since the MiG had been delivered after the truce was signed, many allied officials thought the aircraft should be returned to its owner. However, there were no takers. Additionally, since the Soviets had introduced a superior version of the aircraft, the MiG-17, Kum-Sok's aircraft was less valuable. It was finally decided to keep the aircraft. Once it was at Okinawa, it was reassembled and flown by Capt. H. E. "Tom" Collins. The aircraft was next airlifted to Wright-Patterson Air Force Base in Dayton, Ohio, and given exhaustive flight-testing by USAF test pilots, including Major C. E. "Chuck" Yeager. Once this was completed, the plane was transferred to the USAF Museum in Dayton in 1957 where it remains on display

Sr. Lt. No Kum-Sok, North Korean jet pilot who delivered a Russian-built MiG-15bis fighter to the Far East forces on September 21, 1953, holds the check for $100,000 he received from the U.S. government under terms of an offer by Gen. Mark Clark, then the United Nations Commander. (USAF)

today. Just below the gun sight on the aircraft is the following admonition in red Korean characters: "Pour out and zero in this vindictive ammunition to the damn Yankees."

Kum-Sok spent several months with the USAF providing valuable intelligence regarding Soviet, Chinese, and North Korean capabilities. He and Maj. James Kim, a Korean-American ordered to escort Kum-Sok, arrived in the United States on 5 May 1954. After numerous press conferences and seeing the many sights of San Francisco, they traveled to Washington, DC. During their month's stay in the nation's capital, they visited Congress, where Kum-Sok met Vice President Richard Nixon. They viewed a session of the 83rd Congress, where Kum-Sok was introduced and warmly received by the body of congressional representatives. He received his $100,000 reward later that month and stated that it would be used to pay for technical studies and the care of his mother who had been evacuated to South Korea in 1954.

Major Kim next took Kum-Sok to New York for a whirlwind tour of the many sights and sounds of that exciting city. Since entering the country, CIA personnel looked after the well-being of their celebrated pilot. In September 1954, they assisted him in his enrollment at the University of Delaware. CIA agent Tony Lohmann became his mentor and they became close friends. Lohmann had been in both the FBI and CIA in both World War II and the Korean War. He had resigned from the agencies to join the U.S. Marine Corps and saw combat action in both conflicts.

While attending the university, Kum-Sok changed his name to a more Westernized name, Kenneth Rowe, and met the woman whom he would later marry. After his graduation from Delaware University with an engineering degree, Ken Rowe worked for a number of major companies, primarily defense contractors. These included DuPont, Boeing, General Electric, General Motors, United Technologies, and Westinghouse. He said the reason he worked for so many different companies was that he wanted to see and live in other parts of "this great country."

Ken Rowe returned to Korea in 1970, sixteen years after he defected. He was met by four other North Korean Air Force defectors when he arrived in South Korea. In subsequent meetings with the pilots, Rowe learned that following his escape five of his flying comrades had been executed. One, Lt. Kun Soo-Sung, was his closest friend and a former classmate at the Naval Academy and sponsor of his membership in the Communist Party.[10]

Today, Ken and Clara Rowe live in South Daytona Beach, Florida, where they have raised two sons and a daughter. Their daughter, Bonnie, practices law in Huntsville, Alabama; one of their sons, Edmond, is an aerospace engineer for the USAF at Robbins Air Force Base, Georgia; and their other son, Raymond, who is mentally handicapped, works for the Work-Oriented Rehabilitative Center in Daytona Beach. Ken Rowe retired from Embry-Riddle Aeronautical University, Daytona Beach, Florida, in 2000 after working seventeen years as an aeronautical engineering professor.

chapter nine

MYSTERIOUS DISAPPEARANCE OF COMMANDER LIONEL CRABB, RNVR, 1956

British Commander Lionel "Buster" Crabb, an underwater bomb disposal and salvage diver, disappeared under mysterious circumstances in the frigid waters of Portsmouth Harbor, England, in 1956 while Soviet naval combatants, which included the cruiser Ordzhonikidze, *were visiting the port. British Prime Minister Anthony Eden had arranged the ships' April visit to Britain to improve East–West relations. On board the cruiser were First Secretary of the Communist Party of the Soviet Union Nikita Khrushchev, and Prime Minister Nikolai Bulganin. At the time, Crabb's disappearance produced wild rumors, conjecture, a blitz of media frenzy, and a diplomatic crisis between the two countries. The Soviets lodged voluminous formal complaints against the British government since sentinels on board the cruiser had sighted a diver secretly surveying the hull of the* Ordzhonikidze. *The British Foreign Office responded to Soviet queries by stating that Crabb was engaged in diving tests and was presumed to have met his death while so engaged.[1]*

A year later, a fisherman found Crabb's body on a sandbank off Pilsey Island near Chichester harbor. When the remains were lifted from the water, the head fell off and disappeared in the waters below; the hands were already missing. What was left of the body was clothed in an old-fashioned frogman's dry suit. Crabb's former wife could not positively identify the body and his girlfriend claimed it was not him. A close friend noted the body bore a scar on the left knee similar to what he had seen on Crabb, however. The coroner officially recorded an open verdict but informed British officials he was satisfied the remains were those of Crabb. His mother finally buried her son with the words, "In Loving Memory of My Son, Commander Lionel Crabb RNVR GM OBE At Rest At Last," etched on his gravestone.[2]

Cdr. Lionel Crabb, RNVR GM OBE in "Frogman" diving suit, 1956. (Library of Congress)

The mystery of Crabb's death continued to be the subject of thousands of media stories and some ten books for the next forty years. Rumors such as the following abounded:

- He had been killed by a new antifrogman device fitted experimentally to the Soviet cruiser or by a sniper on deck.

- He was alive and well, living in the Soviet Union or East Germany.
- He had been taken prisoner by the Russians.
- He had talked about defecting to the Soviet Union and did so. A picture said to have been smuggled out of Russia showed Crabb in a Soviet naval uniform, with the caption, "Lieutenant Lev Lvovich Korablov (Crabb) in the Far Eastern Command of the Red Navy at Vladivostoka." When his divorced wife, Mrs. Margaret Crabb, saw the photo she wrote on it, "This looks very like him. I believe it is Crabbie. Margaret Crabb, 26 May 1960."
- He was electrocuted by special steel netting that had been rigged to the underwater hulls of the visiting Soviet ships.
- A Soviet underwater sentinel had cut his throat when he found him attaching a limpet mine to the hull of the cruiser.
- He went missing after taking part in trials of an underwater apparatus in Stokes Bay (several miles from Portsmouth), this according to British Admiralty officials.
- He was later seen in London, Paris, and in a special cancer sanatorium in Russia.[3]

Buster Crabb was a hero during World War II. He was awarded the George Cross of the United Kingdom for bravery and undaunted devotion to duty in the face of enemy action. In 1942, Lieutenant Crabb was appointed officer of mine and disposal at Gibraltar. Several Allied ships had been sunk by Italian frogmen of the Tenth Light Flotilla and British divers were conducting extensive underwater operations checking the hulls of ships for limpet mines. Crabb's job initially was to dispose of any mines brought up by the divers. However, he decided that to do the job properly he should learn to dive himself. At the time, there were no special suits or flippers for divers, and the Davis Submarine Escape Apparatus was used to breathe. Crabb joined the team and found himself diving night and day.

He was successful in removing mines attached to the hulls of a number of ships and was subsequently awarded the George Cross. He was promoted to lieutenant commander and appointed principal diving officer for northern Italy. He was next placed in charge of clearing Venice of mines and opening the port to shipping.

Upon leaving Italy in December 1942, he was honored by being named Officer of the Order of the British Empire (OBE). Crabb was then ordered to Palestine to command an underwater bomb disposal team, whose mission it was "to search ships' hulls for mines planted by terrorists." After completing this tour of duty, he was demobilized in 1947 at the age of thirty-eight. From this point on, most historians assume that Crabb continued to be used by the admiralty for underwater espionage operations. In 1950, he and another frogman dived on the Royal Navy (RN) submarine *Truculent* that had sunk in the Thames Estuary with all hands to rescue any survivors; unfortunately, none survived. The following year he was seen on board a Navy deep-diving ship, HMS *Reclaim,* in search of another downed submarine, the HMS *Affray*. In 1953, he was conducting secret work in the Suez Canal, and in 1954 he dove on the *Tobermory* galleon, but failed to find it.

Though he had been demobilized from the Navy in 1947, his name appeared on the 1955 and 1956 Navy Lists, which also noted his promotion: "Commander (Special Branch) L. K. P. Crabb, RNVR, GM, OBE, HMS *Vernon*." At Vernon, an RN shore establishment at Portsmouth, he was said to have lived in a trailer. He was often seen wearing an RN commander's uniform. He visited Portsmouth frequently, wearing a tweed suit and pork pie cap. He was never without a swordstick with a big silver knob on top, itself engraved with a golden crab.[4]

In October 1955, Crabb was asked by another frogman, Sydney Knowles, to join him on a special mission in Portsmouth. Crabb was recruited through Knowles by the naval liaison office of British Secret Intelligence Service, also known as MI6. The job involved the underwater inspection of the *Sverdlov*, the Soviet cruiser that had arrived in Portsmouth for the Spithead naval review. The ship was of major interest to British intelligence: it was rumored to contain new technology that greatly increased its maneuverability. The divers were asked to look for "blisters" that housed sonar equipment, and to look for a new hull device code-named "Agouti," which reduced the cavitation sound of the ship's propellers. An elaborate plan was developed and put into play to acquire maximum intelligence data on this new warship. Radar equipment was set up in a bunker built into the cliffs of Dover. As the cruiser passed the area, the ship's radar image was recorded while a trailing British submarine took sound, pressure, and echo recordings. RAF reconnaissance aircraft flew numerous missions over the *Sverdlov*, taking hundreds of photographs. Once the cruiser was in port, Crabb and Knowles were able to conduct an extensive underwater investigation of the ship's hull at night.[5]

Upon inspection, they found a large circular opening at the bow. Crabb went up into the hole. It contained a large propeller, which appeared to be designed to be lowered and directed to give increased thrust to the bow. This success led to the decision to use Crabb again to inspect the underside of the *Ordzhonikidze*, which arrived in Portsmouth a year later.[6]

Before the *Ordzhonikidze* arrived, Prime Minister Anthony Eden had forbidden any operations that might prove politically embarrassing. Harold Macmillan (Chancellor of the Exchequer under Prime Minister Eden) recorded the following in his diary:

> *PM [Prime Minister Eden] was asked by the Admiralty about such an under-taking a good few weeks before the visit. Next, he wrote a clear and precise minute, expressly forbidding anything of the kind. After that you would have thought everything would have been all right. Not at all. The Secret Service (without proper liaison) and in touch with minor Admiralty officers, arranged this with Crabb (a retired officer, who specialized in "frogman" work). The Admiralty*

agreed—the PM's [Prime Minister Eden's] order had either been overridden, evaded, or merely not passed down the line.[7]

The Soviet ships arrived on 18 April 1956. The cruiser was moored at the South Railway jetty in the RN dockyard with two Soviet destroyers tied up alongside. Crabb was forty-seven years old at the time, physically out of shape, and drinking heavily. Several associates described him as an eccentric alcoholic. He nevertheless was able to function as a highly skilled diver when called upon to undertake secret missions. Crabb was last seen at the Sally Port hotel on High Street in Portsmouth on 19 April. He had checked in two days before with Ted Davies, a former RNVR (Royal Navy Volunteer Reserve) officer and MI6 operative. Several other MI6 officers were also registered at the hotel. Davies had suffered a heart attack on 18 April, but elected to continue. The following day, Crabb made an underwater dive on the Soviet cruiser but had to return because he needed more weight. He made a second dive and never resurfaced.

MI6 officer Nicolas Elliot suggested Crabb died "from respiratory trouble, being a heavy smoker and not in the best of health, or conceivably because some fault had developed in his equipment." Others felt he should never have been given the mission. Elliot countered that Crabb was a most unhappy man whose private life was in shambles. Elliot claimed Crabb had begged to be allowed to do the job for patriotic and personal reasons.

The matter might have ended there but the Macmillian diary notes went further.

> *He is either killed by the Russians, or drowned by misadventure—we don't know for certain. Then the Russians complain. The Admiral at Portsmouth (knowing nothing about it) denies the charge. Then the Commander's relations ask questions. The Press begin. The Admiralty issues a denial (the most idiotic thing possible, since otherwise we could have refused to know anything about it, as is always the rule with Secret Service work). Then the fat is in the fire. What makes it worst is that . . . nothing was said by officials to Ministers until the Press story broke.*[8]

Although Prime Minister Eden was furious when he heard about the incident, Macmillian advised him to say nothing.

Under enormous pressure, the Admiralty issued a statement to the effect that Commander Crabb was missing and presumed drowned, having failed to surface after a dive while experimenting with secret equipment. Admiralty officials further stated the dive had taken place in Stokes Bay, three miles from Portsmouth harbor. The statement did not satisfy the press and the incident became front-page news.

The media smelled a cover-up. The situation worsened when it was discovered the Sally Port Hotel register pages, which contained the names of Crabb and his associates who had been staying at the hotel at the time, had been torn out of the book. The Soviet ambassador made an official protest to the British Foreign Office about a frogman who had been seen near their warships in Portsmouth and asked for an explanation. Between the press hysteria and the Soviet protest, the Foreign Office issued a response to the Soviet Embassy: "As has already been publicly announced, Commander Crabb was engaged in diving tests and is presumed to have met his death whilst so engaged. The diver, who, as stated in the Soviet note, was observed from the Soviet warships to be swimming between the Soviet destroyers, was presumably Commander Crabb. His approach to the destroyers was completely unauthorized and her Majesty's Government express their regret for this incident."[9]

Before the House of Commons on 4 May, Prime Minister Eden said, "It would not be in the public interest to discuss the circumstances in which Commander Crabb is presumed to have met his death. While it is the practice for Ministers to accept responsibility, I think it is necessary in the special circumstances of this case to make it clear that what was done was done without the authority or knowledge of her Majesty's Ministers. Appropriate disciplinary steps are being taken."[10] With these words, it was clear that Eden was attempting to appease the Russians by distancing the British government from Commander Crabb's activities.

Eden did not speak publicly about the matter again. He did establish, however, a board to investigate the incident. Eventually, Eden made high-level personnel changes within MI6.

Eventually, stories about "Buster Crabb's" disappearance that fateful April night faded. Articles appeared periodically in newspapers and magazines whenever someone came up with a new theory. However, it was not until *Diver Magazine* published a story in its June 1996 online issue about the incident that perhaps the most credible answer to what happened appeared.

An Israeli journalist, Yigai Serna, heard about an immigrant who entered Israel in 1990 professing to have information regarding Crabb's death. The man's name was Joseph Zverkin. He was former head of Soviet Naval Intelligence, and had been an undercover agent in London in the 1950s. Serna met with Zverkin, who was in his nineties, several times. At first Zverkin was hesitant about going on record with what he knew. However, during their third meeting he opened up. Serna wrote that Zverkin spoke in very precise, heavily accented English. He told Serna that when the event happened he was in England using the code name of a German citizen. He told Serna the following:

> Crabb was discovered when he was swimming on the water next to the ship by a
> watchman, who was at a height of twenty meters [sixty-five feet]. An order was
> given to inspect the water and two people on the deck were equipped with sniper

guns—small caliber. One of them was an ordinary seaman, and the other an officer, the equivalent of a lieutenant, who was in charge of an artillery unit on the boat, and an exceptional shot. Crabb dived next to the boat and came up and swam—perhaps because of air poisoning. The lieutenant shot him in the head and killed him. He sank. All the stories about him being caught by us or that he was a Russian spy are not true.[11]

The British Cabinet papers on the Crabb incident will not be released until 2057. Whether they will reveal any information of value regarding Crabb is questionable. More than likely they will provide details of how British officials mishandled the incident to their embarrassment and how their attempts to cover up the affair created an unnecessary crisis within the British government.

chapter ten

HANS CONRAD SCHUMANN
Leap to Freedom into West Berlin, 1961

Following the end of World War II, the Allies split Germany's capital, Berlin, into four sectors. The Allied victors were determined that Germany would never again emerge as a military threat to the world. Eastern European countries liberated by Russian forces remained under Communist domination, and Germany became segmented into West Germany (Federal Republic of Germany, a parliamentary democracy) and East Germany (German Democratic Republic, a member of the Communist Warsaw Pact). Berlin, located a hundred miles inside East Germany and surrounded by East German and Russian forces, remained a joint four sector–occupied territory. The Soviets and their Communists partners in East Germany were determined to drive the Western powers from West Berlin. In June 1959, First Secretary of the Communist Party of the Soviet Union Nikita Khrushchev emphasized this matter in no uncertain terms to W. Averell Harriman, U.S. Ambassador to the Soviet Union: "We are determined to liquidate your rights in West Berlin. What good does it do for you to have eleven thousand troops in Berlin? If it came to war, we would swallow you in one gulp. . . . You can start a war if you like, but remember, it will be you who are starting it, not we. . . . West Germany knows that we could destroy it in ten minutes. . . . If you start a war, we may die but the rockets will fly automatically." [1]

While the U.S., British, and French sectors enjoyed political freedom and grew in prosperity, the Russian sector became stagnant. Since Berlin remained one city, East Germans easily crossed sector borders to the West to enjoy the fruits of a booming economy, much to the dismay of the East German Communist hierarchy and the Soviet Union. By 1961, millions of East Germans crossed into West Berlin and made their way to West Germany. Most of those who fled the Communist sector were young professionals who were desper-

East German soldier Hans Conrad Schumann shown leaping over barbed-wire barrier into West Berlin. Barbed wire was soon replaced by a wall of concrete. (National Archives and Records Administration)

ately needed to build a viable East German state. The Communists decided to close the Berlin escape hatch: on 13 August 1961, the Berlin Wall began with barbed wire fencing that divided the city, street by street, house by house, cutting off East–West communications between neighborhoods and families. The measure was brutal and, in the long run, ineffective. At the time, it created great tension between the United States and the Soviet Union; it was feared that an escalation of the situation might lead to a military conflict.

Within weeks of the erection of the barbed wire fence, construction of a cement wall began, about one hundred yards from the barbed wire fence; the space between these barriers became known as the "death strip." When completed, the city was divided by a heavily guarded cement barrier. The wall stretched for a hundred miles, thirty of which divided the city, with the rest closing off the adjacent East German countryside. Three hundred watchtowers stretched along the wall, manned by guards who had orders to shoot to kill. Behind the barrier wall on the East German side was a "no man's land" that contained an antivehicle crash barrier, the death strip, a line of tall illuminating lights, observation and command towers, surface barriers and "dragon's teeth," a border signal fence, and a hinderland fence, behind which loomed East Berlin.[2]

During the early morning hours of Sunday, 13 August 1961, East German workers and uniformed Stasi troops (the military arm of the Ministry for State Security) erected makeshift barbed wire barriers and fences along a mapped-out line of demarcation across the city. At the same time, the underground railway and city train services connecting the West and East Berlin sectors suddenly stopped. Except for those who walked the streets going to work, most West Berliners were unaware of what was happening. What they witnessed was the initial stage of the isolation of West Berlin. At first, West Berliners noticed no interference in their movement between the sectors, but by 23 August, when the wire had been replaced by the concrete wall, there was a sudden reduction in the number of crossing points. However, between 13 August and 31 August some 25,000 people managed to escape to West Berlin by finding gaps in the barrier wall. The Stasi troops were ordered to shoot to kill refugees. Since most of the troops were Berliners themselves, however, they were more likely to join those escaping. These soldiers were soon replaced by East German forces brought in from other parts of the country. By the time the wall fell in November 1989, approximately 227 individuals had died for any reason either at or because of the wall.[3]

As the barbed wire fences were erected, West Berliners mobbed the border area shouting curses at the East Berlin workers and guards. They became unruly, blaming both the Communists for their treacherous action and the "do-nothing" West. In one instance, a group of West Berliners attacked the Soviet War Memorial situated in the British sector. Bloodshed would have ensued and the Soviet memorial guards killed had it not been for the intervention of British troops.[4]

On 15 August 1961, as the barbed wire was being erected in Berlin, an incident happened that captured the attention of the world. A few miles north of Checkpoint Charlie (the most well-known Berlin Wall crossing point between East Germany and West Germany), there stood a nineteen-year-old Communist German border guard, Corp. Hans Conrad Schumann. Schumann was newly graduated from Non-Commissioned Officer (NCO) training, and had been drafted into the elite "Readiness Police." He was among four thousand provincials who had volunteered for duty in Berlin. Standing on the corner of Bernauer Strasse and Ruppiner Strasse inside East Berlin, he watched a crowd of jeering West Berliners. Behind him, cement slabs were being positioned to replace the three-foot-high roll of barbed wire strung before him. He later wrote, "The people were swearing at us. We felt we were simply doing our duty but we were getting scolded from all sides. The West Berliners yelled at us and the Eastern demonstrators yelled at us. We were standing there in the middle. There was the barbed wire, there was us guards, West Berliners, East Berliners. For a young person, it was terrible."[5]

Schumann was greatly disturbed by his situation. He leaned against a house wall and chain-smoked, periodically glancing at the crowd gathering across the border on the West Berlin side. His evident discomfort was perceived by some of the protestors and they started to goad him into joining them. "Come over! Come over!" they yelled. As their shouts grew louder, a West Berlin police car pulled into sight, its rear door open and engine running, inviting him to desert.[6] "At 2 o'clock I assigned tasks to my soldiers. I was in front and I spread the others out so that it wouldn't look suspicious. Nobody noticed anything. From two until four o'clock I was thinking about the situation and wondering what was the right decision. I would have to leave my parents and my sister. Finally I took the decision. I jumped over the barbed wire at four o'clock. Then I was in the West and they received me with a great cheer. I was the first."[7]

It just so happened that an amateur photojournalist from Hamburg, Peter Leibing, was watching Schumann. "I had him in my sights for more than an hour. I had the feeling that he was going to jump. It was kind of an instinct."[8] Leibing watched as Schumann threw away his cigarette and ran for the barbed wire. Leibing, having learned how to shoot photos of horses in mid-air at steeplechase events, caught the jackbooted Schumann in mid-leap over the wire as he threw off his machine-gun pistol. The iconic image appeared in newspapers around the world. For Leibing, it was the shot of a lifetime. Within a month after the barrier was installed, sixty-eight members of the East German special police had deserted to the West.[9]

Schumann found a home in West Berlin and married a West German woman (Kunigunde Schumann), settling in the prosperous town of Ingolstadt in northern Bavaria. He worked in an Audi factory for twenty years while raising a family. When the Wall came down in 1989, he returned to his hometown located between Dresden and Leipzig to visit his relatives and friends. Thinking he would be welcomed, he found he had become a pariah, instead. He was looked upon as the "Wall Jumper," a traitor and a tool of Western imperialists. Deeply depressed by not being able to renew his connection with those he knew and loved many years before, he hanged himself on 20 June 1998 in an orchard near his home in Ingolstadt at the age of fifty-six.[10]

chapter eleven

YURI GAGARIN
First Man in Space, 1961

On 27 March 1968, Soviet cosmonauts training at the Kirzatch Airfield heard two explosions. One of the explosions sounded like the noise that accompanies a supersonic shockwave. Kirzatch was located seven miles from another airbase, Chkalovsky Airfield, adjacent to Star City (Zvyozdny Gorodok). Star City was a secret compound, and was the main base for Soviet cosmonaut training. On that day in March, the cosmonauts at Kirzatch were forced to abort their training because of the deteriorating weather in the area. Heavy dark clouds, freezing rain, and wet snowflakes filled the air. Flight visibility was near zero. When the air controllers at Chkalovsky heard the muffled explosions, they immediately began calling the pilots of a two-seater MiG-15 UTI jet that was on a training mission in the area, but there was no reply.

A search helicopter was immediately dispatched to the area where the MiG had last been seen on radar. The Soviet pilot located a dark patch of ground emitting steam in a snow-covered wooded area. The helicopter pilot was ordered to land and search the site. Finding a suitable landing area some distance from the blackened patch in the woods, he trudged through deep snow back to what appeared to be a crash site. After surveying the area, he reported back to the base that he had found a large crater, that the earth from the crater had been thrown outwards over a part of the terrain, that surrounding trees were destroyed, and that many pieces of twisted metal were strewn over the smoldering crater. Although it was clear to him he had found the site of an aircraft accident, he could find no signs of the main section of the wreckage—no fuselage or engine parts.

Later in the afternoon, a search team carrying torches arrived at the scene. They found no bodies or parts of the fuselage. They did find bits of clothing and a map case. However, it was not until early morning the next day, as they dug deep into the

Soviet cosmonaut Yuri Gagarin—first man in space. (National Archives and Records Administration)

crater, that they found a piece of a flight jacket. It became apparent the pilots had not ejected, and that their bodies were buried somewhere in the crater.

Several feet deeper into the ground, the recovery team found the engine block of the aircraft. It was apparent the MiG had rammed the frozen ground with enormous force. A mangled landing gear and one wing were retrieved. The searchers subsequently located the crushed fuselage, which held the torn bodies of the pilots. The rest of the day was spent recovering body parts from the crash site. Small pieces of flesh were collected and placed in a surgical bowl. A close friend of Yuri Gagarin inspected a fragment that had a dark brown mole on it. A few days before the incident he had gone with Gagarin to get a haircut and noticed the mole at the base of Yuri's neck. He had mentioned to the barber not to nick the mole. He considered this finding to be proof that Gagarin's body was one of the bodies found.

The Soviet Union had lost in a tragic accident the most famous man in the world at the time, cosmonaut Yuri Gagarin, hero of the Soviet Union, the first man in history to leave the Earth's atmosphere and venture into space.[1]

★ ★ ★

Yuri Alexeyevich Gagarin was born on 9 March 1934, in the village of Klushino in the Smolensk region, one hundred miles west of Moscow. He grew up on a collective farm where his father (Alexei) worked as a carpenter and his mother (Anna) tended farm animals. Yuri was one of four children, an older sister (Zoya), a brother (Valentin), and a younger brother (Boris). Yuri enjoyed family life in his rural town until his father came home one night in the summer of 1941 yelling, "War!" Germany had invaded Russia, and their forces seemed unstoppable. Like previous invaders of Russia, though, they were slowed and then stopped by the fierce Russian winter. Unprepared for such weather and lacking munitions, supplies, and equipment, there followed a two-year retreat by the German army westward. Faced with a massive Russian counteroffensive, the Germans in their retreat overran and occupied the Smolensk region and Klushino. Artillery battles took place daily, and Klushino seemed to bear the brunt of the bombardments. The German invaders threw the Gagarins out of their house and the family was forced to live in a crude shelter.

During the spring of 1943, Yuri's oldest brother and sister were deported on board a "children's train" to Gdansk, Poland, where they worked in labor camps. Valentin and Zoya escaped the camp and hid in the woods waiting for the advancing Russian troops. When rescued, the Russians demanded the children remain with their unit as volunteers. By this time, Valentin was old enough to join front-line service and he became a soldier. Yuri and Boris remained with the family through the end of the war. All had thought that Zoya and Valentin were dead, but near the end of the war both returned home.[2]

Yuri was remembered by his neighbors and teachers as an intelligent, enthusiastic, and hard-working child. One of his teachers who had flown in the Soviet Air Force during the war made a lasting impression on Yuri. However, it was a later experience that captured the imagination of the young man and set him on a course to reach for the sky. Two Yak PO-2 Soviet (plywood) fighter aircraft landed in a marshland near Gzhatsk following a dogfight with German Messerschmitt aircraft. One aircraft was severely damaged and crash-landed, injuring its pilot. Villagers ran to the wreckage and rescued the pilot. They bandaged his badly wounded leg and gave him food and milk. The other Yak landed nearby and its pilot joined the crowd to check on the condition of his flying mate. Yuri and the other boys in the village were subsequently tasked with scavenging whatever petrol they could find to refuel the intact Yak. Before leaving, one of the pilots distributed bars of chocolate to Yuri and his friends. Upon checking the damage to the crippled aircraft the following morning, the pilots decided to burn it. Since the PO-2 had two cockpits (in tandem), the injured pilot was placed in the rear seat, and both fliers departed for their home base. The whole experience was magical for Yuri. He now looked at his teacher, who often wore a faded airman's tunic, with renewed respect and admiration.[3]

When Yuri reached the age of sixteen, he was anxious to leave home. Though he wished to continue his studies, he had only six years of schooling, which limited his potential. He decided to apply for vocational training that would graduate him as an apprentice in a trade. He traveled to Moscow hoping to find work. Eventually, he was accepted at the Lubertsy Steel Plant, which offered training for apprentices. He became a steel foundryman. Always a hard worker, Yuri received a good performance report after his first year and was one of four selected for training at the Technical School in Saratov, a port city on the Volga River. At Saratov, they would learn the many intricacies of maintaining and driving a tractor. Arriving in town, Yuri noticed an Aero-Club sign that urged new members to join. Yuri applied and was accepted. His first flight was in an old canvas-clad Yak-18 training plane; he was thrilled with flying high above the Earth. He recalled later his first flight filled him with pride, and seemed to give meaning to his whole life. His instructor was Dmitry Martyanov, and they soon became fast friends.

As Yuri took more and more to the air, he became disinterested in his training at Saratov. Martyanov recommended Yuri for the Pilot's School at Orenburg, on the Ural River. If Yuri wanted to receive such training, he would have to become a military cadet. Orenburg was the main training center for military pilots. The training there was serious business, since the instructors were active duty soldiers. Yuri met his future wife, Valentina "Valya" Goryacheva, while he was in flight training at Orenburg. Valya was a medical technician who worked on the base. They were married on 27 October 1957, three weeks after the Soviets launched Sputnik 1, the world's first probe into outer space.

Sputnik 1 shocked the United States, which had considered Russia to be a primitive nation, incapable of accomplishing such a feat. Sputnik 2, a more sophisticated artificial satellite, was launched on 3 November 1957. The probe carried a small dog, Laika, that survived the high-gravity forces during blastoff as well as the weightlessness of space, giving the Soviets data that eventually paved the way for humans to travel in space. The Sputnik launches awakened the United States, which accelerated its space program. On 31 January 1958, America launched its first space probe, Explorer 1, atop a Jupiter-C rocket developed by German-born scientist Wernher von Braun. By the end of the 1950s, the United States and the Soviet Union were sending spacecraft-carrying animals and scientific experiments into outer space on a regular basis. Being the first to put a human in orbit became a priority for both countries.[4]

Yuri graduated from flight training and received a lieutenant's commission on 6 November 1957. He was subsequently ordered to the Nikel airbase at Murmansk where he flew reconnaissance missions in Squadron #3, in MiG-15s. Earlier that same year, Soviet scientists, led by Sergei Korolev, had initiated a program to develop a spacecraft for suborbital flights (incomplete orbits) in preparation for Russia's first manned mission. By April 1958, the Soviets had constructed the Vostok one-person capsule. It measured 7.5 feet across and weighed 5.2 tons. It was designed to fly at an altitude of 155 miles. During reentry, it would drop to 6 miles, and the pilot would eject and parachute to Earth separately from the capsule so the Soviets could claim the first manned space flight. The Soviets kept the ejection and parachute phase a closely guarded secret.[5]

In October 1959, Soviet recruiting teams suddenly appeared at all major air stations. No one knew exactly why they were there, but almost immediately they began to interview groups of pilots. As the days went on, the groups became smaller until private interviews were conducted with just one candidate at a time. Those finally selected (including Yuri) were sent to Bordenko Military Hospital in Moscow for health tests. Nine out of ten failed these tests. Ultimately, Yuri was one of twenty cosmonauts selected out of 2,200 candidates. The elite twenty were sent to Star City, the new secret base twenty-five miles from Moscow, for training. Because of financial considerations, the team of twenty was reduced to six. Two candidates made the final cut: Gherman Titov and Yuri Gagarin. Soviet officials decided the cosmonaut to make the first flight would not be informed until the night before the launch, scheduled for 12 April 1961. Both were top performers and of the same body size that the small Vostok capsule could easily accommodate.

A special State Committee selected Gagarin as the commander and Titov as his backup. There were rumors that other factors entered into his final selection. It was thought that his handsome boyish appearance and Russian peasant heritage would result in immediate acceptance by the media. Officials observed that because of his personality and demeanor Gagarin would be able to handle his notoriety with the world press, which would be overwhelming once the mission had been completed. Even the name "Gagarin" gave a touch of czarist aristocracy. Finally, Gagarin's selection was helped along by the First Secretary of the Communist Party Nikita Khrushchev. Gagarin and Khrushchev had much in common: for instance, both were the sons of peasant farmers. Titov, who was middle class, was bitterly disappointed but realized the die had been cast. Long after Gagarin was killed, Titov admitted the government had made the right choice because Yuri turned out to be the man that the people loved.[6]

On 12 April 1961, Gagarin became the first human to travel into space and return. In his book, *Road to the Stars*, Gagarin spoke of his moments during liftoff and early flight in Vostok 3KA-2.

> *I entered the cabin which smelled of the wind of the fields and was placed in my seat; the hatch was closed noiselessly. I was alone with the instruments now illuminated not by sunlight but by artificial lighting. I heard everything that was being done outside the ship, on the earth which had become still dearer to my heart. The iron girders were removed and silence ensued. I reported:*

Support towers break away as Vostok 1 propels Yuri Gagarin on his landmark voyage into space. (National Archives and Records Administration)

"Hallo, 'Earth'! I am 'Cosmonaut'. I have tested the communications. The tumblers on the control panel are in the assigned initial position. The globe is at the point of division. Pressure in the cabin—unity, humidity—sixty-five percent, temperature—nineteen degrees centigrade, pressure in compartment—1.2, pressure in orientation systems—normal. I feel fine and am ready for start."

The technical flight supervisor gave one-and-a-half-hour's notice for the flight. Then an hour's and lastly a half hour's notice. Several minutes before the start I was told that my face could well be seen on the screen of the television device and that my cheerfulness made everybody happy. I was also told that I had a pulse of sixty-four and a respiratory rate of twenty-four.

I answered: "My heart beats normally. I feel fine; I have put on the gloves, closed the helmet and am ready to start."

All the starting commands were also transmitted to me.

"Lift off!"

I answered: "Off we go! Everything is normal."

I glanced at my watch. It was seven minutes past nine Moscow time. I heard a shrill whistle and a mounting roar. The giant ship shuddered, and slowly, very slowly lifted from the launching pad. The roar was not louder than that one hears *in the cabin of a jet aircraft, but it contained a multitude of new shakes and pitches that no composer has ever put down in music or any musical instrument or human voice can as yet reproduce. The rocket's huge engines were fashioning the music of the future which, I imagine, is much more exciting and beautiful than the greatest creations of the past.*

The acceleration of G-forces began to increase. I felt as though some uncompromising force were riveting me to my seat. Although the seat had been positioned to minimize the tremendous gravity pull that now brought all its weight to bear on me, I could hardly move my hands or feet. I knew that this state would not last long, that it would pass as soon as the ship, accelerating, would begin to orbit.

The earth called my attention: "Seventy seconds have passed since the take-off."

I replied: "I hear you: seventy. I feel well. Am continuing flight. The G-forces are increasing. Everything is all right."

I replied in a cheerful voice, but to myself I thought: Is it really only seventy seconds? The seconds seem like minutes.

The earth again asked: How do you feel?"

"All right. How are things going with you?"

The reply from earth was: "Everything's normal." . . .

As soon as the ship passed the dense layers of the atmosphere the head fair-lead was automatically discarded and it flew away. The surface of the earth loomed in the distance through the portholes. Just then the Vostok was flying over a broad Siberian river. I could clearly see the sunlit, taiga-overgrown islands and banks. . . .

The G's were indeed mounting. But I gradually got used to them and was even struck by the thought that they were greater in the centrifuge. The vibration, too, was considerably smaller than what I had to experience during training. In short, the devil is not so terrible as he is painted.

A multi-stage space rocket is such an intricate piece of machinery that it is hard to find a comparison for it, and yet people perceive things by comparison. When each stage burns up its fuel it becomes useless, it is automatically separated and discarded, while the remaining part of the rocket goes on building up the speed of the flight. I never had the occasion to meet the scientists and engineers who developed the splendid, portable fuel for the engines of Soviet rockets. But as I was climbing ever higher to my predetermined orbit I wanted to thank them and gratefully shake hands with them. The intricate engines worked marvelously.

Using up their fuel, the stages dropped off one by one and the moment came when I could report: "The rocket-carrier has separated in conformity with the programme. I feel well. The cabin parameters are: pressure—one; humidity—

sixty-five percent; temperature—twenty degrees; pressure in the compartment—one; the orientation systems are working normally."

The ship entered its orbit, a broad space route, and I found myself in the state of weightlessness. . . . At first I felt uncomfortable, but I soon got used to it, found out how to get about and continued with the flight programme. . . . I left my seat and hung in the air between the ceiling and floor of the cabin. . . .

The earth wanted to know what I saw below me. I reported back that the view I had of our planet was approximately the same as what can be seen from a jet aircraft flying at a high altitude. I could distinctly see mountain ranges, large rivers, big tracts of forests, islands and the coastline of seas. . . . I wanted to observe the moon, to see how it looks in space. Unfortunately, it was not in my field of vision during the flight. "Never mind," I said to myself, "I'll see it next time." . . .

With my eye constantly on the instruments, I determined that the Vostok, which was flying strictly in a predetermined orbit, was about to enter the shaded side of our planet. This happened quickly, it suddenly became pitch black. Evidently I was flying over an ocean because I could not see even the golden dust of illuminated cities. . . .

The automatic orientation system was turned on at 09 hours 51 minutes. After the Vostok emerged from the shadow, the system oriented the ship at the sun. Its rays were piercing the earth's atmosphere, the horizon blazed in a bright orange which gradually changed into all the colours of the rainbow: to light blue, blue, violet, black. . . . The time was 09 hours 52 minutes. I was flying over the region of Cape Horn and sent the report: "The flight is proceeding normally. I feel well. The onboard apparatus is working faultlessly." . . .

The Vostok was flying at a speed of nearly 28,000 kilometers [17,000 miles] an hour. It is a speed that one can hardly imagine. During the flight I felt neither hungry nor thirsty. But at a definite time, keeping to the flight programme, I had a meal and drank water from a special water-supply system. The food I ate was prepared according to a recipe prescribed by the Academy of Medical Sciences. I ate just as I did on earth, but the only trouble was that I could not open my mouth wide. . . . I sometimes could not help listening to my own heart. In the state of weightlessness the pulse and respiration were normal, I felt comfortable and I had full command of my capacity for thinking and for work.

At 10 hours 15 minutes while the ship was approaching Africa the automatic programme arrangement issued commands preparing the ship's apparatus for switching on the braking rockets. I radioed my routine report: "Flight proceeding normally. Am bearing state of weightlessness well." . . .

I was now entering the final and perhaps more responsible stage of the flight than when the ship was placed in orbit and began to circle the earth, for it was the homing stage. I began to prepare for it. Ahead of me was the change from the state of weightlessness to new and perhaps bigger deceleration G-forces and the colossal temperature to which the ship's external plating would be heated when it entered the dense layers of the atmosphere. So far everything had progressed approximately as we had anticipated during our training on earth. But what would the last, final stage of the flight be like? Would all the systems operate normally? Was some unforeseen danger lying in wait for me? With all my respect for automation, I determined the ship's position and held myself in readiness to take over the controls and, if need be, to guide the descent to earth in a suitable region selected for me.

My ship had a solar orientation system fitted with special transducers. These transducers "caught" the sun and, orienting themselves by it, kept the ship in a definite flight attitude with the retrorockets facing in the direction of the flight. The braking system was turned on automatically at 10 hours 25 minutes and worked without a flaw, at exactly the time set in advance. Having climbed to a high altitude, the Vostok now had to descend the same distance. It gradually lost speed, going over from an orbit into a descending trajectory. The ship began to enter the dense layers of the atmosphere. Its external skin rapidly became red-hot and through the porthole filters I saw the frightening crimson reflection of the flames raging all 'round the ship. But in the cabin it was only twenty degrees above zero in spite of the fact that the ship was hurtling down towards the earth like a ball of fire.

The state of weightlessness had passed long ago, and the growing G-forces pinned me to my seat. They kept increasing and were much greater than the stresses I had experienced at the take-off. The ship began to rotate and I reported this to earth. But the rotation which worried me quickly stopped and the further descent proceeded normally. All the systems were obviously working faultlessly and the ship was making for the determined landing area.

The silvery Volga flashed past below. I at once recognized the great Russian river and its banks. At 10 hours 55 minutes, the Vostok, having completed its orbit around the earth, landed safely in a predetermined area, on a ploughed field of the Lieninsky Put (Lenin's Path) Collective Farm, which is situated to the south-west of the town of Engels, near the village of Smelovka.[7]

Gagarin's story of his smooth descent to Earth was the official version released to the world media and Gagarin was careful to stick to his story. However, during his private testimony to a special State Committee to report on the capsule's overall engineering performance, Gagarin explained technical difficulties he encountered that could have cost him his life. There was more to his reentry phase than just his words "the rotation that worried me." As he started to descend, a small service module that provided power and oxygen to the Vostok capsule failed to disconnect before reentry. The umbilical cable containing a dense bundle of wires remained tied to the capsule, causing the reentry vehicle to tumble end over end for several minutes as it rushed headlong toward the Earth. The change in mass distribution distorted the programmed alignment of the capsule, causing it to buck and spin. At one point, Gagarin almost lost consciousness. Fortunately, the outside blazing heat created during the reentry into the Earth's atmosphere burned away the wires and the module separated from the capsule. As the capsule assumed the correct reentry position and the flames that had engulfed the vehicle stopped, Gagarin prepared to eject from the cabin. Soviet scientists correctly determined that a cosmonaut could not survive inside the Vostok cabin as it crashed to the Earth. Gagarin ejected at an altitude of five miles and touched down unharmed. The first man in space had completed his mission in only 108 minutes.[8]

As I stepped on the firm soil, I saw a woman and a girl. They were standing beside a spotted calf and gazing at me with curiosity. I started walking towards them and they began to walk towards me. But the nearer they got to me the slower their steps became. I was still wearing my flaming orange spacesuit and they were probably frightened by it. They had never seen anything like it before.

"I'm a Russian, comrades. I'm a Russian," I shouted, taking off my helmet.

The woman was Anna Takhtarova, wife of the local forester, and the girl, Rita, was her granddaughter.

"Have you really come from outer space?" she asked a little uncertainly.

"Just imagine it, I certainly have," I replied.

"It's Yuri Gagarin! It's Yuri Gagarin!" cried some machine-operators, who had run up from a field camp.

They were the first people I met on earth after my flight. We embraced and kissed as though we were relatives.

A group of soldiers with an officer in command soon arrived. They had been driving along the road in trucks. They embraced me and shook hands with me. One of them addressed me as major. I asked no questions, realizing that the Defence Minister, Marshal of the Soviet Union, had by a special Order of the Day promoted me to the rank of major, skipping one rank. One of the men had a camera and we posed in a big group for a snapshot. This was the first photograph taken after my flight.

The soldiers cordoned the spaceship off. Just then a helicopter arrived for me. It brought specialists from the reception group and also sports commissars who came to register the record space flight. They remained behind and the helicopter took me to the command post of this group so that I could make a full report to Moscow.

When I arrived at the command post, I learned that there was a telegram for me from Nikita Khrushchev. He congratulated me on the completion of the space flight. Before long I received a telephone call from him.[9]

Khrushchev showered Gagarin with words of great praise both from a personal standpoint and on behalf of the Motherland. After a debriefing by Soviet scientists and engineers, Gagarin met with correspondents of the news agencies *Pravda* ("Truth") and *Izvestia* ("Messages") for a full press conference. From that point on, Gagarin entered the surreal world of sudden fame, a world for which he was unprepared.

Two days after his landing, he was flown to Moscow to make his first public appearance. When his aircraft landed at Vnukova Airport in Moscow he walked down a long red carpet to be greeted by Communist Party officials. After making a brief speech, he received the congratulations of Soviet officials after which he was joined by his wife, children, and parents. The group was then driven to Red Square for the official welcoming ceremony. Massive crowds had gathered along the route from the airport and a huge audience filled the decorated Square. That evening, he and his family attended a reception at the Grand Kremlin Palace and Leonid Brezhnev, chairman of the Presidium of the Supreme Soviet, awarded Gagarin two of the country's highest awards: the Order of Lenin and the Gold Star Medal of the Hero of the Soviet Union.[10]

Though continually pressed for public appearances and for press, radio, and television interviews, the young cosmonaut was determined to continue on with his military duties. He returned to Star City and was assigned to head a female cosmonauts' training program. (Though one woman, Valentina Tereshkova, was rocketed into orbit, the program was eventually discontinued.) He soon found himself back in the routine of everyday work, not only with the female program, but also with assisting in the training of cosmonauts scheduled for ongoing Vostok missions. However, his work was frequently interrupted by touring many countries with Secretary Khrushchev by his side. During the summer of 1961, he visited Bulgaria, Czechoslovakia, Hungary, Poland, Great Britain, Canada, Cuba, Norway, Italy (where he was photographed being kissed by the Italian actress Gina Lollobrigida), and East Germany.

Always in demand in the Soviet Union, Gagarin was elected as Deputy for the Supreme Soviet for the Smolensk region in 1962. His new position and military duties ensured that his traveling days would be curtailed, and his higher rank would hinder his chances for another space mission. Russia did not want to lose its most cherished cosmonaut. Gagarin was promoted to lieutenant colonel in June 1962 and to colonel in November 1963. However, Khrushchev's closeness to Gagarin and the first secretary's continual demands for a stronger missile force and space exploration ran counter to the conventional weapons philosophy of the Soviet military. This feud would eventually cause Gagarin's downfall and ultimately his fall from grace.[11]

Gagarin's world began to change with the Foros incident. The Kissely dacha in Foros was located along the coast to the west of Yalta in the Crimea. During the 1960s, it was a luxurious sanatorium that accommodated only the rich and famous.

Soviet Cosmonauts Valery Bykovsky, Yuri Gagarin, and Herman Titov read an edition of *America Illustrated*, an American publication, September 1966. (National Archives and Records Administration)

The best in wine, food, and personal services were offered, along with swimming in the warm waters of the Black Sea. The first cosmonauts and their families were among those who frequented the sanatorium. There were twenty-eight people in the cosmonaut party during their September visit and no one paid much attention to how guests enjoyed themselves at the spacious complex.

From the moment of their arrival in September 1961, it was clear Yuri and his wife were having marital problems. He was rude to her, distracted, and often drove her to tears. Though warned by officials in the group that his behavior was unacceptable for Russia's most famous cosmonaut, Yuri's behavior did not change. He continued to look for distractions and often joined drinking parties with local Crimean dignitaries. The week following their arrival, Yuri took to the sea with some of his companions in a small motor boat, despite being warned by the Foros staff it was against the rules of the sanatorium. Weather conditions deteriorated and swirling winds and rough seawaters made the outing a dangerous venture. As the boat and passengers disappeared over the horizon, a larger boat was sent to rescue Yuri and his friends. In the course of trying to control his boat while manning the steering wheel, Yuri blistered his hands. Once back on shore, he was sent to a medical station for treatment. He took particular note of the attractive blonde nurse who took care of him.

During the final evening of the cosmonauts' stay, a boisterous party took place. During the celebration, Valentina noticed that her husband was missing. Yuri had disappeared in search of the blonde nurse, Anna, who had gone to her room. Various stories have been written as to what happened next: Yuri went into her room, locked the door, and tried to kiss her; or Yuri went into her room and talked to her in a drunken stupor. In any case, there was a knock at the door, Valentina entered, but Yuri was not there. In fact, the cosmonaut had panicked and run out onto a balcony and jumped to the ground below, where he lay unconscious and bleeding. After receiving medical attention (for a gash on his forehead) and spending a week in the clinic, he was flown to Moscow to attend a meeting of the Communist Party Congress. On the fifth day of the meeting, Yuri delivered a short speech. Party officials were unhappy with Gagarin's blunder. Although Khrushchev was disappointed with his protégé's performance at the party Congress, he made light of the moral aspects of the Foros incident. However, high-level Soviet military officials felt otherwise and Yuri's drunken behavior at the sanatorium was the beginning of his fall from grace.

Yuri's world tour resumed in December 1961. He visited Egypt, Greece, India, Ceylon, and Japan. His heavy drinking continued and one of his traveling associates noted the following in his diary:

> He [Yuri] hasn't given up drinking even after the Crimean incident. I don't fancy being a prophet of doom, but it seems to me he's drinking a good deal. He's at the top of his glory, bearing a great moral burden, knowing that his every step is being watched. One or two years will pass, the situation will change drastically, and he'll become dissatisfied. It's obvious in his family even now. He has no respect for his wife, he humiliates her sometimes, and she doesn't have the advantages of education or the social skills to influence him.[12]

Gagarin withstood the pressures imposed by countless visits with foreign delegations that used him for their own political purposes. He was gracious, fun loving, honest, and a credit to the Soviet Union during these tours. Quite often, his social skills were superior to Soviet embassy delegations in foreign countries, which caused resentment that was passed along to Moscow. As previously mentioned, his home life was coming apart, and many of the old- and new-generation cosmonauts were jealous of him because of the attention and privileges he received. Although he had been the first into space and is immortalized by a 120-foot titanium monument of himself in Gagarin Square, Moscow, others followed his path and continued to perform advanced space missions.

In 1963, Gagarin was made deputy director of the Cosmonaut Training Centre at Star City. During the previous years, he had not been able to keep up with his space training because of his numerous administrative duties. Additionally, he had been banned from flying jet fighters because the Soviets did not wish to lose such an important symbol of Russian achievement. In March 1964, Gagarin entered the Zhukovsky Academy in Moscow to attend a special course that he hoped would sway his superiors to put him on the active flight list. Much had changed since 1961: in the mid-1960s, cosmonauts had to complete academic courses that dealt with all aspects of aviation and aerodynamics. Gagarin enrolled in a special course that would earn him a "Pilot-Engineer-Cosmonaut" diploma. He was a conscientious student, working long hours on his area of thesis study, "A Practical Design for a Reusable Winged Space Plane." He became so absorbed in his work that he spent most of his nights at the Yusnost Hotel, neglecting his family and home life. His wife caught him womanizing again and it became apparent he did not belong to her anymore, though she still loved him. He was a favored son of Mother Russia who belonged to everyone.[13]

In the meantime, Khrushchev's star was falling. Although he had proved to the world Russia was a modern technological country now respected by nations of the world, he had failed at home. His agricultural program had failed, which weakened the government's ability to provide the Russian people with one of the primary necessities of life—adequate food. This growing concern was addressed by the Politburo, which decided Khrushchev's fate. In October 1964, he was informed that he had resigned due to age and poor health. Leonid Brezhnev assumed the position of first secretary. Due to the close friendship between the former first secretary and Gagarin, the cosmonaut's life also took a downward turn. Brezhnev was not interested in Khrushchev's space triumphs, nor did he want to be reminded of them by the presence of Khrushchev's protégé. Gagarin's grand tours became a thing of the past, and his communications with the Kremlin were now limited. For all practical purposes, Brezhnev had relegated him to history. The cosmonaut continued to receive enormous amounts of fan mail from his countrymen, however. To them he was still a beloved hero![14]

Gagarin recommitted himself to the country's space program, determined to once again blast off into orbit and someday reach the moon. He worked hard on his diploma and eventually was allowed to train as a backup to a forthcoming space mission. Yuri received his diploma in February 1968, and was made deputy chief of training at Star City. In this capacity, he was possessed with the need to be a first-rate pilot since he was teaching other fliers and had to ensure their respect. Most of the cosmonauts in training at Star City had more than 1,500 hours of flight time. However, due to his career as a cosmonaut, Gagarin had logged only seventy-eight hours of flight time between 1961 and 1968. He had not flown for five months when he took to the air in a MiG-15 UTI jet on 27 March 1968. Flying in the rear cockpit was Vladimir Seregin, a highly experienced pilot whom Gagarin recruited to prepare him to qualify for clearance to fly a MiG-17, a modern version of the MiG fighter series. Tragically, Gagarin and Seregin were killed that fateful day in the accident.[15]

★ ★ ★

Rumors surfaced almost immediately regarding the cause of the accident: that Yuri had lost control of the aircraft trying to avoid a flock of birds, that he had collided with a hot air balloon, that Yuri had been drunk, that he had recently been in a mental institution, that he and Seregin had been shooting at wildlife below them . . . the rumors went on and on. Yuri's friends tried to have the case reopened to defend his reputation, but without success. Some twenty years after the crash all documents pertaining to the incident were declassified. Soviet cosmonaut, Lt. Col. Alexei Leonov, who was one of the investigators in 1968, reviewed the materials and was astounded to find that documents originally written by him while a member of the original commission of inquiry had been falsified and rewritten. His subsequent description as to the cause of the accident is best explained in his own words:

> At the time of the accident, it was known that a new supersonic Sukhoi SU-15 jet was in the same area as Yuri's MiG. Three people who lived near the crash site confirmed seeing such a plane shortly before the accident. According to the flight schedule that day, the Sukhoi was prohibited from flying lower than 10,000 meters [33,000 feet]. I believe now, and believed it at the time, that the accident happened when the pilot violated the rules and dipped below the cloud cover for orientation. I believe that, without realizing it because of the terrible weather conditions, he passed within ten or twenty meters [thirty-two to sixty-five feet] of Yuri and Seregin's plane while breaking the sound barrier. The air turbulence created, overturned their jet and sent it into the fatal flat spin.
>
> To complicate matters, Yuri and Seregin's MiG had been fitted with external, expendable, 260-liter fuel tanks, the purpose of which was to allow a plane to fly much farther in combat. The tanks were designed to be dropped before entering a combat zone, where complicated maneuvering was called for, because they severely compromised the plane's aerodynamic performance. Yuri and Seregin were not expected to perform such maneuvers that day, but it was clear from the way their plane had chopped through the treetops that they had tried to recover from the spin and it seemed they were short of doing so by a matter of just one and a half to two seconds.
>
> The investigating committee would never have admitted at the time that that is what happened because it would have meant admitting that flight

controllers were not adequately monitoring the airspace close to sensitive military installations. I believe ordinary people were unable to accept the real explanation because technical details of Yuri's plane being intercepted by an SU-15 jet were too complicated for most to understand.

But now nobody repeats any nonsense about Yuri being drunk, irresponsible or mad. After the many years I have spent talking about what I believe to be the truth of what happened that terrible day in March, the explanation that it was the result of an approach by a supersonic jet, is, at last, widely accepted.[16]

No matter what one's opinion is or has been about the Soviet Union during the Cold War, there is little doubt that a Russian of peasant stock, Yuri Gagarin, achieved an extraordinary feat in space. The young cosmonaut risked his life in leading the world into a new age. Today, the exploration of space has become a global endeavor. Once dominated by the United States and Russia, new space explorers such as China have emerged, and others will soon follow. In discussions with Russians today regarding the future of space probes they remind us with a smile, "Yes, but we were the first!"

[chapter twelve]

MAJ. RUDOLPH ANDERSON JR.
Cuban Missile Crisis, 1962

At 8:45 AM on 16 October 1962, President John F. Kennedy was awakened by his national security adviser, McGeorge Bundy. As Kennedy sat on a couch in his pajamas, Bundy confirmed what had been a growing suspicion in the intelligence community: the Soviets were installing intermediate-range nuclear missiles in Cuba. This was the beginning of a thirteen-day confrontation between the United States and the Soviet Union that brought the world to the brink of nuclear war, and would come to be known as the Cuban Missile Crisis.[1]

It was not unexpected that a confrontation might take place in Cuba. Ever since Fidel Castro had assumed power in January 1959, then had aligned Cuba with the Soviet Union on 19 December 1960, the United States had been seeking ways to remove Castro from power, culminating with the disastrous invasion by U.S.-backed Cuban exiles at the Bay of Pigs on 17 April 1961. Given Kennedy's pledge five days earlier, on 11 October 1962, not to intervene militarily in Cuba even as forces marshaled for the invasion, it was not surprising that, as Kennedy surveyed the photographic proof that cold October morning, the Soviets were publicly denying the presence of offensive weapons in Cuba.

On 27 July of that year, Castro had announced that he was being assisted by the Soviets in taking measures to defend Cuba. The United States had become suspicious in the summer of 1962 when aerial reconnaissance noted the large number of Soviet ships en route to Cuba, suggesting a military buildup. They rode high in the water, indicating cargo that took up a disproportionate amount of space in relation to its light weight. CIA director John A. McCone, in a memo to Kennedy on 10

August, expressed his belief that the Soviets were placing medium-range ballistic missiles in Cuba.[2]

Many in the U.S. intelligence community disagreed. The Soviet Union had not placed missiles in any Eastern Bloc countries, although it would have been an easy matter to do so. Placing them in the Caribbean, where the United States had military superiority, seemed senseless and would surely provoke an American response. Additionally, there was a steady stream of denials from the highest echelons of the Soviet government.[3]

With offensive nuclear weapons in Cuba, only ninety miles away from the United States, warning time for an attack on Washington, DC, would be reduced from several hours to fifteen minutes. The implications to the strategic balance of power were frightening. Kennedy had difficulty believing the Soviets would engage in such reckless provocation. Perhaps he should have taken counsel of Winston Churchill's description of the Soviet Union as "a riddle, wrapped in a mystery, inside an enigma."[4]

The CIA was conducting twice-a-month overflights of Cuba, and on 29 August returned with film showing construction of SA-2 surface-to-air missile (SAM) sites—distinctive by their six-point star configuration—in eight separate locations. Although the SA-2 was a defensive weapon and clearly within Cuba's rights to possess, McCone speculated over what such missiles were intended to guard. Two days later, Senator Kenneth Keating (R-NY) stood on the Senate floor, and stated there was evidence of Soviet rockets in Cuba, calling on the president to take action.

Curiously, U-2 flights over Cuba ceased on 5 September. The official reason was extremely bad weather, but equally probable was a fear of a U-2 shootdown. On 9 September 1962, Chinese pilot Chen Huai Sheng's U-2 was downed by an SA-2 missile nine miles south of Nunchang, China. It is likely Kennedy's advisers urged caution at that point.[5]

Wanting further proof before proceeding with any course of action, Kennedy ordered the U-2 flights resumed on 9 October. He directed that USAF replace the CIA in operational control of the aircraft, and ordered the CIA to provide their advanced models of the U-2 for the missions, as well as support crews. Responsibility for processing the intelligence gained from the flights would remain with the CIA.

Kennedy's reason for wanting military pilots was to avoid a reoccurrence of the embarrassment Eisenhower endured after CIA U-2 pilot Gary Powers was shot down over Sverdlosk in the Soviet Union on 1 May 1960. If Air Force pilots were shot down, they could be explained as having strayed off course. Whatever the risk, Kennedy needed the photo intelligence the U-2s could provide.

The U-2 was the latest in a long line of aircraft used to gather information on emy forces' disposition and capabilities through aerial surveillance, a mission that s back as far as the use of observation balloons during the American Civil War.

When the CL-282, later redesignated the U-2, was designed by Clarence "Kelly" Johnson at the famed Lockheed "Skunk Works" at Burbank, California, in 1954, the consensus was the design would never work. The intent was to create a craft that could fly at an altitude far beyond the range of radar, missiles, and enemy interceptors. Kelly hoped that by eliminating basic features like most hydraulic systems, structural support, and conventional landing gear, the weight could be sufficiently reduced to allow the craft to attain previously unattainable altitudes of sixty thousand to seventy thousand feet. The only concession to weight was the cameras, capable of a resolution of 2.5 feet from an altitude of sixty thousand feet, and the three hundred pounds of film with which it was loaded.

To achieve range and altitude, the U-2 sacrificed speed: it had a cruising speed of only 460 miles per hour. There was a variance of only ten knots between its maximum and minimum (stall) speed. The air at sixty thousand feet is so thin as to barely support the weight of the aircraft. Too slow an airspeed and the U-2 would stall and go into a nosedive. To complicate matters, the tail and narrow eighty-foot wings of the U-2 (nearly double the distance from nose to tail) were bolted on, rather than being secured by structural supports that ran through the fuselage, making them vulnerable to buffeting at high speeds. As a result, U-2 pilots were required to keep a perpetual vigil on the airspeed indicator. There was an extremely narrow margin of error, so only highly skilled pilots could fly the U-2.[6]

The U-2's maiden flight was on 1 August 1955. The U-2s were introduced into service in 1957, primarily under the control of the CIA's Office of Scientific Intelligence. To avoid "military" incursions into foreign airspace, military pilots resigned their commissions and went to work for the CIA as civilians, a process that came to be known as "sheep dipping."

The Air Force also obtained some U-2s in 1957 and began training selected pilots on a remote airstrip at Groom Lake, Nevada, nicknamed "the Ranch." They also trained pilots in "Area 51," which later was to gain fame as the site of numerous sightings of purported extraterrestrials. The U-2 was an extraordinary aircraft, so required extraordinary pilots able to adapt to flying at the edge of outer space. Those who passed training were fitted for a pressure suit and assigned to the 4080th Strategic Reconnaissance Wing at Laughlin Air Force Base, outside remote Del Rio, Texas. The wing consisted of one U-2 squadron and twenty-five pilots under the command of Col. John A. Des Portes, a World War II bomber pilot.

When Kennedy called for more surveillance on 9 October, most of the squadron's pilots were on assignment elsewhere, sampling air over Alaska or flying reconnaissance missions over Europe or Asia. Two of the more experienced pilots, Maj. Richard Heyser and Maj. Rudolf Anderson Jr., remained at Laughlin, and were ordered to Edwards Air Force Base in California for familiarization in the CIA's U-2Cs, a model superior to the Air Force's U-2As, with a more powerful engine, giving it a five thousand–foot higher ceiling.

Maj. Rudolph Anderson Jr., SAF U-2 pilot, lost his life during the Cuban Missile Crisis on 27 October 1962. He was downed by a SAM SA-2 Guideline missile as he performed aerial reconnaissance. It was on 14 October 1962, during another photo mission, that Major Anderson and Maj. Richard S. Heyser obtained the unmistakable photographic evidence of a Soviet buildup in Cuba. For his heroic actions, Major Anderson was posthumously awarded the Distinguished Service Medal. (National Archives and Records Administration)

Maj. Rudolf "Rudy" Anderson Jr. was typical of the pilots selected to fly the U-2. Born in Spartanburg, South Carolina, on 15 September 1927, he grew up during World War II, and graduated from Clemson Agricultural College in 1948 with a degree in textile engineering. He enlisted in the U.S. Air Force on 6 November 1951, and flew F-86 Saberjets on reconnaissance missions during the Korean War.

Anderson was assigned to the Strategic Air Command (SAC) at Larson Air Force Base in Washington State in 1956 when he was selected to train to fly the U-2. Anderson was lean, athletic, and highly competitive, traits he shared with the other selected pilots. He volunteered for every mission he could get, and was then designated as the standby on other missions. He had hoped to fly the first on over Cuba, but the flight surgeon grounded him until 15 October due to a

Maj. Richard Heyser beside a U-2 high-altitude spy plane at Laughlin Air Force Base, Texas. (AP)

shoulder injury sustained weeks earlier in Alaska, and the mission went to Richard "Dutch" Heyser.

Heyser, like Anderson, was a southerner and Clemson graduate. Born at Apalachicola, Florida, Heyser was a thirty-five-year-old Korean War veteran, a jet instructor pilot, and the squadron's senior pilot. With Anderson sidelined, Heyser was selected for the first USAF overflight of Cuba.[7]

Heyser spent 13 October going over maps with navigators, plotting his course, and receiving updated intelligence on targets and weather. In the afternoon, he took a sleeping pill to guarantee eight hours of uninterrupted sleep and went to bed.

Heyser awoke just after midnight on the morning of 14 October and ate a high protein–low residue meal of steak, eggs, toast, and coffee. He then picked up the latest intelligence briefing and began the preflight protocol, which included a medical check-up, before donning his pressure suit two hours before takeoff. One hour before takeoff, he began breathing 100 percent oxygen to expel any nitrogen. (Nitrogen bubbles during depressurization can cause bends, similar to those of deep-sea divers.)

He was driven through the dark Sunday morning to his aircraft, where he observed that an Air Force insignia had been painted on the fuselage of the U-2. His takeoff, from Edwards Air Force Base in California, was timed to put him over Cuba just after sunrise, approximately a five-hour flight.

At approximately 2:30 AM on 14 October, Mission G3101 lifted off, en route to the Gulf of Mexico, and began climbing into the thin air of the upper atmosphere known as "the chimney." After approaching Cuba from the south, Heyser crossed the Isle of Pines, a small Cuban island that lies south of Havana, at 7:31 AM and activated his cameras.[8]

Heyser flew north across San Cristobal, west of Havana, and exited Cuban airspace twelve minutes later at 7:43 AM. His six-minute photo run yielded 928 photos. Although he vigilantly scanned the sky for contrails of smoke indicating a SAM missile, none was launched. He landed at McCoy Air Force Base outside Orlando, Florida, rather than return to California so the film could be processed more rapidly. He turned the film over to waiting officials, including two Air Force generals, who rushed it to a waiting aircraft that flew it to the National Photographic Interpretation Center in Suitland, Maryland. Heyser would later refer to the flight as a "milk run."[9]

The following day, 15 October, analysis by photo interpreters disclosed signs of heavy equipment in the jungle. Empty missile transporters; cranes; long, narrow, rectangular tents; and special vans used by the Soviets to transport nuclear warheads were all observed, indicating the Cubans were in the final stages of deploying intermediate-range ballistic nuclear missiles (SS-4) in Cuba. Reports of the missiles flowed to Ray Cline, the CIA's deputy director of intelligence, who ordered the film rechecked.

Following confirmation later that evening, Cline notified presidential adviser McGeorge Bundy and Secretary of Defense Robert McNamara, then contacted other high officials in the state and defense departments. Bundy made the decision to allow Kennedy a night's sleep, and did not advise the president of the missiles until early on the morning of 16 October. Bundy later justified his decision, explaining that time had been needed to prepare a presentation and summoning a meeting in the early morning would have jeopardized secrecy.[10]

At 11:45 AM, Kennedy called a meeting of the Executive Committee of the National Security Council, called the "Ex Comm," which included Attorney General Robert Kennedy, his brother; McNamara; Bundy; Secretary of State Dean Rusk; Gen. Maxwell Taylor, chairman of the Joint Chiefs of Staff; Deputy Secretary of Defense Roswell Gilpatrick; Assistant Secretary of Defense Paul Nitze; U.S. Ambassador to the United Nations Adlai Stevenson; Soviet Specialist Llewellyn Thompson; Secretary of the Treasury Douglas Dillon; CIA Director John McCone; Undersecretary of State George Ball; Special Counsel Theodore Sorensen; and Vice President Lyndon Johnson, as well as numerous "unofficial" council members.[11]

After consideration, the committee provided Kennedy with three possible courses of action: a "surgical air strike" on the missile sites, a full-scale invasion of Cuba, or a naval blockade to prevent completion of the sites and force the removal of offensive weapons and components already in place. Possible Soviet responses included invading Turkey to remove (obsolete) Jupiter missiles, blockading Berlin, or a confrontation that could lead to anything from a limited war to a nuclear exchange.[12]

McNamara argued for a blockade as a limited response that could be increased as necessary, and argued that an air strike could never remove 100 percent of the missile sites. Most of the military advisers favored immediate military action. They argued that a blockade would not remove one missile, and that a blockade would create a confrontation between the United States and the Soviet Union. Robert Kennedy recalled in his memoirs that it was the morality of a sneak attack that dominated the deliberations the first five days.

Kennedy would also need to confer with his NATO allies, as well as the Organization of American States, who would need to be convinced there really were offensive weapons in Cuba. As Kennedy and his advisers debated a course of action, construction of the sites accelerated even as Soviet Premier Nikita Khrushchev, Foreign Minister Andrei Gromyko, and Soviet Ambassador to the United Nations Valerian Zorin all insisted there were no offensive weapons in Cuba.[13]

Kennedy ordered saturation aerial surveillance of Cuba, and Anderson and Heyser made several flights before being joined by nine other U-2 pilots: Maj. Buddy L. Brown, Maj. Edwin G. Emerling, Maj. James Qualls, Capt. George M. Bull, Capt. Roger H. Herman, Capt. Charles W. Kern, Capt. Gerald E. McIlmoyle, Capt. Robert L. Primrose, and Capt. Daniel W. Schmarr.[14]

The pilots each flew as many as six flights a day, often ignoring hazardous weather conditions to get the needed photos. "We were just about mapping the entire island," Major Qualls recalled. Tension grew between the Air Force and CIA personnel over who would exercise operational control.[15]

On 17 October, Kennedy flew to Connecticut to campaign for congressional candidate Abe Ribicoff, but was kept informed of events by his brother Bobby. Additional U-2 flights on 17 October uncovered further proof of at least sixteen other installations, and thirty-two more missiles in Cuba. Intelligence estimates gave one week until the missiles were operational. In a meeting on 18 October, Gromyko again assured Kennedy that only defensive weapons were being deployed.[16]

On 20 October, a U-2 brought back film with the first evidence of a nuclear warhead storage bunker. Some reporters had observed the unusual activity, but had been asked to keep quiet in the interests of national security. Kennedy flew back to Washington from campaigning in Seattle and his press secretary, Pierre Salinger, announced the president was canceling his midterm election campaign trip due to an "upper respiratory infection." In fact, Kennedy met with his advisers. The military again strongly recommended an air strike, but Kennedy opted for a "defensive quarantine" of Cuba. The use of the word "quarantine" was deliberate: blockades are an act of war.

On 21 October, Kennedy gave final approval for the quarantine plan even as Gen. Walter Sweeney, Commander of Tactical Air Command, made a last argument for air strikes. But even with hundreds of sorties, Sweeney could estimate only a 90 percent success on missile sites. Fearful the press would break the story prematurely, Kennedy obtained an agreement from the press to hold the story until he prepared a briefing for Congress and an address to the American people. He ordered the U.S. State Department to begin to notify the heads of foreign governments.[17]

The following day, 22 October, after debating the legal justifications of a blockade within the Ex Comm, Kennedy met formally with the National Security Council, then presented photographic proof of Soviet missiles in Cuba to seventeen congressional leaders from both parties at the White House at 5:00 PM.

During the day, SAC had run round-the-clock flights of B-52s armed with nuclear weapons. One-eighth of the bomber force was airborne at all times, and 183 B-47 nuclear bombers were quietly dispersed to thirty-three civilian and military airfields. At 7:00 PM, as President Kennedy began to address the nation, America's military forces worldwide moved to "Defense Condition Three" (DEFCON-3), a designation from "defense readiness condition," indicating war is probable, and putting U.S. forces on an increased level of readiness. On 23 October, SAC was advanced to DEFCON-2, indicating the threat of war was imminent. (DEFCON-1 indicates the nation is at war.)

In his seventeen-minute address to the American people, Kennedy stated that "unmistakable evidence" proved there were Soviet intermediate-range ballistic nuclear missiles and medium-range ballistic missiles in Cuba. He announced the limited quarantine on Cuba and issued a warning to the Soviets: "It shall be the policy of this nation to regard any nuclear missile launched from Cuba against any nation in the western hemisphere as an attack by the Soviet Union on the United States, requiring full retaliatory response upon the Soviet Union."[18]

On the evening of 23 October, as Soviet Ambassador to the United Nations Valerian Zorin called charges of missiles in Cuba "completely false," Castro placed all Cuban armed forces on highest alert, followed by the Soviet Union also going on alert later that evening. American intercontinental ballistic missile crews went on alert and Polaris submarines left port, sailing to preassigned stations. USAF U-2s continued to fly over Cuba as Soviet ships sailed closer to the quarantine line.

On the morning of 24 October, sixteen of nineteen Soviet ships en route to Cuba reversed course, but U-2 surveillance revealed increased efforts to complete intermediate-range nuclear missiles and medium-range ballistic missiles, and nuclear storage buildings. Two Soviet ships, the *Gagarin* and the *Komiles*, continued toward the quarantine line. That evening, Khrushchev called for a summit meeting.

On 25 October, as politicians maneuvered and the aircraft carrier USS *Essex* (S-9) and destroyer USS *Gearing* (DD-710) allowed the Soviet tanker *Bucharest* h the blockade, a U-2 pilot, Capt. Gerald McIlmoyle, reported being targeted by an SA-2 missile near the town of Banes. The yellow light, indicating the plane had been "painted" by enemy radar, came on. He observed two contrails "zip up from beneath" and "explode in the sky above." His report was met with skepticism upon his return to McCoy.[19]

A U-2 reconnaissance on 26 October revealed the Soviets were attempting to camouflage the missile sites and the construction, which was continuing at an accelerated pace. At the same time, Khrushchev sent a letter offering to remove the missiles if Kennedy publicly guaranteed not to invade Cuba.

The morning of 27 October, Anderson persuaded Heyser to let him take his place on the flight roster, and Heyser agreed. After checking the oxygen system, pressure suit, and forty other miscellaneous items, Capt. Roger Herman cleared Anderson for takeoff. Anderson took off from McCoy Air Force Base and turned toward Cuba.

Castro had spent the previous Friday evening in the Soviet embassy in Havana, and had sent a personal cable to Khrushchev urging him to use nuclear missiles if Cuba was invaded. Castro also authorized Cuban forces to fire on U.S. planes.[20]

At 9:15 AM, Anderson's U-2 crossed the northern coastline of Cuba and flew south toward Guantnamo Bay, then headed back northward. He was picked up by radar at the Soviet-manned SAM missile site at Banes, on the northeast coast. With the Soviet commander in Cuba, Gen. Issa Pliyev, away from headquarters, Gen. Stephan Grechko, Pliyev's deputy commander, and Maj. Gen. Leonid Garbuz, chief of staff for military preparedness—believing he had the authority to employ all force short of nuclear weapons—gave the order to fire. At 10:22, two SA-2 missiles impacted with Anderson's U-2, destroying it.[21]

When the Ex Comm received the news of the shootdown, there were fears that Khrushchev had been the victim of a coup by hardliners in the Kremlin. When the USAF put the ten Minutemen One missiles on alert at Malmstrom Air Force Base in Montana, Khrushchev had equal fears that the military would persuade Kennedy to respond with force. As Secretary of State Dean Rusk would later describe it, the two nations were "eyeball to eyeball," and the world sat on the brink of nuclear war.

In 2002, it was revealed the Soviet Foxtrot-class submarine B-59, armed with a nuclear torpedo, almost launched the weapon after U.S. destroyers dropped signaling depth charges near the quarantine line. The B-59, with her batteries running low and her crew suffering from a high level of carbon dioxide in the air within the sub, was forced to surface.[22]

Capt. 2nd Rank Valentin Savitsky, the commanding officer of the B-59, exhausted and desperate, had ordered the torpedo loaded. Unable to establish radio contact with the general staff, Savitsky speculated the possibility the war had already started. Only the arguments of Vasili Arkhipov, the second officer, and the political officer dissuaded the rattled captain from launching the deadly weapon.[23]

President Kennedy meets in the Oval Office with Gen Curtiss, Lemay, Heyser, and other U-2 pilots following the Cuban Missile Crisis. (Photograph provided by the CIA History Staff)

On 28 October, Khrushchev went on Radio Moscow to announce the withdrawal of Soviet missiles from Cuba in exchange for Kennedy's pledge not to invade Cuba. In secret, the United States also agreed to remove the Jupiter missiles from Turkey. The crisis was over. Major Anderson was the sole casualty of the Cuban Missile Crisis.

Laughlin Air Force Base knew only that a U-2 pilot was missing, and there were hopes that Anderson had survived, just as U-2 pilot Gary Powers had survived two years earlier. Those hopes ended a week later when Anderson's body was returned from Cuba. Anderson left behind two young sons and a pregnant wife. He was laid to rest on 6 November 1962, at Woodlawn Memorial Park in Greenville, South Carolina.

On 26 November 1962, President Kennedy presented the Presidential Unit Citation to the 4080th Strategic Wing and the 363rd Tactical Reconnaissance Wing, stating they had "contributed as much to the security of the United States as any unit in history."[24]

Reconnaissance flights on 1 November disclosed that the medium-range ballistic ile sites had been bulldozed. On 20 November, SAC returned to its normal alert

THE WHITE HOUSE
WASHINGTON

28 October 1962

Dear Mrs. Anderson:

I was deeply shocked by the loss of your husband on an operational flight on Saturday, October 27th, 1962.

The courage and outstanding abilities of your husband were evident throughout his career, as witnessed by the award to him during the Korean War, of the Distinguished Flying Cross with two clusters. His tragic loss on a mission of most vital national urgency was once again the sacrifice of a brave and patriotic man. In time of crisis -- the source of our freedom since the founding days of our country.

On behalf of a grateful nation, I wish to convey to you and your children the sincere gratitude of all the people. I have directed the award of the Distinguished Service Medal to your husband.

Mrs. Kennedy joins me in extending to you our deepest sympathy in the loss of your husband.

Sincerely,

Letter of condolence sent to wife of Major Anderson by President John F. Kennedy (John F. Kennedy Presidential Library and Museum)

posture. In 1964, Khrushchev was removed from power, in part due to his handling of the events in Cuba.

On 8 January 1964, Major Anderson was posthumously awarded the Air Force Cross, the nation's second highest award for valor. It was the first time the medal had been awarded. Established by Congress in July 1960, it was created to be the Air Force equivalent to the Distinguished Service Cross and the Navy Cross. Anderson's other awards included the Distinguished Service Medal, three Distinguished Flying Crosses, and a Purple Heart.[25]

Many people believe that it was Anderson's death that caused the two super-powers to step back from the impending confrontation, and have lobbied Congress to posthumously award him the Medal of Honor. Others hold that Anderson's actions were no different from those of the other U-2 pilots who faced the same difficulties and took the same risks.

What cannot be argued is that on that Saturday morning in October, Anderson went aloft in an unarmed and slow-flying jet over hostile territory to obtain vital information, and gave his life in the effort, doubtlessly helping to prevent a nuclear war.

"Top Gun" Aerial Maneuvers Over Cuba
That Really Happened, 1962

★ ★ ★

In the 1986 award-winning movie Top Gun, *starring Tom Cruise and Kelly McGillis, naval aviator Cruise, flying an F-14 Tomcat, encounters an adversary over the skies of the Top Gun fighter pilot school (U.S. Navy Fighter Weapons School) at Naval Air Station (NAS) Miramar in San Diego, California. Cruise's character then performs a rather spectacular maneuver: he rolls his aircraft into an inverted position and flies canopy to canopy with the other plane, both pilots looking up and down at each other. Of course, the scene was staged, but what many are unaware of is that such an aerial maneuver really did happen some twenty years earlier during the Cuban Missile Crisis.*

On 7 March 1963, a Marine F-4 Phantom of Marine Fighter Attack Squadron 531 piloted by Capt. Robert J. Divoky with his "back seater" Radar Intercept Officer (RIO) CWO Zac C. Tomlin was scrambled from their Key West, Florida, base by a USAF air controller against a "hot track" that had originated from Cuba, resulting in the first F-4/MiG engagement.

Tomlin got a radar contact just as Divoky spotted the fastest-moving contrail he had ever seen. It seemed impossible to attempt an intercept with a two thousand–knot closure rate between the two planes, but then Divoky and Tomlin got sucked behind the collision bearing, to wind up one and a half miles in the trail of the bogey.

Divoky worked his speed up to nearly Mach 1.8 to close with the grayish fighter with red Cuban markings doing Mach 1.6 at 35,000–36,000 feet. It was the Soviet bloc's fastest aircraft, a MiG-21 about whose actual performance very little was then known. Despite being sometimes over Cuba, the USAF controller instructed Divoky to continue to follow. One reason may have been that his RIO carried a government-issued Leica camera, and here was a rare opportunity for a close-up photo.

Improbably, the MiG pilot at first seemed unaware of the Marines' presence as they flew close together at Mach 1.6. After Tomlin snapped the MiG's underside, Divoky flew up along the left side of the MiG and then rolled upside down, flying canopy-to-canopy as Tomlin got a remarkable plan view shot of the MiG cockpit while "hanging from his straps." The MiG went on to Havana, while Divoky and Tomlin scooted home with valuable film. The intelligence officers were delighted.

As were the officials in Washington when they received the "one of a kind" photograph.

[chapter thirteen]

THE PALOMARES INCIDENT, 1966

During the early morning hours on 16 January 1966, a U.S. B-52G Stratofortress took off from Seymour Johnson Air Force Base, North Carolina, carrying four type-B28RI hydrogen bombs, in order to maintain a first-strike capability during the Cold War. At the time, U.S. bombers loaded with nuclear weapons circled the globe ceaselessly on air-alert missions as part of Operation Chrome Dome. This particular aircraft followed a routine flight plan that took it across the Atlantic Ocean, over Spain where it was refueled, then northeast across the Mediterranean Sea. After circling near Eastern Bloc borders, it was routinely relieved by another SAC aircraft and turned westward, bound for home. While attempting to hook up with its refueling aircraft, a KC-135A Stratotanker, over the coastal fishing village of Palomares, Spain, on 17 January, the bomber collided with the refueler and both aircraft were destroyed. The tanker blew up, killing its four-person crew and the bomber broke apart as it fell to Earth close to the village. The debris on land was spread over several miles. Four of the seven-person crew of the B-52 parachuted to safety.[1]

Fortunately, none of the bombs was armed. Conventional explosive materials from two of the bombs exploded on impact in fields near the Spanish village, however, creating craters and spreading radioactive plutonium dust over several hundred acres. A third bomb fell to Earth, landing in a dry riverbed. Miraculously, it was found almost intact. Members of the Spanish Guardia Civil took control at the accident site. They were joined by officers and men of the Strategic Air Command's 16th Air Force that was headquartered at the SAC Torrejon Air Force Base in Madrid. Though three of the bombs were found quickly, the fourth had fallen into the Mediterranean Sea. It would be two and a half months before the errant bomb was found and lifted from a 2,550-foot seabed. The cost of the operation was estimated at $50 million to $80 million, and the United States received significant adverse publicity because of the far-reaching international implications.[2]

Thousands of U.S. military personnel and Spanish Guardia Civil swarmed the area, cleaning up the debris on the ground and decontaminating the area. Experienced in handling radioactive cleanups, the American military took the necessary precautions to prevent overexposure to the radiation. However, the Spanish people lacked experience and knowledge in such matters. As a result, many suffered from radiation poisoning. Eventually some 1,400 tons of radioactive soil and vegetation were shipped to the United States for disposal. There were 644 claims filed by Spanish citizens against the USAF for fishing and farming losses and medical injuries.[3]

Locating the lost bomb that fell into the sea posed a serious problem for the American naval recovery fleet. Because it was located so far (3,500 miles) from the U.S. shore, the international press gave continuous coverage to the incident. The world would not believe all four bombs had been recovered until they were indeed again in U.S. possession.

The U.S. Chief of Naval Operations established a Technical Advisory Group to immediately identify what deep-water recovery assets in ships (including robotic submersibles) and personnel were available for recovery of the bomb once it was found. The project, called Aircraft Salvops Med (SalvOpsMed) was headed by Adm. Leroy V. Swanson and included Adm. Odale Waters, oceanographer of the Navy; Capt. E. J. Snyderm Jr., Special Assistant Secretary of the Navy, Research and Development (R&D); Capt. W. F. Searle Jr., Supervisor of Salvage, U.S. Navy; Dr. John P. Craven, Chief Scientist, Deep Submergence Systems Project; and Rear Adm. (Ret.) E. C. Stephan, Submergence Systems Review Group.

Rear Adm. William S. Guest, USN, Deputy Commander, Naval Strike and Support Forces, Southern Europe, was selected to command Task Force 65, an element of the U.S. Sixth Fleet, established for the recovery operation. Its mission was to conduct coordinated surface and subsurface operations in the coastal waters off Palomares to detect, identify, and recover material associated with the aircraft collision. Working with the Technical Advisory Group, the two land and sea elements were tasked to work at maximum effort until the lost bomb was found, placed in its shipping container, and returned to the United States. Admiral Guest raised his flag on board the cruiser Boston and immediately established a security zone around where it was thought the bomb had splashed down. However, the zone could only extend twelve miles seaward before reaching international waters. Soviet minesweepers soon arrived in these waters and began searching for the bomb. Obviously, the fact the weapon might be recovered by the Soviets was of deep concern to the government. In mid-February, the minisubmarine *Alvin* was flown to the by the Reynolds Aluminum Company's *Aluminaut*. The latter was a nersible capable of descents greater than ten thousand feet. Among the

On board the USS *Petrel* (ASR-14), Maj. General Delmar E. Wilson (left), Commander U.S. 16th Air Force, and Rear Adm. William S. Guest, Commander U.S. Navy Task Force 65, observe the fourth and final weapon recovered by Task Force 65 off the coast of Palomares, Spain, at a depth of 2,630 feet. The equipment in the background is a cable-controlled underwater research vehicle, used to attach the lifting lines to the weapon. (U.S. Navy)

areas of best probability was a site identified by a local fisherman, Francisco Simo Orts (sometimes spelled Ortiz), who claimed he had seen the Number 4 bomb enter the sea close to his fishing boat.

U.S. officials drove to the fishing city of Aguilas where Orts resided, and interviewed him. Orts sketched what he had seen fall into the water. He had actually witnessed two chutes—a ribbon parachute and a solid sixty-four foot canopy parachute. After an analysis of the nearby positions of the B-52 crew water landings and the objects Orts had seen, the American team was convinced that Orts had in fact sighted the falling Number 4 bomb case. However, they could not be certain the bomb was still intact. Orts subsequently took U.S. Navy personnel out to the site five miles offshore.

Admiral Guest was briefed. He established a priority list of search areas by which he appropriated search and recovery assets. On 1 March, forty-two days after the collision, an object was sighted by the *Alvin*. The bomb, still attached to its parachute, had initially sunk to a depth of 355 fathoms (2,130 feet), then slid over an underwater ridge and landed another five hundred feet deeper. The bomb was finally located by *Alvin* on 15 March. A recovery robotic device called a cable-controlled underwater recovery vehicle (CURV) tethered to its mother ship, USS *Petrel*, finally brought the bomb to the surface where it was hoisted on board the *Petrel* at 8:40 AM, 7 April 1966.[4]

Early in the search for the bomb, Secretary of Defense Robert McNamara had publicly announced the bomb was valued at $2 billion. His statement would later haunt him: a few months after the bomb had been recovered, Orts and his lawyer, Herbert Brownell, former U.S. Attorney General under President Dwight D. Eisenhower, showed up at the First District Federal Court Building in New York demanding a salvage award for his assistance in finding the bomb. Under maritime law, the person who identifies the location of a ship (or in this case the bomb) can claim the device. The award is usually 1 or 2 percent of the value to the owner of the object salvaged. At a value of $2 billion, Orts was due $20 million. Although Orts filed a claim for $5 million, he eventually was awarded $10,000 for his assistance in finding the bomb. Additionally, he was reimbursed $4,566 for his help in recovering B-52 crew members and the use of his boats during the incident.[5]

[chapter fourteen]

CARL BRASHEAR
An Extraordinary Sailor, 1966

In 1970, Carl Maxie Brashear was the first African American to become a U.S. Navy Master Diver. He died on 25 July 2006 at the age of 75. Although he was not the first U.S. Navy African American Diver, he was the first to attend and graduate from the U.S. Navy Diving and Salvage School. In 1966, he was among the 196 U.S. Navy divers who were rushed to the village of Palomares, Spain, following the 17 January 1966 collision of two USAF SAC aircraft during a refueling attempt. Both aircraft were destroyed and fell to Earth near the coastal fishing village. Four hydrogen bombs carried by a B-52G Stratofortress were among the debris. Three landed in fields around Palomares, and the fourth fell offshore. The U.S. Navy was tasked with recovering the bomb. All recovery assets (ships, deep water submersibles, oceanographers, other scientists, divers, and so on) were quickly brought to bear on the recovery operation. The incident had vast international implications. Within a short period, Soviet minesweepers were roaming the waters twelve miles offshore. The possibility that America's Cold War adversary might find and recover the bomb made the U.S. mission extremely urgent.[1]

The bomb was found by the U.S. Navy on 1 March some six miles off-shore after a search that lasted two and a half months. During the recovery operation, a deck accident on board the salvage ship USS *Hoist* crushed Brashear's lower left leg below the knee. He was subsequently flown by helicopter to the U.S. Torrejon Air Force Base near Madrid and later to the Naval Hospital in Portsmouth, Virginia, where his leg was amputated. Brashear's ordeal, inspirational recovery, and return to active duty is an extraordinary story. A movie, *Men of Honor*, based on Brashear's life, starring Cuba Gooding Jr., was released in 2000. In 1989, Paul Stillwell, Director of the U.S. Naval Institute's oral history program,

BMCS Carl M. Brashear, USN, on board USS *Hunley* (AS-31) while at sea, April 1971. (U.S. Navy)

interviewed Chief Brashear. The following is an excerpt from that interview in the words of Master Chief Brashear, a truly courageous and exceptional man.

> *In September 1965 I got aboard the salvage ship Hoist (ARS-40) and was preparing myself to be a master diver. A few months later, the Air Force lost a nuclear bomb off the coast of Palomares, Spain. This was when the accident happened and I lost my leg. The reason the bomb dropped in the water was that two airplanes had been maneuvering while a tanker was fueling a B-52. According to what people said, the tanker gained on the B-52 too fast, and they collided in midair. Three of the bombs' parachutes opened and landed over Spain. One of the parachutes failed to open, and it fell in the water. [Author's note: The parachute did in fact deploy.]*
>
> *The Air Force asked the Navy to recover that bomb and, of course, the Navy said yes. We searched close to the shoreline for about two-and-a-half months. Then we went out six miles, and on the first pass, there the bomb was, in 2,600 feet of water.*
>
> *The CURV out of Woods Hole (Oceanographic Institution) was going down* ~~*his thing. I rigged what I called a spider, a three-legged contraption with*~~ *ks on each leg. It landed fifteen feet from the bomb. The parachute*

on the bomb had not opened, so the deep submersible Alvin went down and put the parachute shrouds in the grapnel hooks. But the Alvin ran out of batteries and had to surface.

Rear Admiral William Guest, through a radio conversation with our skipper, said to pick it up, so we picked it up to a certain depth. Then we brought a boat alongside to pick the crate up out of the boat and set it on deck. I was picking the bomb up with the capstan when the boat broke loose. The engineer was revving up the engines, and it parted the line.

I was trying to get my sailors out of the way, and I ran back down to grab one, when just as I started to leave, the boat pulled on the pipe that had the mooring line tied to it. The pipe flew across the deck and struck my leg below the knee. I started to run and fell over. That's when I knew how bad my leg was. [The accident, which took place on 25 March 1966, resulted in compound fractures of both bones in Brashear's lower left leg.]

So there I was on the ship with my leg torn up—no doctor, no morphine, six and a half miles from the cruiser Albany (CG-10). While we steamed toward the Albany, I was telling the guys about what I had rigged on the ship, and how to rerig it. I thought I was going to the sick bay on the Albany, but they put me in a helicopter toward Torrejon Air Force Base in Spain. They didn't fuel the helicopter and couldn't make it, so they set me down on a dilapidated runway, waiting for a two engine small plane to come and get me.

The accident happened at 1700, and at 2100 I was still on the runway. I had lost so much blood that I went into shock and passed out.

Now, I'm going to tell you some stuff that my doctor told me later in Torrejon. He said that when I was rolled into the emergency room I didn't have a pulse. Then he said he thought he'd feel on me one more time. He found I had a very faint heartbeat. Right away, he started making arrangements to get some blood. They pumped eighteen pints into me, and I came to.

When they took the bandage off, my foot fell off. So they tried again, and it fell off. It got gangrene and got infected. I was slowly dying from that, so they transferred me to Wiesbaden, Germany, where the doctor said that he could fix me, but it would take three years. I raised all kinds of hell, and he "air-mailed" me to McGuire Air Force Base in New Jersey. Three days later, I came to the naval hospital in Portsmouth, Virginia. The major surgeon there said he could have me fixed in thirty months and have me walking on a brace. I said, "I can't stay here that long. I've got to get out of here. Go ahead and amputate."

He said, "Geez, Chief! Anybody could amputate. It takes a good doctor to fix it."

I said, "I can't be tied up that long. I've got to get back to diving." They just laughed, "The fool's crazy! He doesn't have a the chance of a snowball in hell of staying in the Navy. And a diver? Impossible!"

They did a guillotine-type operation. [A portion of his lower leg was amputated on 11 May 1966.] A while later he said, "We need to cut off another inch and a half." So they cut off an inch and a half.

After that I kept saying, "I'm going to be a deep sea diver, doggone it!" By this time, I was reading about a Canadian Air Force pilot who flew airplanes with no legs. I had also read books that said a prosthesis can support any amount of weight. And I read that you've got to develop an attitude that you're going to accept this. You're going to make it work.

So they got me good enough to go to a prosthetic center in Philadelphia. When I got there, they told me it would be about two months before they could fit me with a temporary cast to shrink my stump. I talked to them a little bit, and about the next week I had a cast on my leg to shrink my stump. And I could walk with a cane. Then I began working out outside the hospital, but I broke my doggone leg, broke it off.

I didn't want anybody doing anything for me, so I started working in the brace and limb shop. When they gave me a leg, I made the statement "Doctor," I said, "I'm going to give you back this crutch, and I'll never use it again." The day they strapped that leg on me, I caught a bus to Portsmouth. I was returned to full duty and full diving—the first time in naval history for an amputee.[2]

From May 1966 to March 1967 Brashear remained at the Naval Regional Medical Center in Portsmouth recovering from and undergoing rehabilitation for his amputations. In March 1967, he was assigned to the Harbor Clearance Unit Two, Diving School, in preparation for his return to full active duty and diving. In 1968, he became the first amputee to be certified as a diver. Two years later he became the first African American to be promoted to Master Chief Petty Officer and Master Diver. Brashear retired from the U.S. Navy in 1979. He then served as a government employee at the Naval Station, Norfolk, Virginia, until he retired a second time in 1993 with the grade of GS-11. During the screening of *Men of Honor* he sat next to President Clinton and remarked, "from the outhouse to the White House," referring to his life as the son of a sharecropper in rural Kentucky in the 1930s.[3]

Chief Brashear was a courageous man who overcame impossible odds, both of racism and of amputation. His fortitude and sheer grit are an inspiration to all. Following *Men of Honor*, he was deluged with invitations to speak to audiences. The Naval Institute was overwhelmed with requests for copies of his oral history. Brashear made contact with numerous people, including amputees and troubled ᵗhs, sharing his experience with them while giving them hope and heartwarming Though he had achieved so much during his lifetime, he remained unpre- ᵗory continues to inspire people today.[4]

chapter fifteen

COMMANDER BUCHER AND THE SECOND KOREAN CONFLICT, 1966–69

Following the Korean Armistice Agreement negotiated between the United Nations Command (UNC), the North Korean People's Army (KPA), and Chinese People's Volunteers (CPV) on 27 July 1953, active combat ceased between Communist North and the Democratic South Korea, initiating a period of covert—and sometimes overt—conflicts that extended several decades following the armistice.

B y agreement, the country was divided across the center at the 38th Parallel, and a DMZ was created along the 155-mile border, with the zone extended two and one-half miles to either side of the military demarcation line (MDL), a six-foot-wide corridor that ran down the center of the DMZ.

As one of the provisions of the armistice, an agency, the Military Armistice Commission (MAC), was created to monitor the terms of the truce, and a section of the DMZ was designated as the Joint Security Area (JSA), an area reserved for negotiations between the governments of North Korea and South Korea.[1]

Referred to as the Truce Village or Panmunjon, due to its proximity to the former village of Panmunjon, the JSA is located on the western end of the 155-mile border, 39 miles northwest of Seoul and 134 miles south of Pyongyang. The village of Panmunjon itself was destroyed in the Korean War, but gained fame as the site of the armistice negotiations between General Nam II for the KPA and Gen. William K. Harrison for the UNC. The formal document was later signed by Gen. Mark Clark, commander of the UNC at Munsan, south of the DMZ, and by Marshal Kim Il Sung for the KPA and Peng The-huai, commander of the CPV at Kaesong, north of the DMZ.

The JSA itself is a section of the DMZ—half a mile wide, roughly circular in shape—that bisects the MDL. In fact, the conference table in the MAC conference room exactly bisects the MDL. The complex also contains a Joint Duty Office (JDO) that maintains a continuous liaison between the two governments, administrative buildings, and facilities for each side's military police performing security duties, no more than thirty-five of whom can be on duty at a time, each manning six guard posts. For the United States, security is provided by the 8th Army's Joint Security Force (JSF) Company whose motto is "In Front of Them All." It is the only site within the DMZ where the two sides come face to face.[2]

The armistice did not mean a cessation of hostility between the two Koreas. Rather, it meant a more subtle expression of that hostility was required. Infiltration, primarily to gather intelligence and establish covert political cells, occurred continuously between 1953 and October 1966. During that period, eight Americans were killed in clashes along the DMZ.[3]

Opening Shots

The first American killed following the armistice occurred when a USAF LT-6 utility training aircraft was downed by ground fire when it accidently crossed into North Korean airspace on 18 August 1955 near the DMZ at Panmunjon, wounding the pilot and killing his observer, Capt. Charles W. Brown. Skirmishes along the DMZ continued, and a second pilot, Lt. Col. Delynn Anderson, was killed in a crash landing south of Seoul after being fired on by North Korean aircraft on 20 April 1961.[4]

On 3 October 1962, Pfc. Richard Rimer, First Cavalry Division, was killed by hostile fire while on guard duty at Hyang Yang on the DMZ, the first American killed on the ground guarding the DMZ. A month later, on 23 November, North Korean troops attacked the 9th Cavalry's A Troop at Outpost Susan, killing one American and wounding another. On 29 July 1963, raiders ambushed a 9th Cavalry jeep patrol, killing two Americans and wounding a third. The fourth member of the patrol was killed while pursuing his attackers.[5]

The nature of the infiltrations changed in the mid-1960s. As America's involvement in Vietnam increased, violations of the armistice increased, as did the violence. Ambushes, sabotage, and assassinations were accomplished by trained raiders on specific missions similar to the guerilla war tactics used by the Viet Cong in Southeast Asia.

In a speech to the Korean Workers Party (KWP) on 5 October 1966, North Korean Premier Kim Il Sung declared, "In the present situation, the U.S. imperialists should be dealt blows and their forces dispersed to the maximum in Asia, Europe, South Africa and Latin America . . . and they should be bound hand and foot everywhere they are. . . . All socialist countries should oppose the aggression of U.S. imperialism in Vietnam and render every possible support to the people of Vietnam . . . the socialist countries should fight more sharply against them."[6]

Whether he hoped to force South Korea to withdraw its three combat divisions from Vietnam, or whether he believed the American commitment in Vietnam would prevent support for South Korea in another conflict since political sentiment against the war in Vietnam would preclude involvement in a second war, Kim Il Sung's clear intent was to instigate conflict.

The beginning of a three-year conflict that would come to be known as the "DMZ War" and the "Second Korean Conflict" began with the attack on an eight-man 2nd Infantry Division patrol in the DMZ four weeks later, on 2 November 1966.

Private Reynolds and the Start of the DMZ War

PVT. ERNEST D. REYNOLDS (KIA)

The President of the United States takes pride in presenting the Silver Star Medal (Posthumously) to Ernest D. Reynolds (US-55881470), Pvt., U.S. Army, for gallantry in action while engaged in military operations, while serving with Company A, 1st Battalion, 23d Infantry Regiment, 2d Infantry Division. Private Reynolds distinguished himself by gallantry in action on 2 November 1966, in the Republic of Korea, by sacrificing his own life in the defense of his fellow soldiers. Private Reynolds was a member of a patrol operating near the southern boundary of the Demilitarized Zone in Korea when his patrol was attacked and overrun by an armed patrol of the North Korean Army. Prior to the attack, as rear security man, he had occupied a concealed position and opened fire upon the enemy, and he continued to fire until he himself was killed. His indomitable courage, determination, and profound concern for his fellow soldiers, are in the highest traditions of the military service and reflect great credit upon himself, the 2d Infantry Division, and the United States Army.

Silver Star citation for Pvt. Ernest D. Reynolds, USA

On 31 October 1966, President Lyndon Johnson went to Korea for a series of meetings with South Korean President Park Chung-hee, placing that country on a heightened state of alert. In the early hours of 2 November, as Johnson slept in Seoul's Walker Hill Hotel, an eight-man patrol of A Company, 1st Battalion, 23rd Infantry was out patrolling the rugged terrain of the DMZ hoping to interdict any infiltrators, unaware that they themselves were being trailed by a North Korean commando team.

Sgt. James Hensley led six experienced GIs and one KATUSA (Korean Augmentation to the United States Army) through the darkness, with Pvt. Ernest Reynolds, a nineteen-year-old new to Korea, bringing up rear security. As they were returning to camp after finishing their patrol, they were ambushed approximately two-thirds of a mile south of the DMZ by intense machine-gun fire and a hail of grenades.

The initial assault wounded or killed seven of the eight men, leaving only Reynolds, who was in the rear, unharmed. Immediately returning fire, he fiercely counterattacked, charging and engaging the enemy to protect his fallen comrades until felled by enemy gunfire, after which he was bayoneted and his corpse mutilated. The same fate befell the others.

Only one soldier, seventeen-year-old Pfc. David Bibee, with forty-eight fragmentation wounds, survived by playing dead as a North Korean soldier stripped him of his watch. Besides Hensley and Reynolds, the others killed were Pfc. John Benton, Pfc. Robert Burrell, Pvt. Morris Fisher, Pvt. Les Hasty, and an unidentified KATUSA. Reynolds defense was so fierce that he was recommended for a Medal of Honor, but instead was presented with a posthumous Silver Star on 4 April 1967.[7]

The ambush made the front page in the United States, but only momentarily distracted the public from the ongoing and escalating conflict in Vietnam. Sixteen Americans were killed in border incidents throughout 1967, and countless others wounded as North Korea worked to create a Communist insurgency in South Korea. Infiltrating North Korean commandos attacked patrols, laid mines, and set out booby traps to harass UNC troops and create havoc.[8]

The year 1967 saw the first use of South Korean artillery since the armistice, attacks on a U.S. barracks well south of the DMZ, the construction of a better border fence, and an increase in the number of firefights and North Koreans killed. Those numbers increased from 371 attempted infiltrations in 1967 to 1,071 attempts in 1968. Land infiltrations through the DMZ were used 83 percent of the time, and infiltrations by sea were used the other 17 percent of the time.[9]

Attack on the Blue House

On 5 January 1968, a thirty-one-man detachment of the North Korean 124th Army Unit went into isolation in Sariwon for eight days of intensive training. Designated "Unit 124," it comprised primarily officers in their mid-20s, fanatical Communists dedicated to toppling South Korea's "puppet regime." They were highly trained for guerilla and terrorist operations in the south.[10]

The unit practiced building seizures on a specially constructed model of the Blue House, the South Korean presidential residence. On 13 January, after more than a week of practical exercises, the commandos staged in a high-security installation just north of the DMZ in the Hwanghae Province. There they met with KPA reconnaissance Chief, Lt. Gen. Kim Chung-tae, who informed them, "Your mission Seoul and assassinate then cut off the head of Park Chung-hee."[11]

As Lt. Kim Shin-jo, the only raider captured alive, later explained, the hope was to create political problems within the South Korean government and cause the South Korean people to rise up against their government.

Early on the morning of 17 January, the North Koreans, dressed in black coveralls, breached the perimeter fence of the DMZ within one hundred feet of a position manned by troops of the 2nd Infantry Division. To avoid detection, they traveled only by night for the next two days.

On the afternoon of 19 January, the commandos stumbled on a party of four South Korean woodsmen. Rather than killing them, they spent the afternoon and evening indoctrinating them about the "oppressed masses" and "people's liberation." Seeing themselves as liberators rather than murderers, they released the men with a stern warning not to go to the police. They reasoned that even if the men did go to the police, they would not be believed, and it was too late in any event. They were incorrect on both points.

The men went to the police that night. By the morning of 20 January, counterguerilla operations were already under way. The police and military were responsible for guarding important sites and people while concurrently searching for the infiltrators, a task complicated by having zero intelligence regarding the target.

That same morning, members of Unit #124 entered Seoul in two- to three-man teams. By monitoring radio traffic, the infiltrators gained valuable information and they hoped to use the confusion of the heightened alert to their advantage. They removed their coveralls to reveal South Korean uniforms with correct insignia for the 26th Infantry Division, a unit assigned to the Seoul area.[12]

On the morning of 21 January, raiders formed into ranks with the intent of marching to the Blue House and posing as a returning counterguerilla patrol. Marching smartly, they made it to within blocks of the presidential mansion, the distance varying in account from 985 to 2,600 feet, before being halted by a group of the National Police. The police commander, Choe Kyu-sik, began to question the soldiers, and became suspicious of their nervous answers. Accounts differ as to whether the police or raiders fired first, but the outcome was a gunfight that killed Choe and two raiders. The rest scattered, throwing a hand grenade into a bus to create confusion as they fled.

A massive ten-day manhunt followed, punctuated by ambushes and attacks as the survivors made their way north toward the border. Eventually, twenty-eight raiders were killed or committed suicide; one, Lieutenant Kim, was captured; and two were unaccounted for and presumed dead. The cost was three Americans and sixty-eight Korean soldiers, police, and civilians killed. Additionally, three Americans and sixty-six Koreans were wounded.[13]

There would be other attempts on Park's life. On 15 August 1974, while Park was making a speech on the twenty-ninth anniversary of Korea's liberation from

Cdr. Lloyd M. Bucher, USN, commanding officer of USS *Pueblo* (AGER-2), shown receiving the Purple Heart medal in 1969 for injuries received while a prisoner of the North Koreans. (U.S. Navy)

USS *Pueblo* (AGER-2) was captured by North Koreans off Wonsan on 23 January 1968. The crew was released on 23 December 1969. (U.S. Navy)

Japanese occupation, a North Korean agent, Mun Se-gwang, fired a shot that missed Park but killed Park's wife.

On 26 October 1979, Park was shot to death by Kim Jae-kyu, director of the South Korean Central Intelligence Agency who declared Park an "obstacle to democracy" and characterized his own actions as those of a patriot.

Two days into the manhunt, a second event occurred off the coast of North Korea that thrust Korea into the focus of the American consciousness when KPN ([North] Korean People's Navy) patrol boats seized a U.S. Navy vessel in international waters.

From the beginning of the Cold War, the gathering of intelligence had been complicated by the closed nature of Communist societies. The United States primarily utilized aircraft, submarines, and low-orbiting satellites for the collection of signals intelligence (SIGINT) and electronic signals intelligence (ELINT). The weakness of this approach was that they were moving rather than stationary platforms, unable to remain on station for long periods, with the exception of submarines, which required the raising of receiving antennas that exposed their position.

The Soviets used fishing trawlers, outfitted as electronic surveillance platforms, that could remain off the coast, outside the twelve-mile limit, gathering intelligence under the cover of fishing in international waters. In response, the U.S. Navy and the National Security Agency (NSA) developed the Auxiliary General Environmental Research (AGER) program as the equivalent of the Soviet trawlers, to utilize small unarmed or lightly armed vessels as ELINT/SIGINT platforms, under cover of oceanographic research. The ships would be manned by U.S. Navy crews, communications technicians (CTs) from the Naval Security Group, and civilian oceanographers.[14]

The United States was already using larger converted World War II Liberty ships, like the USS *Liberty* (AGTR-5), to gather intelligence, but they were conspicuous and expensive to operate. It was hoped that the smaller, AGER-class ships would correct both deficiencies.

The prototype, the USS *Banner* (AGER-1), a retrofitted auxiliary cargo vessel (AKL) experienced success along the Sino–Soviet coastline in 1967, so the conversion of two additional AKLs into AGERs was authorized: the USS *Pueblo* (AGER-2) and the USS *Palm Beach* (AGER-3).[15]

The USS *Pueblo*, built by the Kewaunee (WI) Shipbuilding and Engineering Corporation, was built for the U.S. Army Transportation Corps and launched on 16 April 1944 as FP-344, an 850-ton general purpose supply vessel. It saw service in the Philippines and Korea. Transferred to the Navy in April 1966 as a light cargo ship (AKL-44), it was converted and redesignated AGER-2 in May 1967. Following "shakedown" operations along the West Coast, *Pueblo* departed for the Far East on 6 November 1967 to undertake ELINT collection.[16]

In command of the *Pueblo* was a forty-one-year-old former submariner from Pocatello, Idaho: Lt. Cdr. Lloyd Mark Bucher. Born on 1 September 1927, Bucher was adopted, then orphaned by his adoptive parents, and spent his early years shuttling between family members. In the summer of 1941, at age thirteen, he read a magazine article about Boys Town, an orphanage in Nebraska for boys. After writing a letter to Father Flanagan, he was accepted into the program.[17]

Bucher excelled as a student and athlete at Boys Town, but dropped out of high school during his senior year. World War II was on, and he enlisted in the U.S. Navy, serving from 1945–47. He left the Navy as a Quartermaster 2nd Class with a high school diploma. After working construction and tending bar, Bucher enrolled at the University of Nebraska on a football scholarship in 1949. While he was there, he joined the Naval Reserve Officers Training Corps (NROTC), played halfback on the football team, and met his future wife, Rose. He graduated in 1953 with a degree in geology and a commission as an ensign in the naval reserve.[18]

Bucher was called to active duty in January 1954 and served briefly on board the USS *Mount McKinley* (LCC-7), an amphibious force command ship, before attending the Submarine School at New London, Connecticut, in mid-1955. He served on board the submarines USS *Besugo* (SS-321), USS *Caiman* (SS-323), and the USS *Ronquil* (SS-396), where he served as XO until 1964. After serving as assistant operations officer on the staff of the commander, Submarine Flotilla Seven in Yokosuka, Japan, Bucher was finally given command of his own ship, but it was not a submarine.

When Bucher arrived at the Puget Sound Naval Shipyard at Bremerton, Washington, on 29 January 1967 to take command of the *Pueblo* and its eighty-two-man crew, he noted several deficiencies that affected the ship's seaworthiness. The ship's rudder froze on its first trial run, a problem that frequently recurred. The steering broke down 180 times during trials, and there were problems with internal and external communications. In addition, provisions for destroying sensitive documents and equipment were inadequate: there were only two small hand-fed paper shredders on board, capable of one thousand sheets an hour, and a fifty-gallon incinerator on the deck.[19]

Bucher requested the installation of watertight hatches and a destruction system so that the ship could be scuttled quickly in the event of attack, but neither request was acted upon. On 5 September 1967, *Pueblo* received its final certification from the Board of Certification and Survey that noted, "Deficiencies exist in the ship that substantially reduce her fitness for naval service, but are not of such magnitude to warrant retrial of the ship."[20]

On 6 November, with Herb Albert's "Lonely Bull" playing over the ship's intercom, the *Pueblo* began its trans-Pacific cruise, stopping at Pearl Harbor and weathering a severe North Pacific storm for seven days, before arriving at Yokosuka Naval Base in Japan on 1 December.

The Navy had intended originally for the AGERs to be unarmed, but the attack on the USS *Liberty* on 6 June 1967 had caused that decision to be revised. Although the chief of naval operations had ordered AGERs to be armed with deck cannons, the *Pueblo* was ultimately armed with two .50-caliber machine guns, mounted fore and aft in exposed positions.[21]

While in Yokosuka, the USS *Banner* (AGER-1) arrived, returning from its mission in the Sea of Japan. Although it reported harassment by Soviet and Chinese destroyers that would maneuver as if to ram them, or hoist signals ordering them to heave to (stop) or be fired upon, there were no incidents. They were never bothered by the North Koreans. Also while in port, the steering engine was repaired and the guns installed.[22]

Two Marines, Sgt. Robert Hammond and Sgt. Bob Chicca, joined the crew just prior to its departure from Yokosuka for Sasebo, Japan, on 5 January 1968. They had known each other while attending communications intelligence school, and they had studied Korean together at the Defense Language Institute in Monterey, California. Hammond had served a tour in Vietnam, and now both had been assigned together to monitor and translate Korean radio communications on board the *Pueblo*. The two civilian oceanographers, Dunnie "Friar" Tuck and Harry Iredale, also reported on board at Yokosuka just prior to departure.

It was a cold, gray morning as the ship sailed. It soon ran into another winter storm that stayed with them as the *Pueblo* transited the southern tip of Kyushu and arrived in Sasebo, the other major navy port in Japan, on 9 January. At 6:00 AM on 11 January, after making repairs, the *Pueblo* departed Japan on its mission to monitor North Korean naval activity, monitoring radar and radio communications while observing Soviet naval units operating in the Tsushima Strait.

The plan was to sail north to the Soviet Union–North Korean border, then slowly sail south, remaining fifteen miles offshore while monitoring and recording UHF radio signals. They were ordered to remain on station until 27 January, then return to Sasebo. "My job was to take the ship safely to wherever the spooks wanted to go," Bucher would later recall.[23]

The *Pueblo* sailed north to Operational Area Pluto, between 42 and 41 north latitude, then turned south. A winter storm and freezing temperatures caused ice to form on the deck and superstructure, however, hindering operations that were uneventful, except for the sighting of Japanese and Russian freighters. Only the oceanographers had work as they recorded water temperatures and saline content. They moved south into Operational Area Venus, between 41 and 40 north latitude, off Myang Do.

At twilight on 21 January, a modified Soviet SO-1 type subchaser passed within 1,600 yards of the *Pueblo* but radio silence was maintained and Bucher believed they went undetected. Although the *Pueblo* was not transmitting, it could still receive, but no messages were received updating Bucher about hostile North Korean events on land.

The *Pueblo* then proceeded farther south into Operational Area Mars, off Wonson. The following morning, 22 January, was sunny, and the *Pueblo* began to pick up ELINT. Shortly after lunch, two North Korean (Russian-built Lenta class) fishing trawlers circled the *Pueblo* at about five hundred yards, left, then returned to again circle them, this time from a distance of approximately twenty-five yards. Bucher made the decision to break two weeks of radio silence to send off SITREP 1 (Situation Report 1), the first electronic message to U.S. Naval Security Group (USNAVSECGRU) at Kamiseya.

Unable to raise a response, technicians worked through the night. Fourteen hours later, at 10:00 AM on 23 January, Kamiseya was raised and SITREP 1 was transmitted. The *Pueblo* received no information back regarding the attack on the Blue House two days earlier, but did receive the latest NBA basketball scores.[24]

At 20° Fahrenheit, it was a relatively mild day with light seas, and the *Pueblo* moved to a position fifteen miles offshore of North Korea, near the island of Yo Do. SITREP 2 was transmitted and receipt was acknowledged by Kamiseya before *Pueblo* returned to radio silence. As lunch was being served in the wardroom, Bucher received word of a ship eight miles out and approaching rapidly from the south. Three minutes later, a second report put the ship five miles out and closing. By the time Bucher made it to the flying bridge, the ship, a heavily armed subchaser with crew at battle stations, flying the North Korean flag, was circling the *Pueblo*. "It was like watching a movie, where everyone's behind their guns looking at you . . . the wrong end of a lot of firepower," Chicca later remembered.[25]

Bucher ordered the crew below deck, and had the oceanographers go topside to take water samples. He ordered Ens. Tim Harris, the junior officer on board, to keep a record of events, and had the quartermaster raise the U.S. flag. When the subchaser signaled the *Pueblo* to "Heave To or I Will Fire," Bucher was bemused because they were dead in the water, and he responded with signals stating, "I Am in International Waters" and "I Am Hydrographic."

By now, the subchaser had closed to five hundred yards, and had been joined by three North Korean torpedo boats, as two MiG jets did a low flyover. In the Special Operations Detachment (SOD) hut, Hammond had joined Chicca to monitor the subchaser's communications, and another CT, 1PO Don Bailey, raised Kamiseya on the radio and asked them to keep the line open. Lt. Steve Harris, in charge of the twenty-eight CTs in the SOD hut, asked Bucher if they should begin destroying sensitive material, but was told to hold off, as Bucher still believed it was only harassment. Bucher had radar confirmation they were 15.8 miles out, clearly in international waters.[26]

At 12:10 PM U.S. sources intercepted a message from the subchaser; "The name of the target is GER-2. I judge it to be a reconnaissance ship. It is American guys.

It does not appear that there are weapons and it is a hydrographic mapping ship." When a second subchaser and a fourth torpedo boat were seen approaching, and Bucher saw a boarding party in helmets and carrying AK-47s transferring to one of the torpedo boats, he hoisted flags that said "Thank You for Your Consideration. I Am Now Departing the Area." He ordered the *Pueblo* under way out to sea.[27]

As the *Pueblo* maneuvered to evade the boarding party coming along the starboard side, the subchaser, still displaying the "Heave To or I Will Fire" flags, opened up with her 57-mm cannon, while the torpedo boats raked the superstructure with machine-gun fire. The 57-mm round struck the radar mast and flying bridge, wounding Bucher and two others with shrapnel. Painfully aware this was not typical harassment, Bucher ordered the destruction of all classified material as the ship continued eastward.

The crew worked frantically to destroy all sensitive material, but as Bucher had feared, the facilities were inadequate to the task. "We started burning everything," Chicca recalled. "All we had were trashcans and matches. We didn't have any of the right equipment."[28]

Fireman Duane Hodges came to the SOD hut to assist in the destruction of documents as sailors worked to smash equipment with axes and sledgehammers. Burning documents filled the passageway with smoke and heat, adding to the confusion. Suddenly, the North Koreans opened fire again and an explosion shook the passageway, wounding several men, including Chicca and Hodges, whose leg was nearly blown off. The wounded were carried off to a makeshift hospital on the mess deck. Hodges, who died from his wounds after becoming a prisoner of the North Koreans, was awarded a posthumous Silver Star for what his citation described as "rendering invaluable assistance in the face of intense hostile fire."

The second volley of fire persuaded Bucher to bring the *Pueblo* to a halt. The *Pueblo*'s two .50-caliber machine guns were still wrapped in frozen tarps, with the ammunition stored away below decks. As Adm. John Hyland, former Commander in Chief of the Pacific Fleet, who later convened a Court of Inquiry observed, "He never manned his guns. He didn't go to General Quarters until he'd already been fired upon." Surrounded and outgunned, Bucher reluctantly agreed to follow the North Koreans when he observed one of the torpedo boats uncovering one of its tubes.[29]

The subchaser signaled the *Pueblo* to follow, and Bucher complied, ordering her ahead at one-third speed to give the crew more time to destroy the large volume of classified material on board. Contact was maintained with Kamiseya. Camera gear, machine tools, sidearms, and miscellaneous equipment was jettisoned overboard, and stacks of classified documents were burned, shredded, or thrown over the side in weighted sacks. Bucher fully expected that help was en route, and the last message received from Kamiseya was, "Some birds [are] winging your way."

North Korean photograph of the crew of the USS *Pueblo* (AGER-2) in a press conference after their capture. The ship's commanding officer, Cdr. Lloyd Bucher, is standing at center in the photograph. (National Archives and Records Administration)

Finally out of patience with *Pueblo's* stalling, the North Koreans ordered her to a stop, and a torpedo boat pulled alongside with a boarding party. At 2:50 PM, forty-one heavily armed KPA soldiers boarded under the command of Col. Kim Joon Rok. Rok ordered the crew on deck to the fantail and forward well deck where they were bound and blindfolded and ordered to remain silent as they were punched, kicked, and prodded with bayonets while their personal property was pilfered. Bucher was forced at gunpoint to lead a "tour" of the ship. He later recalled being dismayed at the amount of classified material that remained undestroyed.

The crew was then held below decks in the berthing area for the voyage to Wonson. Thus began eleven months of captivity for the eighty-two surviving members of the *Pueblo* crew. Despite the crew's hopes of rescue, none came. Although four American carriers lay less than an hour's flying time away—and two of them, the USS *Enterprise* (CVN-65) and USS *Oriskany* (CVA-34), put pilots on alert—no assistance was sent. The Air Force in Okinawa did scramble jets, but the response time was too great to be of any use.[30]

Since the mission risk had been rated as "minimal," there was no expectation that there would be trouble. It seems there was no contingency plan in place with which to respond. Subsequent retaliatory actions were shelved as impractical since they would only endanger the welfare of the eighty-two captives. For instance, the commander of the Navy's Pacific command, Adm. Ulysses S. Grant Sharp, proposed sailing the destroyer USS *Higbee* (DD-806) into Wonson harbor, covered by the USS *Enterprise* (CVAN-65) to threaten massive airstrikes if the *Pueblo* was not released. Military action was forced to give way to diplomacy, since the United States was already involved in one war in Vietnam and a second armed conflict was deemed impractical.[31]

The crew was taken off the ship blindfolded in front of a screaming hostile crowd and loaded on board a bus with covered windows and taken to a train, also with covered windows, for the trip to Pyongyang. There, they were brought before the press, the first of what would be many propaganda events.

It was during the eleven months of captivity that the valor of the *Pueblo* crew would be tested and confirmed. Despite severe beatings and torture, the crew retained their cohesiveness. Coerced into false confessions, they did all they could to frustrate the efforts of North Korean propaganda. Denied the means to resist physically, the crew of the *Pueblo* found other means to resist.

Threatened with execution and other psychological torture (their captors had access to each crew member's personnel file), denied adequate medical attention, starved, and physically beaten, the crew nonetheless resisted with nonsensical confessions, false information, and the display of obscene gestures in propaganda photographs. Crew members, aware that their captives had no understanding of "the finger," used the gesture at every opportunity, explaining to their captors that the gesture was a "Hawaiian good luck gesture." When *Time* magazine inadvertently exposed the ruse in the 18 October issue, the beatings were renewed with vigor, a time that came to be known as "Hell Week."[32]

One crew member, Sergeant Hammond, took it upon himself to act as a scapegoat to prevent other, weaker, members of the crew from being beaten. His Navy Cross citation states he "became a symbol of resistance, courage, and dedication to the United States." This infuriated the North Koreans, who singled him out for more frequent and far more severe brutalities than were administered to the other prisoners. When the North Koreans learned the *Pueblo* crew had duped them in their international propaganda efforts, they intensified their efforts to break the will and spirit of the crew through the administration of indiscriminate beatings. Realizing that many of his shipmates were in danger of being permanently injured or killed, Sergeant Hammond willingly attempted to sacrifice his own life in order that his shipmates might be spared further torture. The following day the North Koreans ceased their beatings and torture.

In total, one Navy Cross, two Silver Stars (Hodges and Lt. [jg] Carl F. Schumacher, an operations officer who supervised the destruction of sensitive material under "intense hostile fire"), and six Bronze Stars with combat "V" were awarded to *Pueblo* crew members. All crew members were awarded the combat action ribbon, the Navy Commendation Medal with combat "V," and the Purple Heart, with ten receiving a second award for wounds received in the boarding. Additionally, the POW Medal was retroactively awarded to the crew on 5 May 1990.

Since Navy regulations prohibit the award of military decorations for heroism to civilians, oceanographers Tuck and Iredale were awarded the Distinguished Civilian Service Medal and Superior Civilian Service Medal, respectively.

The crew members were released from captivity only after the United States publically apologized in writing, acknowledging the United States had been spying, and had violated North Korean waters. On 23 December 1968, one by one, the crew members, led by Lieutenant Commander Bucher, crossed the Bridge of No Return into South Korea. The crew was given a hero's welcome upon their return to the United States, and public support continued as the Navy considered its response.

A court of inquiry was called to investigate the circumstances of the *Pueblo's* capture, and a court martial was recommended for Bucher and Lieutenant Harris, the officer in charge (OIC) of the research department, but Secretary of the Navy John H. Chafee rejected the recommendation, stating, "they have suffered enough."

Bucher retired as a full commander in 1973, and wrote his memoirs, *Bucher: My Story*, in 1970. When questioned about the surrender of his ship, Bucher always maintained he was following his orders not to start an international incident. He died in San Diego, California, on 28 January 2004.

Hammond, a Vietnam veteran, retired from the Marines in 1968 and went to work as an adjutant military adviser at the Institute for Molecular Medicine in California.

In 1969, the Navy quietly scuttled the AGER program. The USS *Pueblo* remains in North Korea, docked at Pyongyang, and is a popular tourist attraction. The damage done by the loss of intelligence captured by the North Koreans can only be estimated, but is certainly large.

Both lionized for his actions and vilified for the seizure of his ship, but enjoying the support of the majority of his crew, Bucher said, "I did what I thought was best. I can't change history."[33]

★ ★ ★

January 1968 was not a good month for President Johnson. On 20 January, Communists laid siege to the Marine base at Khe Sanh in Vietnam. The next day, 21 January, an attack on the Blue House in Seoul was narrowly prevented, and on 22 January, a B-52 crashed into the sea near Greenland with four nuclear weapons coming free and unaccounted for. (All were subsequently recovered.) On 23 January, the *Pueblo* was seized and the Tet Offensive in Vietnam broke out 30–31 January.

During the eleven months that followed, as the United States negotiated the release of the *Pueblo* crew, incidents along the DMZ continued. In reaction to increased infiltrations and sabotage, in early 1968 the United States diverted troops bound for Vietnam to Korea and extended the tour of troops already in-country. Infiltrations and attacks continued throughout the year as North Korea worked to establish a guerilla movement in South Korea similar to the one in South Vietnam.

The North's Last Chance: The Ulchin–Samchok Raid

On 24 September 1968, South Korean units engaged in open battle with a battalion of KPA troops that had infiltrated south of the DMZ. A month later, between 30 October and 2 November, the DMZ War hit its high-water mark when 120 KPA commandos of the 124th Army unit landed in eight separate locations in 15-man teams along the South Korean coast between Ulchin and Samchok.

After landing undetected, the teams, dressed in a variety of South Korean uniforms and civilian street clothes, moved inland into the Taebaek Mountains, hoping to create long-lasting guerilla bases in the south and obtain recruits for the KWP. But their efforts to win the hearts and minds of the people were spectacularly unsuccessful. In one village, they gathered the local residents for "educational" sessions, but stoned latecomers to death. At another, they killed ten-year-old Lee Sung-bok because he said he "hated Communism."

Refusing to be intimidated, villagers reported the raiders to a provincial police chief who radioed for assistance. Soon, South Korean forces swarmed into the area. Assisted by helicopters and pilots of the U.S. 6th Combat Aviation Platoon, South Korean Marines, Combat Police, Special Forces, and the newly formed Homeland Defense Reserve Force (HDRF), a force eventually numbering seventy thousand men, were involved in the manhunt.[34]

By 26 December, 110 of the raiders had been killed, with another 7 captured at a cost of 63 South Koreans killed, 23 of whom were civilians. The operation proved the southern forces were capable of containing northern infiltration by themselves.[35]

By the beginning of 1969, the tide was turning in favor of South Korea and the UNC. Troops were receiving increased training in light infantry and counterguerilla tactics. Congress approved $100 million for a special military aid program and another $12 million foreign aid loan. The U.S.–South Korean Operational Planning Staff, created in October 1968 to give the South Koreans a voice in the UNC combined command, was functioning smoothly. And the United States had a new president, Richard Nixon, with a reputation of being tough on Communism.[36]

Concurrently, North Korea's Communist sponsors, the Soviet Union and China, were involved in a series of armed clashes along the Sino–Soviet border. At the same time, the increase of incidents along the Korean DMZ had strengthened rather than weakened the ties between the United States and South Korea.

Early in 1969, North Korean Premier Kim Il-Sung arrested several high-ranking military officers associated with the prosecution of the Second Korean Conflict, including the defense minister, Gen. Kim Chongbong; KPA political bureau chairman, Gen. Ho Pong-haek; chief of the general staff, Gen. Choe Kwang; Reconnaissance Bureau chief, Lt. Gen. Kim Chong-tae; KPN commander, Adm. Yu Chong-gon; KWP guerrilla activities secretary, Maj. Gen. Cho Tong-chol; and the commanders of three frontline KPA corps. Kim Chong-bong, Ho Pong-haek, and one corps commander were executed, and the remainder imprisoned.

At the Fourth KWP–KPA conference, convened in secret at Pyongyang in January 1969, Kim justified his actions by claiming the generals had deliberately sabotaged the campaign and failed to translate the ideology of the KWP into a program palatable to South Korean farmers. Clearly, Kim's unconventional warfare campaign was a failure.

Although incursions and incidents continued, the number decreased from seven hundred incidents in 1968 to a little more than a hundred in 1969. On 15 March, a ten-man working party of the 2nd Infantry Division replacing markers in the MDL was fired on from a North Korean guard post in the JSA. A patrol sent to assist engaged the North Koreans in a four-hour firefight, resulting in one American medic (Pfc. Calvin Lee Lindsey) killed, and two riflemen (SSgt. George T. McKinney and Sp.4 Peter M. Keren) and one KATUSA (Cpl. J. B. Kim) wounded.

After the firefight ended, a medical evacuation helicopter from the 377th Medical Company landed and loaded the dead and wounded on board. Sleet and snow filled the air as the helicopter lifted off, then fell straight down, exploding into flames. Killed was the pilot, Maj. James T. Rothwell; two crewmen, Sp.4 Edwin Stoller and Sp.5 Carroll Zanchi; a doctor with the 121st Evacuation Hospital, Capt. Benjamin Park Jr.; McKinney and Keren of B Company 3/23rd Infantry, 7th ID; and Corporal Kim.[37]

A month later, on 15 April, NKAF fighters shot down the U.S. Navy EC-121M Warning Star reconnaissance aircraft, codenamed "Deep Sea 21" (BuNo 135749), over the Sea of Japan, killing all thirty-one on board and prompting a massive show of naval force.

The aircraft, assigned to Fleet Air Reconnaissance Squadron #1(VQ-1) took off from the Atsugi Naval Air Station in Japan on a routine SIGINT mission, the same route and orbit flown hundreds of times over the previous two years without incident. The mission was graded "minimal risk." Their orders were to fly no closer than fifty nautical miles from the North Korean coast.[38]

On board the unarmed aircraft, under the command of Lt. Cdr. James H. Overstreet, were twenty-nine sailors and one Marine. Besides the flight crew, there was included a cryptologist and linguists. USAF intercept operators in Korea detected two North Korean MiG-21s on an intercept course with Deep Sea 21, but it disappeared from the radar screen at 11:50 PM, its location approximately ninety miles southeast of the North Korean port of Chongjin.[39]

On 16 April, North Korea admitted shooting down an American reconnaissance plane that had intruded into its airspace. A massive air and ship search of the area recovered the remains of only two of the thirty-one crew members. It was the greatest single loss of American lives during the DMZ War.

By 5 June, the last reservists called up and deployed to Korea in response to the *Pueblo* incident departed, and the following month President Nixon announced a reduction of U.S. troops overseas.

On 17 August 1969, Pfc. George Grant, 1/31st Infantry was killed in an ambush while providing security for the 13th Engineers as they cleared brush from suspected infiltration trails. Wounded in the chest by automatic weapons fire, Grant died before help could arrive. The last American casualties of the Second Korean Conflict occurred on 14 October 1969 when four soldiers with the 7th Infantry Division (SSgt. James Grissinger, Sp.4 Charles Taylor, Sp.4 Jack L. Morris, and Pfc. William E. Grimes) were ambushed in daylight in the DMZ while driving a truck clearly displaying a white truce flag. Each man was shot through the head. The attackers fled prior to the arrival of the Quick Reaction Force (QRF).[40]

The year 1969 ended with a decrease in incidents as abrupt as the increase of incursions three years earlier. In three years (1966–69), Americans had suffered 44 killed and 111 wounded in incidents along the DMZ, while 326 South Koreans had been killed and 600 wounded. North Korean losses numbered 715 killed and an unknown number wounded. When one adds in Americans killed before 1966 and since 1969, the number of American casualties in Korea since the 1953 armistice exceeds the number killed in action in the Dominican Republic (1965), Grenada (1983), Panama (1989–90), and Somalia (1993).[41]

While clearly a venue where the Cold War turned "hot," the CIB for veterans of the Korean War is only authorized for those serving since 4 January 1969, and then only under extremely limited circumstances. The Armed Forces Expeditionary Medal is authorized for those soldiers whose service in Korea occurred between 1 October 1966 and 30 June 1974.[42]

[chapter sixteen]

THE USS *FORRESTAL* FIRE, 1967

The aircraft carrier is an awesome combatant that has been a key strategic asset in modern-day naval warfare since the beginning of World War II. Although carriers played a critical role in the Atlantic Ocean and Mediterranean Sea during World War II, it was in the Pacific Theater that carrier warfare turned the tide of battle: its naval aviators soundly defeated their Japanese counterparts, leaving the once-feared Japanese empire on the brink of defeat.

Ith the advent of the Cold War, carriers were unopposed in the Korean and Vietnam wars, acting as floating air bases from which to strike vital enemy targets while supporting American and UN forces engaged in fierce ground fighting. U.S. naval carrier fighters and bombers also saw action in other global conflicts in Lebanon and Libya, and experienced numerous aerial confrontations with Communist aircraft.

Today, American carrier fleets continue to dominate the world's oceans. However, in the future, that domination will perhaps be challenged by a modernized Chinese navy. It is also possible that, with a Russian resurgence, Russian naval warships that will likely include aircraft carriers will once again roam the seas of the world.

Carrier operations are hazardous because of the precision required to launch and recover aircraft on a moving, often pitching, flight deck. Highly trained teams of crew members are responsible for the safety of the planes and pilots of an onboard air group. Their skill and discipline make such complex operations look easy. In fact, the scenario has been equated to a well-rehearsed ballet. It is profoundly dangerous, though: one miscue can spell disaster, especially during combat operations when carrier decks are crowded with fully armed and fueled aircraft. Such an incident occurred on board the USS *Forrestal* (CVA-59) in 1967, nearly destroying the ship as it prepared to launch aircraft during the Vietnam War. The tragic story is

USS *Rupertus* (DD-851) stands by to assist USS *Forrestal* (CVA-59) fighting raging deck fires and explosions while operating in the Gulf of Tonkin, July 1967. (U.S. Naval Historical Center)

best described by author James M. Caiella, currently associate editor of *Proceedings* and *Naval History* of the U.S. Naval Institute in Annapolis, Maryland. Mr. Caiella wrote probably the most accurate and complete account of the happening after interviewing numerous surviving crew members and pilots, including Senator John S. McCain (R-AZ), who as a young Navy pilot attached to Attack Squadron 46 (VA-46) was waiting to launch in an A-4E Skyhawk. Caiella's article, "1051 Hell," was published in the Fall 2003 issue of the Naval Aviation Museum Foundation magazine, *Foundation*, and is reprinted here with the permission of the Naval Aviation Museum Foundation and James Caiella.

"1051 Hell"

James Caiella

On 29 July 1967, a tragic fire on board USS *Forrestal* (CVA-59) nearly sent her to the bottom of the Gulf of Tonkin. Thirty-six years later, the heroes still cry. The sights, sounds, and, most hauntingly, the smells of the carnage they witnessed all those years ago still affects them all. Among the many questions left in the wake of the disaster which befell them, none is more basic than, "What really happened?"

Despite the 7,500 pages of testimony and depositions collected by the Navy board of inquiry and its conclusions, many of those who were witnesses had divergent views of what happened at the time, and conflicting memories of what they believed then and now.

The official report of the investigation into the fire and its aftermath, titled "Manual of the Judge Advocate General Basic Final Investigative Report Concerning the Fire on Board the USS *FORRESTAL* (CVA-59)," was begun within days of the fire and completed on 19 September 1967. The facts cited below are, unless otherwise noted, from that report.

On 29 July 1967, the Newport News–built and Norfolk-based USS *Forrestal*, the first of the Navy's supercarriers, was a newcomer to the Vietnam conflict. She had only been on duty in the South China Sea for five days. The first of the Navy's Atlantic-based carriers to serve in the war, *Forrestal's* captain and crew were determined to show the Pacific fleet what they could do.

At 10:50 AM, *Forrestal* was steaming through placid, steamy waters, preparing to send the second strike of the day toward North Vietnam.

Aft of the angle deck catapult, nineteen aircraft crowded the ship's flight deck with little more than walking room between them. Additionally, seventeen more were positioned on the remainder of the four-acre deck. With the planes fully fueled and armed, aircraft engines were being started and last-minute checks were being made by pilots, plane, and deck crews for the 11:00 AM launch.

Lt. (jg) David Dollarhide of Orange Park, Florida, was in one of the attack jets armed with two old bombs. His A-4E of VA-46 was parked next to and forward of that of squadronmate Lt. Cdr. John McCain, now the senior senator from Arizona.

"We manned aircraft at 10:30 AM, being spotted on the usual place on the port quarter aft. I started up and went through my checks. The plane captain saluted and left the flight deck," the now-retired Delta Airlines pilot had written in his diary.

One minute later, the 5,400 sailors and airmen of *Forrestal* began a fight for their lives and their ship.

1051

Dollarhide's diary continues, "Seven minutes before launch, I heard a muffled explosion above the noise of the engines and looked back to the right of my aircraft to see a mass of flames from my right wing going aft, down through the other A-4s. There were several people in flames, rolling on the flight deck and running to put out the flames on their bodies."

Photographer's Mate Dave Stanbrough, of Burns, Oregon, the petty officer in charge of photography on the flight deck, remembers that, "It seemed only a minute or so after I got my coffee that the fire call came over the ships intercom. 'Fire! Fire! . . . Fire on the flight deck!' Then the first explosion shook the ship and the alarm for 'General Quarters, all hands man your battle stations' came over the intercom, then another explosion."

An errant electrical charge had ignited the motor of a five-inch Zuni rocket mounted on an F-4B Phantom II fighter. The rocket whooshed one hundred feet across the deck, severing the arm of a crewman in its path, before striking and rupturing the fuel tank of an A-4E Skyhawk attack bomber.

From the official report: "A review of the voluminous material contained in the Report of Investigation establishes the central fact that a Zuni rocket was inadvertently fired from an F-4 aircraft (#110) and struck the external fuel tank of an A-4 aircraft (#405)."

The VF-11 F-4B was crewed by Lt. Cdr. James E. Bangert, the pilot, and RIO Lt. (jg) Lawrence E. McKay. Lt. Cdr. Fred White, of VA-46, who died in the fire, was the pilot of A-4E #405, just aft of McCain's #416.

As four hundred gallons of jet fuel were both blasted and spilled from the tank to the deck, it ignited and spread beneath other aircraft.

"I saw one of our plane captains . . . reeling backward just out of the fire, his entire body charred and still burning. His left arm was almost completely severed and he was trying to hold it on," Dollarhide's diary continues.

As a result of the impact, the explosion or an electrical short caused by the incident, at least one of the two Korean War–vintage one thousand–pound bombs under the bomber's wing fell to the deck and split open. Witnesses reported seeing its internals burning with a white-hot ferocity.

Just feet from the epicenter of the fire, Dollarhide, "Started getting out of the aircraft. . . . I leaped out the left side because of the fire on the right. My feet caught on the canopy rail and I did a three-quarter twist, landing on my right hip. My right hip and elbow were broken. I couldn't get up and rolled on the deck for a few seconds 'til a kid came over and helped me up."

As those in the midst of the spreading flames tried to escape, others manned fire hoses and extinguishers to battle the fires. Fifty-four seconds after the initiation of the fire, Chief Gerald W. Farrier, the head of the fire-fighting crew, arrived at the scene and immediately began battling the blaze around the cracked bomb with a hand-held fire extinguisher.

About twenty seconds later, the first of the hose crews arrived, playing salt water on the forward boundary of the fire.

Dollarhide's diary continues, "I rolled over and looked back to see everything from the plane next to mine on down [the deck] engulfed in fire. I wondered if the pilot [John McCain] had gotten out or if he was leaning forward in the cockpit."

Slightly more than ninety seconds into the fire, the bomb exploded.

Aviation Boatswain's Mate Third Class Gary L. Shaver remembers, "There was a one thousand–pound bomb lying on the deck surrounded by burning fuel. I emptied the extinguisher to no avail. Several feet away from me was flight deck chief, Chief Farrier, who also had an extinguisher and was applying it right on the bomb.

"Suddenly there was an explosion. Chief Farrier disappeared.

"I felt like I was going to come apart as the bomb's concussion and shrapnel hit me. I was blown into the air, out of my shoes and helmet and struck by shrapnel in the left shoulder, stomach, arms, and head."

The two fire crews first on the scene were decimated.

Bill Boote, a VA-46 squadron member, related that he "then ran over to the Number 4 elevator and catwalk to retrieve a fire hose to fight the fire. We ran back out to the fire and yelled back to the sailor in the catwalk to charge the hose. Well, no water came, so I ran back to the catwalk and asked them why they didn't charge the hose. They told me that they were working on this unit and couldn't give us any water. I ran back to the other sailors to tell them that there was no water available and to get out.

"That's when the first one-thousand pound bomb went off.

"I was only sixty feet away, and it threw me another sixty feet through the air and I landed face down on the flight deck. I heard a voice in my head say 'don't move.' That's when the main landing gear from an A-4 hit the deck two feet from my head. I then moved forward to the area where the A-5s were parked and into the catwalk."

Dollarhide's diary continues, "I had a renewed fear that debris was going to fall on us and I began to get up. . . . The green shirt that I had knocked down helped me. . . . We turned our backs on the scene and began to scramble up the flight deck for cover as more bombs began to go off."

Nine seconds later, a second bomb exploded with even more ferocity. Bodies and debris were hurled nearly a thousand feet forward to the bow of the ship.

Fighting for the Ship

Within the first five minutes, the aft end of the 1,039-foot ship was rocked by seven more major explosions of the one thousand–pound weapons. Minor explosions were too numerous to count. The fires were fed by forty thousand gallons of highly volatile jet fuel spilling from tanks and fuel cells ripped by blasts and shrapnel.

The explosions smashed holes in the armor plate that formed the flight deck. Flaming and unburned fuel, water, and foam cascaded into the compartments, which were primarily crew berthing areas, below.

Fighting below-deck fires was even more dangerous than the flight deck fires due to the confined spaces, low light, thick black smoke, and toxic fumes.

Steve Andersen of Minneapolis, an Illustrator Draftsman Seaman working in the Integrated Operational Intelligence Center, could have stayed in the relative safety of the bow of the ship, where he had been evacuated. His job with a Top Secret clearance made him hard to replace. However, he chose to fight the fires in the compartments.

Crewmen fight the series of fires on the *Forrestal* flight deck as the USS *Rupertus* directs her hoses at the blaze from the other side. The holocaust was caused by an errant missile fired from an F-4 Phantom jet that struck another aircraft as heavily armed, fueled aircraft were being readied for launch on combat missions over North Vietnam. (U.S. Naval Historical Center)

"Standing in water that seemed, at the time, hot enough to cook meat in was the immediate sensation. It was soon replaced, however, with far worse experiences. . . . The smell of burnt flesh mixed with aviation fuel and burning rubber is something that I think I will likely never forget."

Although the fire on the flight deck was contained within an hour, those below raged until 4:00 AM the next day.

Simply moving through passageways and up or down ladders was dangerous enough, as photographer Mate Dave Stanbrough related.

Explosions continued as I climbed the ladders, working my way up. Other sailors were in scramble mode, also moving up and down the ladders, getting into battle positions. Each explosion would jolt or knock us down as we scrambled. Hatches were being closed and the ship being made watertight. As I moved up the last few decks, I had to crawl through the smaller screw hatches, re-screwing each one as I passed through it.

Reflection

As the day ended and the tasks of fighting for survival turned to recovery and clean-up, and as the last fires were being squelched, some took time to reflect on the day.

Senator McCain recalls: "I went to sick bay to have my burns and shrapnel wounds treated. There I found a horrible scene of many men, burned beyond saving, grasping the last moments of life. Most of them lay silently or made barely audible sounds. They gave no cries of agony because their nerve endings had been burned, sparing them any pain. Someone called my name, a kid, anonymous to me because the fire had burned off all his identifying features. He asked me if a pilot in our squadron was OK. I replied that he was."

At this moment, McCain was standing by Dollarhide's bed, who had been brought to sickbay for treatment. Dollarhide relates that the burned sailor was Airman Robert Swerlein, a VA-46 plane captain who was later evacuated to the hospital ship, USS *Repose* (AH-16). He died three days later.

Stanbrough, the photographer's mate, was realistic in his thoughts. "As dark fell on the ship, compartment fires still raged in the aft part of the ship. That's where my compartment was. That was home and where everything I owned was in a locker. All was lost except the smoky uniform I was wearing, but I was not in one of the 134 body bags.

"I was nineteen years old and I would turn twenty in two more days, on the 31st. On my birthday, we held memorial services for our fallen shipmates."

For others, it was a time to reflect upon fate.

Bob Shelton, of White Oak, Texas, has lived with these thoughts for thirty-five years.

I served on board USS Forrestal *as a quartermaster third class. I was scheduled to stand the port after-steering watch on 29 July 1967, but a buddy, James Blaskis, talked me into trading watches with him. I took his watch on the bridge. The resulting explosions killed a lot of brave sailors that day. James was trapped below decks [at my post] and died.*

He made the wall in Washington, and I made Life *magazine.*

The Toll

It verges on the callous to use numbers as replacements for the human cost, but it is virtually the only way to comprehend the enormity of the event.

As a result of the fires and explosions, 134 sailors and airmen died and 161 were seriously wounded. Many more went unreported because their wounds were less severe. Of those who died, only twenty-eight had been on the flight deck. Fifty died where they slept.

Seaman Andersen spoke of the gruesome job of recovering shipmates' bodies. "All the while, we were, of course, terrified that another bomb was going to go off right next to us. I am not as certain about the issue of courage as I am about the notion of being totally stunned by fear, mixed with the shock and disbelief that one witnesses in a truly horrific situation."

Twenty-one aircraft were destroyed, with another forty damaged. There were seventy-three aircraft on board when the fire started.

The ship suffered $72 million in damage. Destroyed aircraft accounted for another $44 million, while damaged aircraft accounted for another $10 million. Ordnance lost was worth $1.95 million, and supplies and equipment were valued at $3.15 million.

Those severely traumatized have never been counted.

Aviation Boatswain's Mate Third Class Gary L. Shaver of the V-1 Division was operating a starter tractor that morning.

> *I saw the A-4 behind the aft cat explode. I ran to the crew locker, grabbed a PKP fire bottle and ran to the fire. I saw men on fire, bombs on the deck surrounded by fire. I saw hell in the making.*
>
> *In 1972, after returning to civilian duties, I was medically retired. Two years ago, I was hospitalized and recognized as suffering all these years with the memories, nightmares, and hell of that day called PTSD [post-traumatic stress disorder], I will be on medication and in therapy forever.*

The Board

The investigation board focused on the Zuni rocket and its LAU-10 launching pod. Those on board that day generally agreed that the rocket started the fire, but that it was confinable, fightable, that they had a chance until that first bomb went off.

The final report found that there were shortcomings in the Zuni launching pod. Attachment cords between the pod and its mounting rail on the aircraft, called "pigtails," carried the electrical firing charge from the pilot's finger on the button to the rocket's igniter. Pins on the pigtail could be bent, causing a short circuit.

Furthermore, there were two separate safety procedures to prevent an inadvertent firing of the Zuni. One was that the pigtails were not to be plugged in until immediately before the aircraft's launch. With the high tempo of flight deck operations, the delayed connection of pigtails slowed down launches such that they caused conflicts with the launching of one mission and the recovery of a previous mission. The veterans of the experienced Pacific-based carriers passed this information to the newly arrived *Forrestal* squadrons. The ship's safety committee chose to bypass this safety procedure because there was another significant device that was highly effective.

That device, essentially a safety pin, mechanically and electrically prevented a rocket's launch. Standard procedure was for that pin to be pulled only immediately before launch.

However, in some instances, again in the interest of getting the aircraft off the deck as soon as possible, crews began pulling pins before the aircraft got to the catapult.

The Navy report determined that the rocket fired when the pilot of the F-4B carrying the Zuni switched power sources.

Once one of the engines in the twin-engined Phantom II was at a certain power level after being started by a "huffer," the pilot would switch from the external source to the internal source powered by the running engine. When the pilot switched power sources, it caused a brief spike of electrical energy.

By itself, it would not have launched a Zuni. However, with the pigtail connected, the electricity had a route to the rocket. With the safety pin pulled, the Zuni was electrically and mechanically free to be fired.

While the board determined that to be the cause of the rocket's firing, and its subsequent impact with another aircraft's fuel tank caused the fire, it needn't have been the cause of many—if any—deaths.

The Bombs

There were eighty bombs on board fifteen attack aircraft, totaling 24.5 tons of high explosives, for the 11:00 AM mission. Eight tons consisted of sixteen old AN/M65A1 one thousand–pound bombs. The seven that exploded did so in a catastrophic "high order" fashion, as they were designed to do against an enemy. The nine others were listed as missing or jettisoned.

The "old" bombs, which caused so much death and destruction, according to the official report, were manufactured in 1953 and had been stored on Okinawa.

One crew member, Bill Boote of Sparta, New Jersey, recalls that the night before, "I was sitting on the starboard side next to Elevator 1, near our line shack for the plane captains and troubleshooters, with my friends John Pasko, Richard Hatcher, and a few of the plane captains. Our conversation that night, after USS *Diamond Head* (AE-19) had started to off-load ordinance, seemed to me, that those bombs looked old."

The bombs were old, filled with Composition B explosive. Unlike more-modern explosives, "Comp B" becomes unstable with age and hot, humid storage conditions. At the least, these weapons were fourteen years old and had been stored in the open in the hot, humid climate of Guam.

The M65s were "thin skinned," just thick enough to hold the explosives and their shape. The more modern MK 80-series bombs on board had thicker skins, which provided significantly more insulation for the explosive from heat and shock.

Of the sixty-four "modern" bombs prepared for launch, only two exploded at high order and two at low order. The rest either burned, melted, or were jettisoned.

Experts estimated that the firefighters needed but three minutes to contain the fire.

The first of the M65s blew at ninety-four seconds into the fire. None of the modern weapons detonated until more than five minutes had elapsed.

The issue of the old bombs was never significantly addressed in the final report. However, one notation in it indicates that "cook-off tests of ordnance involved in the *Forrestal* fire confirmed that the cook-off time for the AN-M65A1 bomb is on the order of eighty-five to one hundred twenty seconds. This time is significantly less than for other bombs tested."

Firefighting

The report also addressed firefighting issues. While praising the crew for its courage and tenacity in fighting the fires, its conclusion was that firefighting should be left to professionals.

It found that 57 percent of the ship's company "had attended a firefighting school of at least two days duration within the past thirty-six months," but further "that numerous personnel who were near the fire fighting stations at the outset of the fire on the flight deck were unfamiliar with fire fighting procedures and therefore unable to contribute to the fire fighting efforts."

The most effective means of fighting a fuel fire on board ship is with foam. The foam blankets the flames and fuel source, effectively smothering the fire. Water serves only as a cooling agent. It tends to spread the fire around because the fuel floats on top of the water.

The first explosion decimated the two main firefighting crews of *Forrestal*, taking with them the initial foam hoses on the scene. The water used by later crews spread the fire rather than put it out.

Fixes

The board appended a list of sixty-two recommendations. The first nine dealt directly with the LAU-10 launcher, Zuni rocket, and Triple Ejector Rack. The next four focused on weapons systems and testing equipment. Numbers fourteen through thirty covered procedures and documentation at levels from the CNO to shipboard. Fully half of the recommendations, thirty-one of them, addressed firefighting issues, from training to the development of "revolutionary new firefighting equipment and procedures."

Zuni rockets were relegated to ground-based operations. Safety procedures were reevaluated and strengthened. "Old" bombs were removed from the munitions pipeline. Newly manufactured bombs were given a plastic-like coating as a further insulation against fire. Firefighting school, at a facility named after Chief Farrier, became mandatory for sailors.

Before the fire, pilots had received no training or instructions in what to do in such emergencies. With the introduction of "zero-zero" ejection seats, they had an alternative to simply running through flames.

Although the report cited the errors of safety checks on the rocket, it found no one on board the ship directly responsible for the fire and subsequent explosions.

Its final recommendation, Number sixty-two: "That no disciplinary or administrative action be taken with regard to any persons attached to USS *Forrestal* (CVA-59) or Carrier Air Wing 17 as a result of the fire which occurred on board USS *Forrestal* on 29 July 1967."

Aftermath

Heroism was, and is, a word carefully chosen by the men of *Forrestal*.

The ship's skipper, Captain John K. Beling, never used the word lightly. "I am most proud of the way the crew reacted. The thing that is foremost in my mind is the concrete demonstration that I have seen of the worth of American youth. I saw many examples of heroism. I saw, and subsequently heard of, not one single example of cowardice."

Andersen added a crewman's perspective.

Although I only witnessed a few, I know that there were many heroes who gave up their lives that day. Many sacrifices were made so that others might live or be served first.

I carried one guy to sick bay for help, and while I was there, witnessed a Marine with a badly mangled leg holding onto a tourniquet. He was very calm and seemingly of quite clear mind in spite of having the knowledge that he was almost assured of losing the leg. Regardless, he was demanding that others he considered to be more seriously injured than he be treated before him. Although I'm unclear what happened to him, I am confident that, at the least, he lost the leg.

Thirty-five years later, for many who were there off the North Vietnamese coast, it was only yesterday.

Forrestal received emergency repairs over eight days in the Philippines, which gave limited aircraft operational capability. She then went on to her homeport, where she spent nearly nine months in repair at the Norfolk Naval Shipyard in Portsmouth, Virginia. From there, the ship went on to serve until 11 September

USS *Forrestal* as seen from the air after her arrival at Cubi Point, Republic of the Philippines, for temporary repairs before returning to her stateside home port. (U.S. Naval Historical Center)

1993, when she was decommissioned after completing a total of twenty-one deployments. She never made another Vietnam cruise.

Today, *Forrestal* remains in storage in Newport, Rhode Island, awaiting final disposition. Her crew is trying to save her from being turned into scrap by having her preserved as a museum ship in Baltimore Harbor.

Authors' Note: James M. Caiella is associate editor of *Proceedings* and *Naval History* magazines of the U.S. Naval Institute in Annapolis, Maryland. Mr. Caiella is an Army veteran, having served as an artillery communications sergeant in the Republic of Korea from 1969 to 1970.

chapter seventeen

THE PANMUNJON AX MURDERS AND OPERATION PAUL BUNYAN, 1976

In the 1970s, there were still 42,000 American troops stationed in South Korea. Following the DMZ War of 1966–69, the number of incidents decreased, but continued to occur.

On 12 October 1970, a shoving match escalated into a brawl between UNC and KPA guards armed with shovels, clubs, and rocks. Reinforcements arrived from both sides. It was only after two KPA guards emerged from a guard post armed with AK-47s that the fighting ceased, leaving one American with a skull fracture, and seven UNC guards and an unknown number of KPA guards injured.[1]

On 3 March 1974, KPA soldiers harassed a UNC tour inside the DMZ, near Observation Post 5, and attacked a UNC officer accompanying the group, kicking him in the groin. As twenty-five to thirty KPA soldiers moved in to isolate the officer, they were dispersed by a UNC QRF who rescued the injured officer. KPA soldiers then vandalized Check Point 4. When the QRF redeployed, the KPA responded by sending one hundred soldiers to KPA Guard Post 7, at the west end of the Bridge of No Return. The arrival of the UNC JDO prevented further escalation when he proposed an immediate Security Officers (SO) meeting. His sedan was attacked, and he was injured as he withdrew from the area. (His arrival and proposal of an immediate SO meeting prevented further escalation. Nonetheless, he was attacked and injured as he withdrew.)[2]

On 30 June 1975, Maj. W. D. Henderson, the commander of the U.S. Army Support Group, was accosted and spit on by a North Korean journalist in the DMZ. When he tried to defend himself, he was attacked from behind by a KPA guard, who knocked him unconscious and stomped on his throat, crushing his larynx. UNC

Joint Security Area (JSA) Panmunjon, Korea. (U.S. federal government)

and KPA guards rushed to the area, and fighting broke out as UNC guards tried to prevent the KPA from inflicting further injury to Major Henderson. A UNC newswoman was also attacked. (Major Henderson recovered and retired from the Army.)

Tension was high along the DMZ all summer, but it was the events on 18 August 1976 surrounding a tree that threatened to again turn the Cold War "hot" in Korea. A forty-foot poplar tree located within the JSA in the vicinity of the Bridge of No Return blocked the view between UNC Checkpoint (CP) 3 and UNC Observation Post 5. A survey team recommended the tree be removed. When a six-man Korean (South) Service Corps (KSC) team with saws entered the JSA on 6 August to remove the tree, however, a large KPA guard force ordered them to leave the tree alone. The team withdrew.

With the intention of avoiding a confrontation but still addressing legitimate security concerns, the detachment commander of the JSF, Lt. Col. Victor S. Vierra, ordered the tree be trimmed and lower branches removed. On 18 August, five KSC workers entered the JSA, accompanied by a ten-man security detail made up of American and KATUSA military police infantry; the JSF commander, Capt. Arthur G. Bonifas; his deputy, 1st Lt. Mark T. Barrett; and a South Korean Officer, Capt. Kim Moon-Hwan, acting as interpreter. (The UNC troops, although infantry, wore military police brassards, as required by the armistice agreement.)

Bonifas, West Point class of 1966, was a popular officer from Newburgh, New York, and was familiar with the difficulties in dealing with the North Koreans. He had been involved in several earlier confrontations, having been assaulted by KPA guards in the JSA on one occasion, and leading a detail to rescue successfully a group of U.S. soldiers being held at gunpoint near the Bridge of No Return on another.[3]

Bonifas was preparing to depart in three days to return to his wife and child in the United States and his new post at Hunter Army Airfield in Georgia. His replacement, Capt. Ed Shirron, had already reported in, and Bonifas had left him at UNC CP 5 to observe the operation. Barrett was newly arrived, having been in-country only a few weeks. At a little over six feet, Barrett, who was from Columbia, South Carolina, was relatively inexperienced with KPA provocations. Bonifas had the foresight to have a twenty-man QRF moved up to UNC CP 2, just inside the JSA, ready to respond if the KPA harassed the work detail.

At 10:30 AM, a UNC jeep and a "deuce and a half" truck entered the JSA, and the KSC workers set up their ladders and began pruning the lower branches. Five minutes into their work, a truck drove up and two officers and nine enlisted KPA soldiers dismounted. The senior officer, Lt. Pak Chol, had a reputation for provoking UNC personnel. He strode up to Captain Kim and demanded to know what was going on. Kim explained that the workers were only trimming the tree. Pak responded, "That is good," then went over to watch the work and began supervising and giving directions. Bonifas, annoyed, ordered the men back to work.

Twenty minutes later, Pak strode over to Bonifas and abruptly ordered the work halted. Bonifas refused, stating they would complete their work, and withdraw. Pak shouted that any further work would bring "serious trouble." He said, "The branches that are cut will be of no use, just as you will be after you die." When Bonifas ignored him, Pak whispered to a soldier, who departed in a jeep for reinforcements.[4]

Ten additional KPA guards arrived by truck and others trotted over from nearby guard posts, bringing the number to thirty KPA surrounding the thirteen UNC troops and five KSC workers. Pak began screaming that any more cutting would result in "death." The QRF was monitoring the situation by radio, and had the area under telephoto camera surveillance, but did not move in to avoid escalating the situation.

Bonifas turned his back on Pak to order the detail to hurry up and finish the trimming, and did not see the KPA officer remove his watch, or the other officer roll up the sleeves of his jacket. As an NCO advanced to warn Bonifas, Pak shouted in Korean, "Kill the U.S. aggressors!" and the KPA guards, wielding pickax handles, clubs, and knives, attacked the smaller party.[5]

Pak kicked Bonifas in the groin, knocking him to the ground, where he was bludgeoned to death by three KPA guards armed with crowbars and metal pipes. Barrett was chased by six KPAs around the truck and over a low retaining wall, where he was attacked and beaten. A soldier broke free to get to the truck, which he drove into the crowd, scattering the KPA and providing cover to the prone Bonifas. The KPA attacked the UNC guards systematically, in teams, and only withdrew

Distant photo of tree pruning incident of 18 August 1976 during which two U.S. officers were killed. Some thirty North Korean security guards can be seen around a truck where they attacked KSC personnel who were pruning a tree that hindered the surveillance of the area. Using axes, the Koreans hacked to death UNC officers Maj. Arthur G. Bonifas, USA, and 1st Lt. Mark T. Barrett, USA. (U.S. Army)

after the arrival of the QRF. Bonifas was dead at the scene. Barrett died in the arms of a South Korean soldier on the way to the hospital. Total casualties were two American officers killed, and three KATUSA, four Americans, and Captain Kim injured. The attack had lasted four minutes.[6]

Believing this to be a provocation rather than a spontaneous act, the American response had to be carefully calculated. Only four hours after the attack, Kim Jong-Il, son of Kim Il-Sung and North Korea's chief delegate to the Conference of Non-Aligned Nations, meeting in Colombo, Sri Lanka, announced an unprovoked attack on North Korean guards by American officers and called for a withdrawal of all U.S. forces from Korea.[7]

It was the middle of a presidential election year in the United States. The humiliating withdrawal from Vietnam a year earlier influenced American foreign policy and morale in the military. Additionally, with the downsizing of U.S. military assets, the 7th Infantry Division had been withdrawn from Korea, leaving only the 2nd Infantry Division, while the North Koreans had been increasing the size of their forces.

That evening, Gen. Richard Stilwell, the American commander of UNC forces who was hurriedly called back from Japan, met with his senior officers to devise an operational plan (OPLAN) for the American response. Not responding was not an option, and a massive response could trigger an invasion of the south by North Korea. Some rated the likelihood of war as fifty–fifty. As Gen. John Singlaub, an officer on Stilwell's staff recalled, "If North Korea unleashed a massive armored assault on Seoul, we would have no choice but to request authorization for the first use of nuclear weapons since World War II."[8]

It was decided that the American response would be the removal of the poplar tree from the JSA. The plan, code-named Operation Paul Bunyan, would demonstrate American and South Korean resolve and forcefully reassert UNC rights in the DMZ by a massive show of force. The necessary elements involved surprise, speed of execution, and withdrawal, while avoiding a direct engagement with KPA troops. The key objective, as expressed by General Stilwell was, "That damn tree must come down." He understood the destruction of the tree would be a great loss of face for the North Koreans.

The following day, 19 August, the JCS ordered all American forces in Korea to DEFCON-3, an increased level of readiness indicating war is probable, followed by a similar announcement by the South Korean military thirty minutes later. All U.S. personnel in Korea on pass or leave were recalled, and high-altitude reconnaissance flights by SR-71 aircraft were increased, recording North Korean preparations for war. South Korean air bases at Osan, Kunsan, and Taegu began receiving additional aircraft flown in from the Philippines and Japan, all visible to North Korean radar as the 2nd Infantry Division and the First South Korean Army troops deployed into forward positions along the DMZ. Naval presence in the Sea of Japan was increased, and F-111 nuclear-capable bombers began flying toward Korea. By that evening, it was confirmed North Korea was in a wartime posture, but the character had changed from offensive to defensive.

Operation Paul Bunyan was scheduled to begin at exactly 7:00 AM on Saturday 21 August, and would involve a force of more than eight hundred men. Task Force Vierra, named for Lieutenant Colonel Vierra, commander of the U.S. Army Security Group (USASG), would be the force responsible for cutting down the tree. Two thirty-man platoons of combined American and South Korean guards armed with pistols and ax handles would guard two eight-man teams of engineers as they worked with chain saws. All the South Korean troops were Special Forces and Black Belts in Tae Kwan Do.

A company of 1st South Korean Division reconnaissance troops would be staged just outside the JSA, mounted on trucks and armed with M-16s, machine guns, and mortars. Overhead, elements of the 9th Infantry regiment would circle just south of the DMZ in twenty Bell UH-1 Iroquois helicopters, commonly called "Hueys," supported by twelve AH-1G Cobra attack helicopters. Above them would be F-4 Phantom fighters, and higher still, F-111 medium-strategic bombers, all visible to North Korean radar. The USS *Midway* would launch combat aircraft, and six batteries of 105-mm artillery would deploy in full view of the North Koreans with, as Stilwell put it, "rounds in the tubes and hands on the lanyards."[9]

At 11:45 PM Friday, authorization was given and the OPLAN became an operational order. At 6:48 AM Saturday, 21 August, as B-52s took off from Guam, and forty combat aircraft launched from the carrier *Midway*, a large convoy departed Camp Kitty Hawk toward the JSA. An officer in a jeep pulled out of the convoy and drove to the quarters of the Neutral Nations Supervisory Commission, where he informed Swiss Maj. Gen. Claude Von Muyden and Swedish Maj. Gen. Lage Wernstedt of the operation under way to cut down the poplar and remove illegal barriers, and asked them to notify their Czech and Polish counterparts.

The surprise was complete. As the Hueys hovered just south of the DMZ, Task Force Vierra's 2nd Platoon deployed north and blocked the south end of the Bridge of No Return, the most obvious route for reinforcement from the north. At the same time, the 3rd Platoon formed a cordon around the tree, and two teams from B Company, 2nd Engineer Battalion, commanded by Capt. Patrick Ono cut down the tree, leaving only a stump. A force of about 150 KPA troops arrived in a bus and two trucks, and deployed but took no action.

Stephan Sprague, a twenty-one-year-old private in Alpha Company, 2/9 Infantry, was among those detailed to stand guard around the tree. He recalled, "We were told that whatever we did was going to start a major confrontation between the North and South. . . . We knew there was a chance of some of us going to war and . . . not coming back." Pvt. Michael Brouilette in the same unit remembered being told that Operation Paul Bunyan could lead to World War III. "We were really scared. . . . We thought [this] was it, we're all going to die."[10]

The first cut was made at 7:18 AM, and the task was complete by 7:45 AM. At that point, the force withdrew. A demonstration had been made, and war was narrowly averted. Heavily armed infantry remained in place the remainder of the day. By that afternoon, Kim Il-Sung had issued a statement of regret over the killings of 18 August, the first time in twenty-three years that North Korea had accepted even partial responsibility for an incident.

Camp Kitty Hawk was later renamed Camp Bonifas in honor of one of the murdered officers, and a stone monument stands at the site of the murder, its brass plaque memorializing the sacrifice of Captain Bonifas and Lieutenant Barrett. The stump was removed in 1987, and replaced by a monument.

chapter eighteen

CAPT. BERT K. MIZUSAWA, USA

The Firefight atPanmunjon, 1984

The world was a busy place on 23 November 1984. In Zimbabwe, two rebels were convicted and sentenced to death by hanging for taking part in the kidnapping of six foreign tourists. Paraguayan officials were conducting a nationwide manhunt for Nazi fugitive Josef Mengele. Libyan troops agreed to withdraw from Chad, and Israeli police shot a Palestinian demonstrator to death in the West Bank. The Soviet Union and the United States announced the resumption of talks to limit nuclear arms, even as the Soviet Union performed a nuclear test at Eastern Kazakh, in Semipalitinsk. And in the United States, as Americans enjoyed the Thanksgiving holiday, Quarterback Doug Flutie, in the last seconds of the fourth quarter of the Orange Bowl, tossed a forty-eight-yard "Hail Mary" pass for a touchdown, giving Boston College a 47–45 victory over Miami. A small but significant skirmish in the Korean DMZ that day went virtually unnoticed by most Americans.

Within the DMZ, the JSA is the only area where forces from both sides come face to face with no barriers. This is also the site, more popularly known as "Panmunjon," where negotiators from the UNC and the KPA can meet to resolve issues that arise over the 1953 Armistice Agreement. The JSF is responsible for protecting the UNC personnel, including visitors, and property within the DMZ and, in particular, the JSA. In 1984, this force of approximately two hundred specially selected infantrymen was a 60–40 mix of U.S. and South Korean soldiers under an American command structure. The JSF Company was divided into four platoons. Duty rotated between three primary missions. One platoon had the "north mission," that of guarding the JSA by checkpoints, providing surveillance of North Korean activities, and providing 24/7 security on the border, officially known as the MDL. A second platoon was the "training platoon," with a

Capt. Bert K. Mizusawa, USA, Silver Star recipient. (Mizusawa collection)

primary mission of conducting reconnaissance and ambush patrols in the DMZ areas adjacent to the JSA. A third platoon was the JSF's QRF, which remained combat ready to provide no-notice reactions to any incidents. The fourth platoon was off duty, and usually provided soldiers to augment the other three platoons. The usual rotation was two successive days each for QRF–North–Training–Off.[1]

Both sides give DMZ tours of their area of the JSA, but the predominant number of visitors and tours are from the south, with tours conducted in the north restricted to the most reliable and privileged visitors to the insular Communist regime. On 23 November 1984, the North Koreans were conducting a tour with one such group in their sector of the JSA when one of the visitors broke from the group and dashed across the MDL into South Korea.

The defector, Vasily Yakovlevich Matuzok, was twenty-two years old. He was a Soviet citizen and a diplomatic trainee at the Soviet Embassy at Pyongyang, the capital of North Korea. The son of a Red Army officer, he had been planning to defect for more than two years, and the tour of Panmunjon gave him the chance. He later stated it was his "very first opportunity to go to the West."[2]

As Matuzok raced between the MAC and JDO buildings, which straddle the border with a few other buildings on Conference Row, and headed into the brush south of the Sunken Garden in the UNC sector, he was pursued by eight KPA guards who unholstered their sidearms and fired at the fleeing figure with the intention of killing him, or at least stopping him from defecting. They were joined by other KPA guards from the PanMunGak building and barracks to the north, as other KPA soldiers in the KPA checkpoints laid down suppressive fire on the soldiers in the UNC checkpoints.[3]

Two JSF soldiers, Pfc. Michael A. Burgoyne, a twenty-year-old from Portland, Michigan, and his South Korean counterpart, Pfc. Chang Myung Gi, were escorting a civilian work crew in the vicinity of UNC Checkpoint 4 when they observed KPA guards chasing and firing at a civilian. Although out in the open, Burgoyne and Chang drew their .45 pistols and fired at the pursuing KPA guards, which allowed Matuzok time to reach a position of concealment in the brush south of the Sunken Garden.

The KPA returned fire, striking Chang on the right side of his nose, killing him instantly. Another shot struck Burgoyne in the jaw, knocking him down. By this time, the 4th Platoon, housed in CP 4, had been alerted and began suppressive fire on the KPA soldiers, pinning them down in the area of the Sunken Garden. During this action, Sp.4 John Orlicki laid devastating fire on the pinned-down North Koreans with his M-203 grenade launcher, resulting in at least one KPA casualty.[4]

At the Tactical Operations Center (TOC) at Camp Kitty Hawk, located on the southern boundary of the DMZ and the base camp for the UNC Security Force (UNSF)–JSA, Capt. Henry Nowak was completing an orientation tour for a newly assigned NCO when he was advised by the duty NCO that shots were being fired in the JSA. Nowak alerted the JSF commander, Capt. Bert Mizusawa. Captain Mizusawa ordered his driver to take his jeep to the TOC with helmet, flak vest, and weapons, and then ran to the TOC. The QRF's combat-loaded vehicles were located outside the TOC. Mizusawa gave the vehicle guards the order for the QRF to mount while he received a quick situation report from Captain Nowak.

★ ★ ★

Bert Kameaaloha Mizusawa was born in Honolulu, Hawaii, in January 1957, to a Nisei (second-generation Japanese) father and Dutch mother, the second of six sons. Two uncles were members of the renowned 442nd Regimental Combat Team and had been wounded in action in Italy during World War II. Another uncle was killed in action while serving with the 2nd Infantry Division in the battles of Heartbreak and Bloody ridges during the Korean War. His father met his mother while serving in the Army while on occupation duty in Europe in 1953.

Capt. Bert Mizusawa in the Joint Security Area, Panmunjom, Korean DMZ. (Mizusawa Collection)

Although his father left the Army, he later enlisted in the Air Force. Mizusawa spent his early years in stateside USAF bases and overseas in Japan and Germany. In 1975, when Mizusawa entered the U.S. Military Academy at West Point, he was the first member of his family to attend college. He excelled at West Point, graduating first in the class of 1979, which was the last all-male class at the U.S. Military Academy.

After graduating from the Infantry Officer Basic, Airborne, and Pathfinder Schools at Fort Benning, Georgia, and from the Air Assault Course at Fort Campbell, Kentucky, 2nd Lieutenant Mizusawa was assigned as a platoon leader in Company B, 1st Battalion, 509th Infantry (Airborne) at Vicenza, Italy, in February 1980. While with the 509th, he served as rifle and mortar platoon leader, Assistant Battalion S-1 (personnel and administration), Assistant Battalion S-4 (Logistics), and as XO of Company A. After returning to Fort Benning in July 1983 to attend the Infantry Officer Advanced Course, Mizusawa was selected to command the JSF at Panmunjon and reported to Korea the following March.[5]

It was around 11:40 AM on 23 November that Mizusawa scrambled to assemble the QRF. Since the platoon leader and platoon sergeant were not immediately located, Mizusawa took command of the QRF's deployment. He has very vivid memories of that day.

> *I was in my office that morning reviewing an incident that occurred the previous evening. I was alerted by our operations center that there was shooting up north. The information was spotty, but obviously significant enough to deploy the Quick Reaction Force, which that day was the 1st Platoon.*
>
> *As we raced up the road to the JSA, I was able to get a situation report from the 4th Platoon, which was up on the border. During the quick ride up, which only took a few minutes, I learned from Lt. Tom Thompson, the 4th Platoon Leader, that the North Koreans had come across into our sector, we had at least one man down, and there was a civilian in the area, a fact that didn't seem significant at that time. The key information I needed was where the North Koreans were so I could determine how to maneuver the QRF into the area. The North Korean disposition was not clear, but I was able to confirm that Checkpoint 2, the entrance into the JSA, was not yet engaged.[6]*

Based on this information, Mizusawa dismounted the QRF 328 feet south of CP 2. The QRF consisted of three eleven-man rifle squads and three machine-gun crews. Mizusawa quickly directed Staff Sergeant Lamb, Sergeant Gissendaner, and Sergeant Diaz, the three squad leaders, on objectives: Lamb's 1st Squad to a berm in the center to provide defilade fire, Gissendaner's 2nd Squad to move until contact on the left flank to engage the enemy in their concealed approach route and Sergeant Diaz's 3rd Squad to initially hold in reserve at CP 2 and then to move to an overwatch position at Helipad 128 that provided cover and linked the 1st Platoon with the 4th Platoon firing positions just south of CP 4.

As the 1st and 2nd Squads moved to their positions, the 4th Platoon was laying down devastating fire with automatic rifles and grenade launchers from CP 4, about five hundred feet to the right front. The 1st Platoon leader, Lt. Steve Tryon, entered the fight and took tactical control of the platoon as it deployed to cover the western and southern flanks of the Sunken Garden area. At this point, Captain Mizusawa coordinated the fire of the 4th Platoon with the assault of the 1st Platoon in order to close with and destroy the KPA force in the UNC sector, and to prevent their reinforcement by additional KPA troops.[7] Mizusawa remembered, "Sgt. Jose Diaz's 3rd Squad, with two of the machine guns, [advanced and] secured the high ground on the east end of Conference Row in the area of the UNC Helipad 128. This position provided a clear field of fire on Conference Row and the Sunken Garden while neutralizing two KPA checkpoints. Additionally, this position prevented infiltration from the swampy area in the vicinity of the Neutral Nations Camp."[8]

Mizusawa maneuvered the two remaining squads in traveling overwatch north toward Conference Row. Sgt. Curtis Gissendaner's 2nd Squad moved north along the left side of the Sunken Garden while Mizusawa remained with SSgt. Richard Lamb's flank and 1st Squad maneuvering to the right of the KPA force that had crossed the MDL into the UNC sector, estimated to number as many as thirty.

"It was all very fluid," Mizusawa remembered. "The North Koreans were coming in and setting up positions on our left side to avoid the 4th Platoon fire, and the 1st Platoon squads literally crashed into their flank and rear. We had a berm that provided some cover and concealment until we were right on top of the main North Korean position. From this berm you could see a couple of North Korean bodies out in the open."

As Lamb later recalled, "The platoon came on line in a wooded area approximately seventy-five meters [246 feet] southeast of the Sunken Garden and secured the southern side of the access road to the Bridge of No Return and Checkpoint 3. We posted flank security and prepared to cross the road with increasing automatic weapons fire coming from the vicinity of Conference Row and the Sunken Garden. As elements began bounding across the road, the Soviet defector, Mr. Matuzok, was spotted hiding in the underbrush."[9]

Matuzok requested help in Korean, and Tryon ordered him secured and sent back to Mizusawa.

While I was maneuvering with the middle squad through a wooded swampy area, QRF soldiers ran into a Caucasian in civilian clothes lying down in the muck and speaking rapidly in Korean. This was about ten meters [thirty-three feet] from where I was. Everything was happening rather quickly and I directed a Korean soldier to tell the civilian to crawl towards us and to search him for weapons.

At this point, I realized the civilian was a defector and knew that I was responsible for him as well as for my soldiers. After he was searched, I pulled the defector down to the ground next to a small mound that provided some protection from direct fires. The defector was trembling and began reaching into his leather jacket and handing me rolls of 35 mm film. I assumed that he was shaking because it was cold and he was soaking wet from the swamp. (He later told me he was sure that I was going to kill him.) I stuffed the film into my jacket pocket. Then he handed me a passport and said in English, "I am a Soviet citizen and I wish to seek asylum in the United States."

I opened up the passport and [saw] the Cyrillic writing of a Soviet passport. With bullets flying over our heads, I remember thinking it was just like in the

movies. And for some reason what was happening didn't seem unusual. I wasn't
sure why he was giving me the film but I pocketed all seventeen rolls. Later I
understood it was intended to convince me to spare his life.[10]

Mizusawa then called the 1st Platoon sergeant, SFC Howard Williams, forward
and directed him to run with Matuzok 330 feet south through the woods, then
cut east to the road to get the defector on a jeep back to Camp Kitty Hawk. After
a debriefing by the operations officer, Captain Nowak, Matuzok was put on a helicopter sent from Seoul and transported to the UNC and Combined (U.S.–Korea)
Forces Command headquarters in Yongsan.

Mizusawa returned to the 1st Platoon at the berm, and ordered Gissendaner's
squad farther forward on the left flank. By maneuvering to make effective use of
terrain, the 1st Platoon had the KPA force in a "C" shaped encirclement, with all
avenues of escape cut off or covered by direct fire. Lamb recalled,

> *Continuing pressure from the base squad and our occupation of the Sunken*
> *Garden forced the enemy to surrender or be annihilated. Sgt. Lee Kyong Tae,*
> *Pfc. Mark Deville and myself moved across the last fifty meters [164 feet] of open*
> *terrain under fire to occupy the Sunken Garden. . . . We cleared the garden area*
> *literally chasing and flushing enemy soldiers from covered positions and routing*
> *them across an access road into a small confined area. At one point, enemy fire*
> *became so intense it shredded small scrub bushes being used for concealment.*
> *While covering the enemy, we closed to within ten to fifteen meters [thirty-two*
> *to forty-nine feet] and forced them to raise their hands above their heads in*
> *surrender.*[11]

About forty minutes into the firefight, KPA officials requested a cease-fire
via landline to the UNC JDO, who maintained a "hotline" from an office on
Conference Row. While the JDO was a Navy lieutenant commander, the senior
person on duty was the JDO NCO, an Air Force staff sergeant. Although the JDO
NCO came running out yelling "cease-fire," Mizusawa did not immediately have
his troops stand down.

> *One of the sergeants from the JDO came running out yelling "cease-fire." We*
> *didn't cease fire at that point because nobody had talked to me about it, and the*
> *situation was still volatile. You could see the JDO NCO falling to the ground*
> *because of the firing. We were also preparing to capture some North Koreans.*
> *There were about three bodies lying out and eight surrendering. I called for a*
> *QRF truck to enter to pick up those we had captured. But then my driver told*
> *me that Lt. Thompson, who had landline communications in the north platoon's*

operations center, needed to speak with me on my Motorola [walkie-talkie]. He
informed me that "CP Seoul has authorized the North's request for a cease-fire."

I knew that the North Koreans didn't have much choice, but was wary of
a cease-fire. I wanted to preserve the tactical advantage. I also knew the north
would lie about things and I didn't want them to bring their dead and wounded
back until it could be documented. They were about one hundred meters [328
feet] on our side of the border so I told my driver, Pfc. Warren Choate, to drive
me up to the border to intercept the North Korean soldiers. Doing this was risky,
but I thought it was important to try. They had about thirty soldiers come across,
and I didn't know how many they had on their side of the border but their unit
had one hundred men or so.[12]

Accompanied only by his driver, Mizusawa advanced five hundred feet in the
open to the MDL—fully exposed to potential enemy fire from KPA checkpoints
and under minimal covering fire from the JSF platoons—to demand an immediate
SO meeting.

As the JSF commander, I wore a second hat as the UN Command Security
Officer, the lowest of only three positions authorized to conduct dialogue with the
North. I called an immediate meeting with the North Korean Commander. I
had never called for a security officer meeting before because the North Koreans
would just use it as a propaganda forum. Calling a meeting on the spot gave me
a reason to stop the North Koreans from evacuating the "evidence."

The North Koreans delayed their response to my demand while they carried
their dead and wounded back across the border. Since I was informed that CP
Seoul had given the North permission to remove their dead and wounded, I had
to live with that. I wanted to try to stop it, but it was just my driver and me
in a precarious position. We expected to be shot at since the withdrawing KPA
were very agitated and likely indifferent to the cease-fire if they were even aware
of it.[13]

As Nowak later wrote, "Fully aware that the KPA had just committed an unprecedented violent violation of the Armistice Agreement and with no indication that
the KPA had accepted or would honor the cease-fire, Capt. Mizusawa demonstrated
exceptional courage in the face of imminent danger and risk to his personal safety by
walking the approximately seven hundred feet distance between UNC Checkpoint
4 and UNC Checkpoint 5 and back to determine the status of his soldiers, stabilize
the intensely charged situation, and restore order in the JSA."

At approximately 12:50 PM, three pistol shots were fired from behind the
PanMunGak building. A Neutral Nations Supervisory Commission (NNSC)

member reported the shots as a KPA officer's execution of two KPA soldiers. Mizusawa later said,

> I was contacted by an NNSC Major General. I don't recall if it was the Swiss or Swede, but he reported that when he heard the gunshots, he went to see what happened and saw two KPA bodies being put in a vehicle and it was pretty clear to him that the North had summarily executed them. After that, I never saw my counterpart commander again, and I heard he was one of those executed. I have no knowledge on who the other person was, but there was speculation it was Capt. Pak-chol, nicknamed "Bulldog," the officer responsible for Capt. Bonifas' murder in 1976.[14]

Mizusawa remained on Conference Row for the next forty-eight hours, as the 1st Platoon rotated in to relieve the 4th Platoon in place, because of North Korean threats to retaliate. The 1st Platoon would be three nights in a row deployed in the JSA on an alert. The previous evening, 22 November, at approximately 9:00 PM, Mizusawa deployed with the QRF on a report of North Korean infiltrators in the UNC sector.

> We had a new night vision device in one of our key checkpoints, observation point 5 [OP 5], which was the checkpoint that observed and photographed the 1976 ax murder of Capt. Arthur Bonifas, one of my predecessors as JSF commander. We had been running ambush patrols in the DMZ at night because there was evidence that the North Koreans were infiltrating across the border after dark. As JSF commander, I was always alerted when they thought North Koreans came across the border, and many were unconfirmed detections based on military intelligence assets located outside the DMZ. But that night, the report was from my soldiers who were observing an infiltration inside the JSA, and had a position on two humans. In this case, we were sure.[15]

After the sighting was confirmed by the JDO and the battalion commander, Lt. Col. Chuck Viale, Mizusawa deployed his QRF, which he split into three squads.

> I had a brand new platoon leader, Tom Thompson. It might have been his first week. I formed two of his squads into an L-shaped ambush position, with the squad at the left with its back to the border and the squad to the right blocking further ingress into the south. With Lt. Thompson to the right and SFC Taylor to the left, I positioned myself at the apex of the L, which was at the base of the famous poplar tree [the site of the ax murders]. The third squad, accompanied by Lt. Col. Viale, was sent into the reeds [tall grass common to wetlands], leaving from OP 5 to engage the North Koreans or to flush them into our ambush kill zone.

We were all on the radio listening as OP 5 vectored and reported the closing distance of the third squad, from a point about two hundred meters [656 feet] from the apex, with the enemy soldiers about halfway in between. The chance for fratricide was high, and we had never trained on vectoring forces based on thermal imagery. Also, the enemy soldiers had to know they had been detected and were being surrounded, and would rather die than surrender given past precedent. So we took our time. I was lying next to the poplar tree with my driver for over an hour in the cold trying to hear anything moving to our front. During this time, we received several reports of an increasing number of North Korean soldiers with automatic weapons lining up on the border. Then without warning there was a burst of automatic fire about fifty meters [164 feet] in front of us.[16]

The firing came from the point man for the third squad.

Surprise was no longer an issue since the "cat was out of the bag," so I had my jeep brought up and the lights turned on, pointing in the direction of where we believed the North Koreans were. This could have given us the visibility needed for a clean engagement, with minimal risk of hitting our own soldiers, but it turned out to be a mistake. Even though the lights were angled down, the thick reeds were about ten feet high, too high to see anyone. It was like turning your high beams on in the fog, and it obviously didn't help our night vision. Lesson learned.

After things settled down, at least as much as they could under the circumstances, we waited quietly for the night vision device to recycle and to reacquire. This was not an easy wait, especially since I had given away my position, but my driver and I hunkered down at the base of the tree. Lt. Col. Viale was pushing point, with me at the funnel point of the ambush and two desperate North Korean soldiers in between. Lt. Thompson reported that the North Koreans were moving toward my location and not too long afterwards I could hear movement. My driver and I put our weapons on automatic; I remember my fingers being numb from the cold. It crossed my mind that it would be ironic if I was the second JSF commander killed at the base of the poplar tree.

After that we didn't hear anything more, and didn't want to recon by fire. We lay in wait another hour, and decided to stand down after being convinced the North Koreans managed to somehow slip back north. In retrospect, getting the 4th Platoon back for some rest was good given their central role in the intense firefight the next day.

This 22 November incident was very significant, although it was overshadowed by the next day's events. It was the first shots fired in Panmunjon since 1953 and we expected the North to launch a major protest of the unprecedented hostile firing. I was in my office the following morning preparing a response when I was alerted for the other firefight.[17]

Even though the firing of small-arms weapons within the JSA was a major violation of the 1953 Armistice Agreement, the North Koreans did not lodge a protest over the incident, nor subsequently publicize it, which suggests a tacit admission that they had initiated a hostile infiltration into the UNC sector.[18] More likely, 23 November was a dividing point in the history of the JSA.

On 1 December 1984, Pfc. Chang Myong Gi was posthumously presented the Bronze Star with a Combat V, and was promoted to corporal.[19] Mizusawa and four others also were awarded Bronze Stars with Combat Vs. Additionally, Army Commendation Medals were awarded to several other soldiers. A monument was erected memorializing Chang's sacrifice, and a memorial, including taps and a last roll call, is held every year at Freedom House in the JSA on the anniversary of his death. New barracks were dedicated as "Chang Barracks" at Camp Kitty Hawk, which was renamed Camp Bonifas in 1985 to honor the JSF commander who similarly sacrificed his life.[20] The Sunken Garden was later filled in and renovated.

Vasily Matuzok was granted asylum in the United States and eventually studied at the Fletcher School at Tufts University under an assumed name. While there, he was reunited with Bert Mizusawa, who was a student a few miles away at Harvard University.

Because of political considerations, including the glut of medals awarded following the invasion of Grenada in 1983, valor along the Korean DMZ went too long unrecognized by the military and the American government.

In July 2000, after years of petitions by veteran groups and individuals within the military, the Pentagon approved the award of the Silver Star to Captain Mizusawa, SSgt. Richard Lamb, Sp.4 John Orlicki, and Pfc. Mark Deville, and the award of the CIB for all who participated in the firefight.[21]

Mizusawa finished his time in Korea, and on active duty, as assistant operations officer assigned to the UNC Military Armistice Commission MAC in Seoul, leaving Korea, and active duty, on 1 November 1985. He remained in the Army Reserve, and was promoted to brigadier general in a ceremony attended by former Army Chief of Staff Gen. Eric Shinseki in a ceremony at Fort Belvoir, Virginia, on 27 January 2006.[22]

After leaving active duty, Mizusawa returned to school, earning a master's degree in Public Policy from the Kennedy School of Government and a law degree from Harvard Law School, as well as a master's degree in strategic studies from the Army War College. He held senior positions in private industry and in the government, serving on the staff of both the secretary of the Army and the Senate Armed Services Committee. He deployed twice on active duty—to Afghanistan in 2005, and to

Iraq in the second half of 2006, where he served as deputy to the commanding general, Multinational Corps in Baghdad.

The "Soviet Defector Incident," as it has come to be known, has been called "the most serious and most violent incident in the fifty-five year history of the JSA,"[23] and Mizusawa has become known as the "Last Veteran of the Korean War." But as he is quick to point out, the armed confrontation along the DMZ continues to this day.

chapter nineteen

SSGT. GREGORY FRONIUS AND THE EL SALVADOR INSURGENCY, 1987

On 5 May 1996, a sunny spring day, a group of families gathered on the green lawns of Arlington National Cemetery to witness the unveiling of a memorial dedicated to the twenty-one U.S. servicemen killed in El Salvador during its civil war from January 1981 to February 1992. Speaking to the crowd, William G. Walker, the U.S. ambassador to El Salvador from 1988 to 1992, acknowledged the appropriateness of recognizing the service of more than five thousand U.S. veterans in an unacknowledged, "secret" war. "For too long, we have failed to recognize the contributions, the sacrifices of those who served with distinction under the most dangerous conditions. Only today, a full four years after the achievement of peace, are we finally and officially proclaiming that those who served and those who died did so for the noblest, the most unselfish of reasons." [1]

Following a military coup in El Salvador in 1979, political stability disappeared, replaced by a series of military and civilian juntas incapable of restoring order. A Communist-inspired insurgency, the Farabundo Martí National Liberation Front (Frente Farabundo Martí para la Liberación Nacional; FMLN), formed to oppose the government. Concerns about the Sandinista regime in Nicaragua and the funneling of weapons from Vietnam through Nicaragua to leftist insurgents caused the Reagan administration to increase military assistance to El Salvador in 1981. [2]

In January 1981, the FMLN launched its final offensive to overthrow the government, and was barely defeated by the El Salvadoran Army, which was too weak to solidify the victory. This allowed the insurgents to escape into the countryside to begin a guerilla war. Pro-Cuban Marxist insurgents waged a series of attacks on government troops, police stations, power stations, and other symbols of national authority.

SSgt. Greg Fronius training an indigenous soldier. (Courtesy of Celinda Carney)

To counter the spread of Communism in Central America, the Reagan administration sent U.S. advisers to El Salvador to train the El Salvadoran Army in counterinsurgency methods beginning in October 1980. To combat the insurgents, a series of Immediate Reaction Battalions (IRBs) were formed and trained by U.S. Special Forces troops, the famed Green Berets. In 1982, the United States established a regional training center in Honduras to train Salvadoran units without bringing them to the United States. In 1983, a similar facility was established within El Salvador.

Besides training troops, the U.S. Army sent advisers to the brigade headquarters of each of El Salvador's six military zones. Teams of advisers lived, worked, and trained with Salvadoran troops for six-month tours of duty. Because of an agreement between the El Salvadoran government and the U.S. State Department, the number of "official" advisers was limited to fifty-five in country at any one time, and the selected officers and NCOs were thinly deployed throughout the country.[3]

To avoid the appearance of taking an active role in another civil war, reminiscent of Vietnam a half-dozen years earlier, advisers were officially prohibited from participating in combat operations, and field commanders were told in no uncertain terms not to nominate soldiers for combat awards. Yet they carried weapons, earned combat pay, and frequently came under fire as they accompanied troops in the field. Additionally, they were targeted and attacked by guerillas.[4]

Between 1982 and 1987, the El Salvadoran Army grew from 20,000 to 65,000 men and saw U.S. security assistance grow from $42.2 million to $704.7 million. But attacks on Salvadoran *cuartels* (fortified army camps) continued to occur.

The most publicized attack was the assault by FMLN guerillas on the headquarters of the 4th Infantry Brigade in El Paraíso ("paradise" in Spanish), Chalatenango, on 31 March 1987. The attack, which destroyed buildings, killed sixty-four Salvadoran soldiers, and wounded an additional seventy-nine, also resulted in the first U.S. combat casualty of the conflict: SSgt.Gregory A. Fronius.

It was not the first time an American had been killed in El Salvador. On 25 May 1983, Lt. Cdr. Albert Schaufelberger, the senior U.S. Naval representative in country, was murdered by gunmen while picking up a friend from the grounds of the University of San Salvador. Two years later, on 19 June 1985, four off-duty Marines from the Marine Corps Security Guard Detachment in San Salvador were gunned down as they sat at an outdoor café in the Zona Rosa District. Both were targets of the insurgents, but Fronius was the first American killed in combat in El Salvador at a time when the Republican administration was working hard to convince the American public that no Americans were in combat in El Salvador.[5]

★ ★ ★

Gregory Fronius was born in Plainsville, Ohio, on 3 November 1959, the day JFK was elected president. The youngest of three brothers, he grew up wanting to be a soldier, a goal he achieved upon his enlistment in the U.S. Army in 1977 at the age of eighteen.

In 1980, while assigned to an infantry unit in Panama, Fronius met Celinda Ortega, a Panamanian woman whom he courted and married despite his inability to speak Spanish. Their first son, Gregory Jr., was born in September 1981. The couple returned to the United States where Fronius graduated from Special Forces training at Ft. Bragg, North Carolina, in 1983 and attended the Defense Language Institute (DLI) in Monterey, California, in 1984, studying Spanish in preparation for his reassignment to Central America.[6]

In 1985, Fronius was assigned to the 3rd Battalion, 7th Special Forces Group (Airborne) based at Ft. Gulick in the Canal Zone in Panama. In January 1987, he was assigned as an adviser to the El Salvadoran Armed Forces (ESAF) to teach small-unit tactics and small-arms marksmanship to Salvadoran soldiers. Known as Sergento Rojo (rojo is "red" in Spanish) because of his bright red hair, Fronius was popular with the troops. He was one of three Americans attached to the 4th Brigade headquarters at El Paraíso.[7]

El Paraíso was located about thirty miles from San Salvador, the capital of El Salvador, deep in the heart of FMLN-controlled territory. El Paraíso's garrison was kept busy patrolling the highways and guarding power plants and bridges. The compound itself was designed by American Special Forces teams and was considered impregnable, protected by a minefield, razor wire fences, and other physical barriers. It was a showpiece of Salvadoran military strength and determination for visiting military dignitaries. As such, the facility was a prime target for the FMLN.

Rules of engagement for American advisers required them to remain within the compound except for training or humanitarian missions. U.S. advisers were explicitly prohibited from going on combat patrols. Furthermore, they were admonished to use good judgment and avoid placing themselves in danger.

Early in 1987, there was a resurgence of political and military activity by the FMLN with the intent of destabilizing President José Napoleón Duarte's Christian Democratic government. In what was obviously a well-thought-out and meticulously planned operation, the insurgents attacked El Paraíso early on the morning of 31 March.

At 2:00 AM, three teams of FMLN sappers, each made up of 10–15 men, infiltrated through the minefield surrounding the camp to penetrate the perimeter fence and eliminate the sentries, possibly assisted by collaborators inside the compound. Unobserved and unopposed, they entered the camp carrying eight hundred–gram explosive satchels while a fourth team set up machine-gun and mortar positions on a hill overlooking the base and zeroed in on preselected targets. The teams, trained by Cuban and Nicaraguan advisers, were clad in black and armed with H&K MP-5 .9-mm submachine guns.

The attack was a complete surprise and took the government troops unaware. It began with a mortar barrage that continued for two hours, targeting command buildings, administrative offices, and barracks with incredible accuracy. Explosive satchels were thrown into officers' quarters and barracks. Machine-gun fire raked panicked figures running confused in the open, silhouetted in the darkness by the flames, and the base was thrown into chaos.[8]

Although the base normally had 1,000 troops, only 250 were present, with the rest out on operations. Fronius was the only American on base at the time. He grabbed his weapon and gear and raced out into the darkness, only to be wounded in the shoulder almost immediately on exiting the barracks. Knocked into a ditch by the impact, Fronius applied a dressing to his wound and rejoined the fight.

Crossing the compound, he attempted to organize the confused ESAF troops into a defensive posture, but the confusion was too great and he was unsuccessful. He then raced to the TOC, a bunkered command and control center constructed to withstand enemy assaults, where most of the ESAF officers had taken refuge.

Across from the TOC was an elevated berm, control of which could put the TOC in jeopardy. Deciding to preemptively seize the high ground, Fronius climbed the stairway to the top of the berm only to come into close combat with three guerillas. Fronius killed one, and likely wounded another, before being shot himself and knocked down the stairs.[9]

As he lay wounded at the bottom of the stairs, two ESAF soldiers tried to reach his position to render aid, but enemy fire was too intense. Fronius waved them away as shrapnel from mortar air bursts rained down on him. He was incapacitated from his wounds or already dead when FMLN sappers detonated an explosive charge under his body, perhaps in retaliation for his stiff resistance.[10]

Posthumously awarded the Silver Star, his citation states Fronius "rallied the defense in action that resulted in many casualties among the attacking forces, before he was himself mortally wounded."[11]

After three hours, as daylight approached, the insurgents became vulnerable to an aerial counterattack and withdrew, leaving sixty-four Salvadorans and one American adviser killed in action and another seventy-nine Salvadorans wounded. The insurgents left behind eight dead and political humiliation for the Duarte administration. It was the most successful attack by FMLN forces to date.[12]

Was it a coincidence that an attack occurred at the time the base was undermanned and vulnerable? How were the attackers able to circumvent the minefield and other defensive measures? How was their intelligence on the base so accurate? In his book, *True Believer*, DIA (Defense Intelligence Agency) counterintelligence investigator Scott Carmichael suggested a possible answer. He believed a senior DIA analyst, Ana Belen Montes, was at least partially responsible for the security breach.

Montes, an agent for Cuban intelligence, was subsequently arrested, tried, and convicted for espionage in 2002. She was at the time an analyst on El Salvador and Nicaragua and may have passed information about the secret base to her Cuban handlers. She took an official trip to El Salvador in February–March 1987, and visited the base at El Paraíso where she was briefed extensively, just weeks before the attack.[13]

Under investigation for five years, Montes was arrested on 21 September 2001, just ten days after 9/11, the day she would have gained access to information about the pending military incursion against the Taliban in Afghanistan. She was convicted of spying for Cuba and sentenced to twenty-five years in prison.

As for Fronius, his family originally was told he had been killed in his barracks by a mortar attack; they learned the truth only much later. He was denied a posthumous Bronze Star at the time because El Salvador was not considered a combat zone. Only in February 1996, after President Clinton signed the 1996 Defense Authorization Act, did the truth about his (and others') actions in El Salvador come to light. Through the efforts of Rep. Robert K. Dornan (R-CA), all veterans who served in El Salvador from January 1981 to February 1992 were authorized the award of the Armed Forces Expeditionary Medal. This facilitated the award of other combat decorations, including Fronius' Silver Star.[14]

A second attack on El Paraíso in 1988 was less successful because the guerillas fought against more-prepared and better-trained ESAF forces. Certainly the professional training imparted to the ESAF by U.S. advisers was a factor in its ultimate victory over the guerillas. When the FMLN launched its last offensive in 1989, it was soundly defeated. Free elections supported by a majority of the people forced the FMLN to seek a political solution. This resulted in a signed peace accord between the government and the FMLN, which was recognized as a legitimate political party, and land and judicial reform measures were enacted.[15]

Explaining the purpose of the memorial to those gathered at Arlington that Wednesday morning, Greg Walker, a former Special Forces staff sergeant who led a veterans' campaign to gain official recognition of the U.S. military's role in El Salvador said, "We wanted to correct history. We wanted to recognize the sacrifices of those who served . . . [and] we wanted to honor our dead and bring closure to their families."

[appendix i]

AIRCRAFT DOWNED DURING THE COLD WAR

Note: The following compilation of shootdown information is not all inclusive. It does not include aerial combat losses incident to and during the Korean and Vietnam wars.

1945

- Soviet Yak-9 Frank damaged U.S. Army Air Force B-29 Superfortress dropping supplies to a POW camp near Hamhung, Korea, and forced to land. Crew experienced no injuries. (29 August)
- Soviet fighters fire on U.S. Navy 7th Fleet air patrols in Manchurian airspace. (2–16 September)
- U.S. Navy PBM-5 Mariner attacked by Soviet fighter twenty-five miles south of Darien (Port Arthur) Manchuria. No damage inflicted. (15 November)

1946

- Yugoslav Air Force Yak-3 forced down a Royal Air Force Dakota transport flying over southern Yugoslavia, near Niš.
- U.S. Navy PBM-5 Mariner based in Tsingtao, China, on unauthorized flight over Darien (Port Arthur), Manchuria, fired on by Soviet fighter. No damage inflicted. (20 February)
- U.S. Army Air Force C-47 shot at near Vienna, Austria, but managed to escape. (22 April)
- U.S. Army Air Force C-47A transport shot down by Yugoslav Air Force Yak-3 over northern Yugoslavia. Four American crew members and four passengers survived and were released by the Yugoslavian authorities. (9 August)

- U.S. Army Air Force C-47 transport shot down by Yugoslav Air Force Yak-3 over northern Yugoslavia. Five-man crew were killed. (19 August)
- U.S. Army Air Force A-26 Invader of USAF 45th Reconnaissance Squadron, Furth, Germany, became lost in heavy weather while on a mission to Amsterdam, the Netherlands, and eventually landed in a village northeast of Budapest, Hungary. Aircraft was undamaged and flyable but low on fuel. Soviet Air Force officers questioned pilot and crewman. Once they had developed the onboard film, Soviets were satisfied there was nothing of consequence on the images. Later an American arrived in Budapest with enough fuel to get the A-26 in the air. After a refueling stop at the regular Budapest airfield, the crew and aircraft returned to their home base. (1–2 December)

1947

- USAF B-29 Superfortress of the 28th Bomber Squadron disappeared over the Bering Sea. The crew of twelve were presumed dead. (24 February)
- U.S. Marine Corps aircraft crashed in China and the four-man crew was captured by Communist forces. They were released in July 1948. (29 December)

1948

- Soviet pilots claimed to have downed a USAF B-25 Mitchell over the Black Sea. USAF AT-6 was shot down over Greece by Communist guerrillas. The pilot was killed. (22 January)
- Two Turkish Supermarine Spitfires were shot down by small-arms fire when they entered Bulgarian airspace at low altitude. The pilot of one of the aircraft was killed when his plane fell into the Black Sea. The other was captured and later returned to Turkey. (9 February)
- U.S. observation plane was shot down near Kaesong, Korea, by North Korean forces. The pilot was wounded in the attack. (19 February)
- British European Airways Vickers Viking (G-AIVP) circling Gatow Airfield, Berlin, in preparation for landing, collided head-on with a Soviet Yak-3 fighter, which was performing aerobatics. The Soviet pilot and all fourteen on board the Viking were killed. (5 April)
- U.S. Navy plane crashed near Tsingtao, China. Two crew members were held prisoner by the Communist Chinese for nineteen months. (19 October)
- USAF RB-29 Superfortress was attacked by Soviet fighters over the Sea of Japan. RB-29 crew suffered no injuries. (22 October)
- Italian Air Force P-38 Lighting (NN4175) was shot down over Yugoslavia. (27 October)

1950

- Republic of China (RoC) Air Force F-10 (a photo reconnaissance B-25 Mitchell) was shot down by a People's Republic of China (PRC), People's Liberation Army Air Force (PLAAF) aircraft. The crew of six was killed. (14 March)
- RoC Air Force P-51 Mustang was shot down by PRC PLAAF ground fire. The pilot was killed. (16 March)
- Soviet pilot P. Dushin claimed to have downed a USAF B-26 Invader. (April)
- Soviet pilot V. Sidrov claimed to have shot down a USAF B-26 Invader. (April)
- Soviet pilot Nikolai N. Guzhov claimed to have shot down two USAF F-51 Mustangs. (April)
- RoC Air Force P-51 Mustang was shot down by Soviet aircraft stationed in Shanghai. The Mustang pilot was killed. (2 April)
- U.S. Navy PB4Y-2 Privateer from VP-26, Det A. was shot down by Soviet La-11 Fangs piloted by Boris Dokin, Anatoliy Gerasimov, Tezyaev, and Sataev over the Baltic Sea off the coast of Latvia. Ten crewmen were lost. (8 April)
- Soviet pilot Keleinikov claimed to have shot down a USAF P-30 Lightning (F-82 Twin Mustang). (24 April)
- Soviet pilot V. S. Yefremov, flying an La-11 Fang, claimed to have shot down a USAF F-51 Mustang over the Chukotka Peninsula. (May)
- Soviet pilot I. I. Shinkarenko claimed to have downed a USAF B-24 Liberator. (11 May)
- USAF RB-29 was shot at near Permskoye airfield in the Soviet Union, but escaped. (14 July)
- RoC Air Force P-47N Thunderbird was shot down by PRC ground fire over Xiamen. The pilot was killed. (29 July)
- Soviet pilot Kursonov shot down a PRC PLAAF Tu-2 Bat that he mistook for a B-25 Mitchell after it strayed over a restricted area near Shanghai. (9 August)
- U.S. Navy P2V Neptune of VP-6, piloted by Arthur Farwell, was intercepted at night by four MiG-15 Fagots, near Vladivostok. The Neptune's tail gunner opened fire and one MiG exploded. (October–December)
- Soviet MiG-15 Fagots shot down an RB-45C Tornado of the USAF 91st Strategic Reconnaissance Squadron, forty-five miles east of Andung, PRC (just across the Yalu River from Sinuiju, North Korea). Four crewmen were lost. (4 December)
- Two Soviet MiG-15 Fagots, flown by S. A. Bakhev and N. Kotov, shared in the downing of a USAF RB-29 Superfortress. (26 December)

1951

- USAF RB-45C Tornado of the 323rd Strategic Reconnaissance Squadron, based in Yokota, Japan, conducted a night overflight five hundred miles into

Manchuria. The crew reported they were attacked by MiG-15 Fagots while approaching their target in Harbin, PRC. They managed to escape damage by outrunning the intercepting fighters. (4 July)

- Italian Air Force P-38L Lightning was shot down over Yugoslavia. (13 October)
- U.S. Navy P2V-3W Neptune of VP-6 was shot down by Soviet aircraft over the Sea of Japan off Vladivostok. (6 November)
- RoC Air Force P-47N Thunderbolt failed to return from a reconnaissance mission over Guandong, PRC. (8 November)
- USAF C-47 transport, with a crew of four, flying from Munich to Belgrade, became lost over Yugoslavia and entered Hungarian and then Romanian airspace. It was fired on by Hungarian and Romanian border guards and finally forced down by a MiG-15 near the Yugoslav frontier. One crew member survived. (18 November)

1952

- A U.S. Navy patrol bomber was damaged by gunfire from an unidentified trawler one hundred miles southeast of Shanghai, PRC. One crew member was injured and the plane returned safely to Taiwan. (4 April)
- Air France DC-4 was shot at by two MiG-15 Fagots when approaching Berlin. The aircraft was damaged and three passengers wounded. (29 April)
- USAF RB-29 Superfortress of the 91st Strategic Reconnaissance Squadron, based in Yokota, Japan, was shot down by Soviet fighters over the Sea of Japan, 18 miles from the Soviet coast near Hokkaido. 12 crew members were lost. (13 June)
- Swedish SIGINT C-47 Hugin was shot down over the Baltic Sea, near Ventspils, Latvia. Everyone on board the C-47 was killed. The only wreckage found at the time was a life raft. The C-47 was one of two (the other being Munin, both named after Odin's ravens), together with a Ju 86 called Blondie, which supposely belonged to the so-called 6 Transportflyggruppen, which at the time had a staff of twelve. In reality they were used for SIGINT duties, the C-47s were fitted out with five operator stations, the operators belonging to FRA (Forsvarets Radioanstalt; the Radio Establishment of the Defense). In June 2003, Swedish searchers found the wreckage of the C-47 on the bottom of the Baltic in international waters near Gotska Sandoen island, about 75 miles (120 kilometers) east of the Swedish coastline. The wreckage was raised during the night of March 19/20 2004 and returned to Sweden. (13 June)
- Swedish PBY Catalina was downed by Soviet aircraft outside the island of Dago. The PBY was looking for survivors of the Swedish SIGINT C-47 lost on 13 June. After taking hits in the fuselage and the engines, the PBY was forced to

land on the water with two of the crew of seven injured. The crew was rescued by a German merchant ship. (16 June)

- U.S. Navy PBM-5S2 Mariner from VP-731 was attacked by two PRC MiG-15 Fagots over the Yellow Sea. Two crew members were killed and two were seriously injured. The seaplane suffered extensive damage, but was able to make it safely to Paengyong-do Korea. (31 July)
- U.S. Navy PB4Y-2S Privateer of VP-28 was attacked by two Chinese MiG-15 Fagots off the coast of the PRC. The Navy aircraft was able to safely return to Naha, Okinawa. (20 September)
- USAF RB-29 Superfortress was shot down over Kurile Islands by two Soviet La-11 Fang fighters. Crew of eight lost. (7 October)
- USAF C-47 was fired on near Berlin. (8 October)
- USAF B-47 photo reconnaissance flight, authorized by President Truman and staged out of Eielson Air Force Base, was flown over the Chukotsky Peninsula. It confirmed the Soviets were developing Arctic staging bases on the peninsula from which their bombers could easily reach targets on the North American continent. (15 October)
- U.S. Navy PB4Y-2S Privateer of VP-28 was attacked but not damaged by a Chinese MiG-15 Fagot off Shanghai, PRC. (23 November)
- U.S. CAT (CIA airline) flying from Seoul, South Korea, on a mission to pick up an agent in Manchuria was shot down in Jilin province, PRC. The C-47 pilots were killed but two passengers (CIA officers) survived and were captured. Fecteau and Downey were imprisoned for two decades before being released. (29 November)

1953

- USAF B-29 Superfortress on a leaflet drop mission over Manchuria was shot down by a swarm of enemy fighters. Aircraft crew bailed out. Three of the fourteen-man crew died during the attack; the rest were captured and released in 1956. (12 January)
- U.S. Navy P2V-5 Neptune of VP-22, based at Atsugi, Japan, was fired on by Chinese antiaircraft guns near Swatow, PRC, but was able to ditch in the Formosa Strait. Eleven of the thirteen crewmen were rescued by a U.S. Coast Guard PBM-5 Mariner, which came under fire from Chinese shore batteries on Nan Ao Tao island. While attempting to take off in heavy seas, the PBM crashed. Ten survivors out of nineteen were rescued by the destroyer USS *Halsey Powell* (DD-686). Nine crewmen were lost. (18 January)
- A PRC pilot claimed to have shot down a U.S. Navy F4U Corsair on Qianlidao in Qingdao. (6 March)

- Two USAF F-84G Thunderjets of the 36 TFW, based in West Germany, crossed into Czechoslovakian airspace. They were intercepted by Czech MiG-15 Fagots, and one F-84G was shot down. The American pilot ejected and survived. (10 March)
- Royal Air Force Avro Lincoln MK2 was shot down by a Soviet MiG-15 Fagot in the Berlin air corridor, near Boizenberg, twenty miles NE of Luneburg. Seven fliers were killed. (12 March)
- Pilot of a Soviet An-2 Colt, flying from East Germany, became lost and landed in a small field near Irmelshausen, West Germany. The pilot realized where he was and took off and returned to East Germany before West German border police arrived to question him. (14 March)
- USAF WB-50 Superfortess reconnaissance aircraft of the 38th Strategic Reconnaissance Squadron, 55th Strategic Reconnaissance Wing was attacked by two Soviet MiG-15 Fagots twenty-five miles off the Kamchatka Peninsula, near Petropavlovsk. The Soviet aircraft opened fire on the Superfortress which returned fire. The MiGs broke off and returned to their base. (15 March)
- British European Airways Viking was shot down by Soviet MiG-15 Fagots near Berlin. (17 March)
- USAF B-50 was attacked by Soviet MiG-15 Fagots. (22 March)
- U.S. Navy P4M-1Q Mercator was attacked by two MiG-15 Fagots while flying off the Chinese coast near Shanghai. No damage was done to either the Mercator or the MiGs. (23 April)
- Soviet MiG-15 Fagot opened fire on a USAF WB-29 Superfortress off the Kamchatka Peninsula. WB-29 gunners returned fire. There were no casualties. (15 May)
- RoC Air Force P-47N Thunderbolt was shot down by PRC ground fire over Dongshan Island. The P-47 pilot was killed. (16 June)
- U.S. Navy PBM-5S2 Mariner of VP- 46 was fired on by PRC surface ship in the Formosa Strait. No damage inflicted. (28 June)
- U.S. Navy P2V-5 Neptune of VP-1 was fired on by PRC antiaircraft artillery near Nantien, PRC. No damage inflicted. (8 July)
- Two Chinese MiGs damaged a U.S. Navy PBM-5 Mariner in an attack that took place over the Yellow Sea. (21 July)
- Aeroflot Il-12 Coach was shot down by USAF F-86F Sabre fighter near Kanggye, North Korea, shortly before the Korean War armistice went into effect. All twenty-one people on board were killed. (27 July)
- USAF RB-50G Superfortress based in Yokota, Japan was shot down south of Askold Island, Vladivostok, by Soviet pilots flying MiG-17 Frescos. One crewman survived, and seventeen were lost. (29 July)

- Royal Air Force Canberra, a modified B Mk.2, suffered damage during a recon-naissance flight over Kapustin Yar missile base in the Soviet Union. Aircraft aborted its mission and landed in Iran. (August)
- USAF T-6 was shot down over the Korean DMZ by North Korean ground fire. One crewman was killed, and one survived. (17 August)
- U.S. Navy PBM-5 Mariner of VP-50 was intercepted by two PRC MiG-15 Fagots thirty miles east of Tsingtao, China. MiGs made numerous firing passes but hit Mariner only twice in tail with 37mm cannon shells, causing little damage. No crew casualties. PBM returned safely to base. (2 October)
- U.S. Navy PBM-5 Mariner of VP-50 picked up an unexpected tail wind while approaching Shanghai. The aircraft got close to the coast of the PRC before crew determined their position. After plane turned away from coast, it was attacked by two MiG-15 Fagots. Three firing passes were made. PBM took no hits and returned to base. (18 November)
- RoC Air Force P-47N Thunderbolt was shot down by PRC ground fire over Jejiang, China. The pilot was killed. (17 December)

1954

- U.S. Navy P2V-5 Neptune of VP-2 departed NAS Iwakuni in Japan and headed toward the west coast of Korea. The flight continued north across the Korean DMZ, then along the North Korean coast to the coast of China before turning south. After reporting engine difficulties, the aircraft headed toward the Kimpo (K-13) airbase at Suwan. The engine difficulties might have been a result of a hostile attack on the Neptune. The aircraft reached the vicinity of K-13 before crashing. All ten crew members were killed. (4 January)
- USAF RB-45 Tornado flying over the Yellow Sea with an escort of F-86 Sabres was attacked by eight MiG-15 Fagots. One MiG was shot down. (27 January)
- An RoC Air Force P-47N Thunderbolt was shot down by PRC ground fire. The pilot was killed. (9 February)
- Czech Air Force fighter shot down a twin-engine aircraft. (10 March)
- An RoC Air Force P-47N Thunderbolt was shot down by a PRC Air Force MiG-15 Fagot. The pilot was killed (18 March)
- Two U.S. Navy AD-4 Skyraiders, from VA-145 and VC-35 Det F, launched from the USS *Randolph* (CVA-15) on a simulated strike mission against a West German airfield. They were attacked over or near the Czechoslovak border by a Czech MiG-15 Fagot. One AD-4 received damage to its tail. (21 March)
- U.S. Navy P2V Neptune from VP-2 was attacked by a Chinese MiG-15 Fagot while on patrol over the Yellow Sea. The MiG made three firing passes and the crew of the Neptune returned fire. There was no apparent damage to either aircraft resulting from the encounter. (9 April)

- An RB-45C Tornado operated by the Royal Air Force narrowly escaped being shot down by antiaircraft fire near Kiev, Soviet Union. The mission was aborted. (29 April)

- One of a flight of six CAT C-119 Flying Boxcars was hit twice by ground fire as it was about to drop ammunition to beleaguered French Foreign Legion troops at Dien Bien Phu, Vietnam. The plane crashed in Laos near the Nam Het River. Two pilots were killed. Of the four French crewmen on board, two survived the crash. One died later of his injuries. The lone survivor was subsequently taken captive by Pathet Lao forces. He was released 13 October 1954. (6 May)

- Three USAF RB-47E Stratojet reconnaissance planes took off from RAF Fairford, England; two of the Stratojets flew as airborne spares and turned back before the overflight began. The remaining plane penetrated Soviet airspace at Murmansk. The plane flew over numerous Soviet airfields and naval facilities conducting photographic reconnaissance and making radar scope images of the various facilities. The RB-47E continued to Arkhangelsk before turning west and heading back to England. The plane was intercepted by MiG fighters after being over Soviet territory for about fifty miles. Initially, MiG-15 Fagots were spotted, but a short time later a flight of MiG-17 Frescos appeared. The operational deployment of the MiG-17 was a significant surprise to the crew of the RB-47. When the MiG-17s climbed to approximately the same altitude as the reconnaissance plane (38,000 feet) the Soviets opened fire. The Soviet fighters each made single shooting passes at the RB-47. The reconnaissance aircraft was equipped with a tail gun controlled by the copilot; it returned fire but did not hit any of the Soviet planes. One MiG was able to hit the Stratojet with several rounds and caused moderate damage to the wing and fuselage. Before the MiGs were able to shoot down the USAF plane, it crossed the border into Finland and the MiGs broke off the attack. However, during the attack the RB-47's fuel tanks were hit and the plane nearly ran out of fuel before it was met by a Boeing KC-97 tanker for in-flight refueling. The RB-47 landed safely in England a short time later. (8 May)

- Two RoC Air Force P-47 Thunderbolts engaged two PLAAF MiG-15 Fagots and claimed one as damaged. (11 May)

- USAF RB-47 Stratojet of the 51st Strategic Reconnaissance Wing flying photo reconnaissance over northern Soviet Union exchanged gunfire with MiG-17 Frescos. The RB-47 was slightly damaged but the aircraft returned safely to home base. (22 May)

- RoC Air Force B-17 was shot down by ground fire near Fujian, PRC. Four crewmen were killed. (26 May)

- Belgian transport aircraft was shot down by MiGs over Yugoslavia. One crew member was killed. (3 June)

- RoC Air Force P-47N Thunderbolt was shot down by a PRC Air Force La-11 Fang and the pilot was killed. (3 June)
- RoC Air Force P-47N Thunderbolt was shot down by a PRC Air Force MiG-15 Fagot and the pilot was killed. (6 July)
- A Cathay Pacific Airways DC-4 on a flight from Bangkok, Thailand, to Hong Kong, was shot down by PRC La-9 Fritz fighters near Hainan Island, China. Of the eighteen people on board (including six Americans), ten were killed. (22 July)
- Two U.S. Navy AD-4 Skyraiders from VF-54 were launched from the USS *Philippine Sea* (CVA- 47) to look for survivors from the Cathay Pacific DC-4 shot down four days previously. They were attacked by two Chinese La-7 Fins. A number of other VF-54 AD-4 Skyraiders and an F4U-5N Corsair of VC-3 came to the aid of the Navy aircraft. Both Chinese fighters were shot down by the American fliers. (26 July)
- Two U.S. training planes were shot down over Czechoslovakia. The pilots were captured and held for several months. (12 August)
- U.S. Navy P2V-5 of VP-19, operating from NAS Atsugi, Japan, was attacked forty miles off the coast of Siberia by two Soviet MiG-15 Fagots. The aircraft ditched and one crew member was lost. The surviving nine crewmen were rescued by a USAF SA-16 amphibian. (4 September)
- Bulgarian fighter intercepted and fired on an unknown intruder at night. The plane that had been fired on crashed in Greek territory. There was no official Greek comment on this, but Greek newspapers published memorials for dead pilots, without connecting their deaths to a specific event. (9 September)
- RoC Air Force PB4Y was shot down by ground fire near Xiamen, PRC. The crew of nine was killed. (12 September)
- RoC Air Force P-47N Thunderbolt failed to return from mission over the PRC. (15 October)
- RoC Air Force P-47N Thunderbolt crashed while on a bombing mission in Fujian, PRC. The pilot was killed. (1 November)
- USAF RB-29 Superfortress reconnaissance aircraft was shot down by Soviet fighters near Hokkaido Island in northern Japan. The plane carrying a crew of eleven was conducting routine photographic reconnaissance near Hokkaido and the southernmost of the disputed Kuril Islands. The plane was attacked and seriously damaged, forcing the crew to bail out. Ten crewmen were successfully rescued. The eleventh man drowned when he became entangled in his parachute lines after landing. (7 November)
- RoC Air Force RT-33A crashed into mountains in Fujian, PRC, while evading a PLAAF MiG-15 Fagot. The pilot was killed. (17 November)

1955

- U.S. Army L-20 Beaver was shot down by North Korean fire over the Korean DMZ and the crew of two was killed. (19 January)
- RoC Air Force F-84G Thunderjet was shot down by PRC ground fire. The pilot was killed. (19 January)
- U.S. Navy P2V sustained wing damage after it was fired on by PRC antiaircraft artillery while over Formosa Strait. (February)
- RoC Air Force P-47N Thunderbolt was shot down by PRC ground fire. The pilot was killed. (21 January)
- USAF RB-45 Tornado of the 91st Strategic Reconnaissance Squadron was attacked over the Yellow Sea, forty miles west of Pyongyang, by two North Korean or Chinese MiG-15 Fagots. An air battle involving eight USAF F-86 Sabres and twelve MiG-15s followed. Two MiGs were shot down. No Sabres were lost. (5 February)
- U.S. Navy AD-5W Skyraider of VC-11 Det. H from USS *Wasp* (CVA-18) sustained damage from Chinese antiaircraft artillery. The AD was covering the evacuation of Chinese Nationalists from Tachen Islands. The aircraft ditched and the three-man crew was rescued by RoC patrol boats. (9 February)
- RoC Air Force P-47N Thunderbolt was shot down by PRC ground fire. The pilot was killed. (20 February)
- Two PRC MiG-15 Fagots downed a USAF RB-47E Stratojet of the 4th Strategic Reconnaissance Squadron, flying from Eielson Air Force Base, near Kamchatka. Three air personnel were lost. (17 April)
- Eight USAF F-86 Sabres were attacked by twelve PRC PLAAF MiGS off the Korean coast. One F-86 was claimed to be shot down by a PRC pilot. USAF pilots claimed two MiGs destroyed on same day, fifty miles southwest of Simuiju. (10 May)
- RoC Air Force RT-33A was shot down over Jiangxi by a PRC Fresco. The RT-33A's one crew member was killed. (22 June)
- U.S. Navy P2V-5 Neptune of VP-9 flying a patrol mission from Kodiak, Alaska, was attacked over the Bering Strait by two Soviet MiG-15 Fagots. The aircraft crash-landed on St. Lawrence Island after an engine was set afire. Of the eleven crew members, four sustained injuries due to gunfire and six were injured during the landing. The United States demanded $724,947 in compensation. The Soviet Union eventually paid half this amount. (22 June)
- Four RoC Air Force F-84G Thunderjets engaged four PRC MiG-15 Fagots, downing one. (4 July)
- A RoC Air Force F-84G Thunderjet was shot down by PRC ground fire near Kinmen, killing the pilot. (16 July)
- El Al Airlines Lockheed 049 Constellation, flight 426, flying from London to Tel Aviv via Vienna and Istanbul, strayed into Bulgarian airspace, likely due to

strong winds in very bad weather. The aircraft was intercepted in early morning darkness at 17,500 feet by Bulgarian MiG-15 Fagot fighters and was shot down near Petrich, Bulgaria. The aircraft crashed near the Strumitza River, close to the Yugoslav and Greek borders in southwestern Bulgaria. All fifty-one passengers and seven crew members on board were killed, including six American nationals. (27 July)

- USAF LT-6 utility/training aircraft was shot down by North Korean ground fire after the aircraft inadvertently overflew the DMZ into North Korea. The pilot was wounded and the observer was killed. The body of the observer and the pilot were returned by the North Koreans on 23 August. (18 August)
- RoC Air Force F-86 Sabre was shot down by a PRC MiG-15 Fagot. (15 October)
- An-2 Colt carrying Polish UN observers along the Korean DMZ was shot down by South Korea. (7 November)

1956

- One MiG-15 Fagot was claimed when four RoC Air Force F-84G Thunderjets engaged four MiG-15 Fagots of the PRC PLAAF. (14 April)
- PRC PLAAF MiG-17 Fresco shot down an RoC Air Force B-17 during a nighttime interception. The B-17's crew of eleven was killed. (22 June)
- One MiG-15 Fagot was claimed when four RoC Air Force F-84G Thunderjets engaged four MiG-15 Fagots of the PRC PLAAF. (20 July)
- Four RoC Air Force F-84G Thunderjets engaged three MiG-15 Fagots of the PRC PLAAF. Two MiGs were shot down. (21 July)
- RoC Air Force claimed two MiG-15 Fagots shot down when four F-86 Sabres engaged three MiG-15 Fagots of the PRC PLAAF. (21 July)
- U.S. Navy P4M-1Q Mercator of VQ-1 disappeared after a nighttime attack by the PRC PLAAF thirty-two miles off the coast of Wenchow, China, and 180 miles north of Formosa. There were no survivors of the sixteen crew members. The bodies of two crew members and some wreckage were recovered by the USS *Dennis J. Buckley* (DDR-808). Additionally, the bodies of two crew members were recovered by the Chinese and returned to the United States. (22 August)
- USAF RB-50G Superfortress was lost over the Sea of Japan. The sixteen crew members were all presumed to be killed. It is suspected that the aircraft was lost due to a powerful storm, Typhoon Emma, which was in the area. (10 September)
- PRC PLAAF shot down a RoC Air Force F-84 over Shantou. (4 October)
- RoC Air Force C-46 Commando was shot down over Jejigxi by a PRC PLAAF MiG-19 while on an airdrop, killing the crew of nine. (10 November)

1957

- RoC Air Force RF-84F Thunderflash crashed while being pursued by a PRC PLAAF MiG, killing the pilot. (15 April)
- Four U.S. Navy AD-6 Skyraiders from VA-145 launched from the USS *Hornet* (CVA-12) and overflew the coast of the PRC. They encountered antiaircraft fire; one aircraft sustained slight damage. (12 June)
- RoC Air Force P-47 was shot down by PRC ground fire and the pilot was killed. (1 July)
- RoC Air Force B-26 Invader was shot down over the PRC and the crew of three was captured. The crew was released eight months later. (5 November)
- T-33, with one crew member on board, was lost over Albania. (23 December)
- USAF RB-57 was shot down over the Black Sea by Soviet Fighters. (24 December)

1958

- RB-57D operated by the RoC Air Force was shot down over Shandong, PRC, by a People's Liberation Army Naval Air Force MiG-15 Fagot. The pilot was killed. (18 February)
- USAF F-86 Sabre fighter was shot down by antiaircraft artillery over North Korea when it accidently flew across the DMZ into North Korea. The pilot bailed out and was returned uninjured by North Korea. (6 March)
- Indonesian Air Force F-51D Mustang shot down a CAT B-26B Invader that had already been damaged by antiaircraft fire. The B-26 had just bombed the Ambon Island airstrip in the Moluccas, in support of a revolt in Sulawesi aimed at overthrowing the government of President Sukarno. The CIA pilot and his navigator were captured by Indonesian forces and the pilot was held captive for nineteen months before being brought to trial in a military court. He was accused of six bombing raids that killed twenty-three Indonesians, including seventeen members of the Indonesian armed forces. The pilot was found guilty and sentenced to death. The death penalty was not carried out and he was released in 1962. (18 May)
- RoC Air Force RF-84F Thunderflash crashed near Fujian, PRC, while being pursued by PLAAF MiG-15bis Fagots. The pilot was killed. (17 June)
- USAF C-118, reportedly on a regular supply flight from Wiesbaden, West Germany, to Karachi, Pakistan, via Cyprus and Iran, crossed the Soviet border near Yerevan, Armenia. Two Soviet MiG-17P Frescos shot the aircraft down eighteen miles south of Yerevan. Five crew members parachuted to safety and four others survived the crash-landing on a half-finished airstrip. The nine crewmen were captured and later released by the Soviets on July 7, 1958. The aircraft was reported to be the personal aircraft of Allen Dulles, then director

of the Central Intelligence Agency. The C-118 had carried senior CIA aides to Europe on an inspection trip, and it was in Turkey when it was diverted. (27 June)

- USAF RB-47, flying from Iran, was intercepted by Soviet fighters over the Caspian Sea 130 miles east-southeast of Astara. The RB-47 evaded the fighters and fled to safety. (26 July)
- Four F-84G Thunderjets from the RoC Air Force 1st Wing in Tainnan were on patrol near Nan Ao Island when four PRC PLAAF 54th Regiment MiG-17 Fescos attacked. PLAAF pilots were credited with shooting down one F-84. (29 July)
- RoC Air Force F-86F Sabres shot down three PRC PLAAF MiG-17 Frescos. One F-86 failed to return from engagement. (14 August)
- RoC Air Force F-86 Sabres shot down two PRC PLAAF MiG-17 Frescos. (25 August)
- USAF C-130A Hercules flying from Adana, Turkey, was shot down near Sasnashen, Soviet Armenia, about thirty-four miles northwest of the Armenian capital of Yerevan by Soviet MiG-17 Frescos. The C-130 was a Sun Valley SIGINT aircraft. Seventeen C-130 crewmen were killed in the shootdown. (2 September)
- RoC Air Force F-86 Sabres shot down seven PRC PLAAF MiG-17 Frescos. One F-86 Sabre was lost in the engagement. (18 September)
- RoC Air Force F-86 Sabres shot down eleven PRC PLAAF MiG-17 Frescos. In this air battle, one of the AIM-9B Sidewinder missiles fired by the F-86s hit a MiG-17, but the warhead did not explode. The MiG-17 returned safely to its base and the missile was extracted. The missile was delivered to the Soviet Union, and from there was sent to the Toropov engineering office to be copied. The product of this process being the AA-2 Atoll, long the most prolific Soviet air-to-air missile. (24 September)
- Three crewmen were killed and two were captured when an RoC Air Force C-46 Commando was shot down over the PRC. The captured crew members were released on 30 June 1959. (29 September)
- Five crewmen were killed when an RoC Air Force C-46 Commando was shot down by ground fire over Kinmen, PRC. (2 October)
- RoC Air Force F-86F Sabres shot down four PRC PLAAF MiG-17 Frescos. One F-86F was damaged by debris from an exploding MiG-17. The pilot bailed out and was taken captive. He was released on 30 June 1959. (10 October)
- USAF RB-47 Stratojet was attacked by Soviet fighters over the Black Sea. The crew of three was not injured and the aircraft returned safely to base. (31 October)

- USAF RB-47 Stratojet was attacked by Soviet fighters, east of Gotland Island over the Baltic Sea. The crew of three was not injured and the aircraft returned safely to base. (7 November)
- USAF RB-47 Stratojet was attacked over the Sea of Japan by Soviet fighters. The crew of three was not injured and the aircraft returned safely to base. (17 November)

1959

- RoC Air Force B-17 was shot down by a PLAAF MiG-17PF near Guandong, PRC. The B-17 crew of fourteen was killed. (29 May)
- While flying a patrol mission over the Sea of Japan, a U.S. Navy P4M-1Q of VQ-1 was attacked fifty miles east of the Korean DMZ by two North Korean MiG-17 Frescos. During the attack, the aircraft sustained serious damage to the starboard engine and the tail gunner was seriously wounded. The aircraft made it safely back to Miho Air Force Base in Japan. (16 June)
- Four RoC Air Force F-86 Sabres battled 24 PRC PLAAF MiG-17 Frescos, over the Straits of Taiwan, claiming two. (5 July)
- RoC Air Force RB-57D was shot down near Beijing, PRC by an SA-2 Guideline missile. The RB-57D pilot was killed. (7 October)
- Czechoslovak MiG-17 Fresco and MiG-19 Farmer forced an Italian F-84 to land. (12 October)

1960

- RoC Air Force PB4Y was shot down by Burmese fighter aircraft, near Thai-Burmese border, killing five crew members. Two other crew members were taken prisoner. The aircraft was carrying supplies for Chinese Kuomintang forces fighting in Northern Burma. (15 February)
- Four RoC Air Force F-86 Sabres engaged 20 PLAAF MiG-17 Frescos, over the Straits of Taiwan, claiming one shot down. (16 February)
- During an overflight of the PRC by an RoC U-2, more than thirty Chinese fighters attempted unsuccessfully to intercept the U-2. (March)
- RoC Air Force RB-69A was shot down at night over the PRC, en route to South Korea. All thirteen crew members were killed. (25 March)
- Cuban Hawker Sea Fury and T-33 aircraft shot down five CIA B-26C Invaders operating in the Bay of Pigs invasion. (18 April)
- Cuban T-33 aircraft shot down two CIA B-26C Invaders operating in the Bay of Pigs invasion. (19 April)

- U.S. aircraft was fired on by North Korean fighters. The pilot was killed when the aircraft crashed while attempting an emergency landing south of Seoul. (20 April)
- CIA Lockheed U-2C flown by Francis Gary Powers from Peshawar, Pakistan, was shot down by an SA-2 Guideline missile, near Sverdlovsk, Soviet Union. Evidence indicated that Powers was shot down by the first of three missiles fired by a battery. A Soviet MiG-19 Farmer pilot was inadvertently shot down and killed by another SA-2 Guideline fired later in the incident. Powers bailed out and parachuted to safety. He was taken captive and later tried in a Soviet court. After serving some time in prison, he was released in exchange for Soviet Spy, Rudolf Abel, on 10 February 1962 in Berlin. (1 May)
- USAF C-47 was forced to land in East Germany by Soviet MiGs. The nine crew members were held captive until July 1960. (25 May)
- USAF ERB-47H Stratojet of the 38th Strategic Reconnaissance Squadron, 55th Strategic Reconnaissance Wing, flying over the Barents Sea was downed by a Soviet MiG-15 Fagot. Two crewmen survived and were taken prisoner. Four others were killed. Survivors were released from Soviet captivity on 25 January 1961. (1 July)
- RoC Air Force RF-101 Voodoo was shot down by ground fire near Fukien, PRC. The pilot was captured. (2 August)
- An Iran Air DC-4 returning to Tehran from a cargo flight to Beirut was attacked by Soviet fighters after it strayed into Soviet airspace. The aircraft sustained damage to the left wing and both outboard engines. The crew of three made a safe wheels-up landing on the southwest coast of the Caspian Sea. (4 August)
- Thirteen crew members were killed when an RoC Air Force RB-69A was shot down by an SA-2 Guideline missile over Shantung province, PRC. (6 November)
- USAF F-102s out of Galena, Alaska, made the first intercept of a Soviet aircraft, a Tu-16 Badger, in Alaskan airspace. (5 December)

1962

- Bulgarian MiG-17 reconnaissance aircraft was reported to have crashed into an olive grove near one of the U.S. Jupiter missile launch sites in Italy, after overflying the site.
- During an overflight of the PRC by an RoC U-2, a Chinese missile guidance radar locked on the U-2. The pilot took evasive action and escaped without harm. (28 May)
- In Operation Coldfeet two U.S. military officers parachuted from a CIA B-17G into the abandoned Soviet arctic ice station NP 8. After searching the station, they were retrieved using a Fulton Skyhook system. (28 May)

- RF-101A Voodoo of the RoC Air Force was lost near Fukien, PRC. (August)
- RoC Air Force RB-69A was shot down over PRC, killing the crew of thirteen. (1 August)
- RoC Air Force U-2A was shot down by an SA-2 Guideline missile over the PRC, nine miles south of Nunchang. The pilot bailed out of the aircraft and was captured. He later died in a hospital. (9 September)
- USAF RB-47H was intercepted over the Baltic Sea by a Soviet MiG-19 Farmer. (24 September)
- USAF U-2A of the 4080th Strategic Reconnaissance Wing was shot down by an SA-2 Guideline missile over Cuba. The pilot was killed when shrapnel punctured his pressure suit, causing the suit to decompress at altitude after the cockpit had already decompressed. He was posthumously awarded the Distinguished Service Medal. (27 October)
- A Russian-flown MiG-21 Fishbed intercepted two USAF F-104C Starfighters from the 479th Tactical Fighter Wing on a reconnaissance sortie near Santa Clara, Cuba. The F-104s disengaged and retired northward. (4 November)

1963

- Soviet MiG-17F Fresco shot down an Imperial Iranian Air Force Aerocommander 560. The IIAF crew members and a colonel of the U.S. Special Forces were killed. (May)
- A U.S. Army OH-23 Raven helicopter was shot down over the Korean DMZ. The crew of two were captured and not returned until a year later. (17 May)
- RoC Air Force RB-69A was shot down near Nanchang, PRC, killing the crew of fourteen. The aircraft was shot down by a PLAAF MiG-17PF Fresco. (14 June)
- U.S. Army "LT" was lost over Korea. (6 August)
- RoC U-2C was shot down by an SA-2 Guideline missile over Jiagxi, PRC. The aircraft had been on a mission to photograph the Lanzhou nuclear weapons plant and the Jiayuguan missile test site. After overflying these sites, the aircraft was approaching the coast of China when it was shot down. After evading one missile, a second tore off the aircraft's right wing. The pilot survived and was captured. He was released on 10 November 1982. He was refused entry into the RoC and eventually was admitted to the United States. (1 November)
- USAF U-2 crashed off the southwest coast of Florida while returning from Cuban overflight. The pilot was killed. (20 November)
- A Soviet pilot shot down an Iranian civilian L-26B aircraft. (20 November)

1964

- USAF T-39 Sabreliner, based in Weisbaden, West Germany, was shot down by a Soviet fighter over Thuringia, about sixty miles inside East Germany while on a training flight. The crew of three was killed. (24 January)
- USAF RB-66 Destroyer from the 10 TRW, based at Toul-Rosières, France, was shot down over East Germany by Soviet MiGs. The aircraft was shot down near Gardelegen after straying out of the Berlin air corridors. The three crew members parachuted to safety and were released several days later. (10 March)
- RoC Air Force U-2C pilot was killed when his aircraft experienced an equipment failure and came apart over the Taiwan Straits. (23 March)
- RoC Air Force RB-69A was shot down near Yantai, Shantung Peninsula, killing fourteen crew members. This nighttime interception was made by a PRC PLAAF MiG-17F Fresco, aided by an Iluyshin Il-28 Beagle, which dropped flares. (11 June)
- RoC Air Force U-2G was shot down over Fujian, PRC, by an SA-2 Guideline missile. The pilot was killed. (7 July)
- Soviet Tu-16 Badger crashed in the Sea of Japan near the USS *Bennington*, USS *Cunningham*, and USS *Eversole*. (15 July)
- Soviet MiG-17F Fresco shot down an Imperial Iranian Air Force Aerocommander 560. (August)
- USAF aircraft was attacked over the Korean DMZ. (14 November)
- RoC Air Force U-2C narrowly avoided being shot down while photographing the Lanzhou nuclear weapons plant in the PRC. Several SA-2 Guideline missiles flew by so close to the aircraft that the pilot was temporarily blinded. (27 November)
- RF-101A Voodoo of the RoC Air Force was shot down by a PLANAF J-6 over Wenzhou in Zhejiang Province of the PRC. The pilot was taken prisoner by fishermen after bailing out over the ocean. He was released from captivity in July 1985. (18 December)

1965

- One of three CIA operated P-3 Orions is rumored to have shot down a MiG over the PRC with an AIM-9 Sidewinder missile. These P-3s conducted low-level nocturnal intelligence gathering missions over mainland China. (1964–65)
- RoC Air Force U-2C was shot down over the PRC southwest of Beijing by a SA-2 Guideline missile. The aircraft was on a mission to photograph the Paotow nuclear weapons plant. The pilot survived and was released from captivity into Hong Kong on November 10, 1982. He was refused entry into the RoC and eventually was admitted to the United States. (10 January)

- While flying over the PRC, an RoC Air Force U-2 was intercepted by a MiG-21 Fishbed in a zoom climb. The MiG fired two missiles; both missed. (March)
- RF-101C Voodoo of the RoC Air Force was shot down near Shantou in Guangdong Province in the PRC by a MiG-19 Farmer. The Voodoo pilot was killed. (18 March)
- USAF ERB-47H Stratojet of the 55th Strategic Reconnaissance Wing was damaged in an attack by two North Korean MiG-17 Frescos over the Sea of Japan. The B-47's tail gunner returned fire, possibly shooting down one MiG. The B-47 made an emergency landing at Yokota Air Base in Japan with two engines inoperative and severe structural damage. The six-man crew escaped injury. (27 April)
- U.S. Army aircraft was shot down by North Korean ground fire. (18 May)
- RoC Air Force C-123B Provider was shot down over South Vietnam by the Viet Cong. (27 June)
- USAF RB-57F, operated by Pakistan Air Force 24th Squadron, was damaged by an SA-2 Guideline missile over India while it was beginning its descent toward Peshawar from Ambala. The missile exploded near the RB-57F, causing extensive structural damage, but the aircraft was able to make a successful forced landing at Peshawar. The aircraft was repaired by Pakistan and later returned to the United States. (11 September)
- RoC Air Force U-2C crashed off the northwest coast of Taiwan, killing the pilot. (22 October)
- USAF RB-57F of the 7407 Support Squadron at Wiesbaden, West Germany, was lost over the Black Sea, near Odessa. The crew was presumed killed. Recent investigations indicate there might not have been any Soviet activity related to this loss. The crew probably perished from an oxygen system failure, since it took more than an hour for the aircraft to spiral down from altitude and fall into the Black Sea. After seven or eight days spent searching for the aircraft, only small bits and pieces of wreckage were ever found. (14 December)

1966

- HU-16 of the RoC Air Force was shot down by a PRC PLAAF MiG-17 over Matsu while transporting defectors to Taiwan. (10 January)
- South Korea Air Force F-5s intercepted a Soviet An-8 Camp flying near North Korea. This An-8 was likely an environmental monitoring aircraft, taking air samples from the nuclear test conducted by the PRC two days earlier. (11 May)

1967

- USAF ERB-47H Stratojet of the 55th Strategic Reconnaissance Wing, flying over Iran, near the Soviet border, was reported to have been hit by a Soviet SAM missile. The damaged aircraft managed to reach the mountains north of Tehran, but crashed before being able to land, killing the entire crew. (1967)
- Twelve PRC PLAAF MiG-19 Farmers fought four RoC Air Force F-104G Starfighters over the Straits of Taiwan. One MiG-19 was downed. One Starfighter failed to return to base. (13 January)
- Soviet fighter forced an Iranian L-20 to land. (28 June)
- RoC Air Force C-123B Provider was reported to have been shot down over the South China Sea. (22 August)
- RoC Air Force U-2C was shot down over Jiaxing, killing the pilot. (9 September)

1968

- U.S. Navy A-1H Skyraider from VA-25 on a ferry flight from the Philippines to an aircraft carrier in the Tonkin Gulf was shot down by a MiG interceptor after accidently violating airspace of Hainan Island, PRC. The pilot was killed. (14 February)
- U.S. Navy P-3B from VP-26 on a coastal surveillance photoreconnaissance mission, shot down, possibly by a Cambodian naval vessel, crashing in the Gulf of Thailand. Twelve crew members were killed. (1 April)
- Soviet TU-16 Badger buzzed a group of U.S. Navy vessels, including the USS *Essex* (CVS-9) off the coast of northern Norway. Shortly after passing low over the *Essex*, the Soviet bomber banked and one wing tip hit the sea. The plane then cart wheeled and exploded. There were no survivors. (25 May)
- A Seaboard World Airlines DC-8 carrying 214 U.S. troops to Vietnam, from McChord Air Force Base, Washington, via Yokota Air Base, Japan was forced to land on Etoforu Island in the Kuril Island chain by Soviet fighters. The pilot of the DC-8 was warned by a Japan Self-Defense Force radar site on the northern island of Hokkaido that he had strayed off course and was headed for the Soviet Union. The warning came too late: the aircraft had already been intercepted by MiGs. A day later, after the Soviets received an apology for the incident, the aircraft and passengers were released. (1 July)

1969

- A U.S. helicopter, evacuating wounded from a firefight in the Korean DMZ crashed, killing five crewmen, two U.S. infantrymen, and a South Korean infantryman. (15 March)

- While flying a patrol mission over the Sea of Japan, a U.S. Navy EC-121M of VQ-1 was attacked and shot down by two North Korean MiG-17 Fresco fighters ninety miles off the coast of Korea. All thirty-one members of the crew were killed in the attack. Two bodies and some wreckage was recovered by search vessels. (15 April)
- Two U.S. Army UH-1Bs from HAL Detachment 3 shot down in Sway Rieng Province, Cambodia, by Cambodian antiaircraft fire. (28 April)
- RoC Air Force U-2 aircraft crashed south of Cheju Island, Korea. (16 May)
- U.S. Army OH-23 Raven of the 59th Aviation Company was shot down over the Korean DMZ. The two-man crew and one other man were captured by the North Koreans and released 108 days later (17 August)

1970

- U.S. Army helicopter was fired on by North Korean gun positions along the Korean DMZ. (1 October)
- USAF U-8 was lost over the Soviet Union (Armenia). The crew of four were all rescued. (21 October)
- USAF KC-135R was intercepted by Soviet MiG-17 Frescos, while conducting a SIGINT flight over international waters near Vaygach Island. One of the MiGs fired warning shots, but the KC-135R ignored them and continued on its mission. The MiGs continued to escort the KC-135R, but did not fire on it again. (17 November)

1971

- USAF C-130 Hercules was reported to have crashed near the Soviet border, in Iran. (1971)

1973

- Soviet Tu-16 Badger overflew the USS *John F. Kennedy* (CVA-67) in the Norwegian Sea. While attempting to escort the bomber away from the area, a U.S. Navy F-4 Phantom II collided with it. The Tu-16 safely returned to base and the F-4 landed at Bodo, Norway. (4 October)
- RoC Air Force U-2R crashed near Taiwan, killing the pilot. (23 November)
- Soviet MiG-21SM Fishbed intercepted an Imperial Iranian Air Force RF-4E Phantom II in Soviet airspace. After an unsuccessful attempt at firing an AA-2 Atoll missile at the Phantom, the MiG destroyed the Phantom by ramming it. The Phantom's crew bailed out safely and were captured by Soviet border guards. They were released sixteen days later. (28 November)

1974

- Soviet An-24 Coke reconnaissance aircraft, low on fuel, made an emergency landing at Gambell airfield in Alaska. The crew remained on the aircraft overnight and were provided with space heaters and food. The next day they were refueled and departed for home. (27 February)
- The crew of a Soviet Border Guard Mi-4 Hound on a scout mission along the Soviet Union–PRC border became lost and crossed the border into China south of Belesha. The helicopter ran out of fuel and landed in the PRC. The three crew members were imprisoned in China until December 1975, when the crew and helicopter were returned to the Soviet Union. (March)
- Two U.S. helicopters came under North Korean ground fire along the Injin River. (9 May)

1977

- Imperial Iranian Air Force F-4E Phantom II was reported to have damaged a Soviet MiG-25G Foxbat over Iran with an AIM-7 Sparrow missile. The damaged Soviet aircraft managed to make it back over the Soviet border before crashing. (1977)
- U.S. Army CH-47 Chinook was downed over Korean DMZ by a North Korean MiG-21 Fishbed. The Ch-47's pilot was captured and the other three crew members were killed. The pilot was released after fifty-seven hours of captivity. (14 July)

1978

- A Korean Air Lines Boeing 707-321B flew over Murmansk while on an Anchorage–Paris flight, due to a navigation error. A Soviet PVO Su-15 Flagon fighter intercepted it and fired an air-to-air missile at the airliner. The missile blew off part of the 707's wing and showered the fuselage with shrapnel, killing two passengers. The pilot of the 707 reported that when he caught sight of the Soviet interceptor he reduced speed, lowered his landing gear, and flashed his navigation lights on and off, all ICAO procedures signifying willingness to follow the Soviet interceptor. After his airliner was damaged, he descended through clouds to a lower altitude and in doing so he became separated from the Soviet interceptor. For more than an hour the airliner flew at an altitude of several thousand feet across the snow-covered terrain, seeking a safe landing place. The Soviets had no idea where he was. Several approaches to possible landing sites were aborted when obstructions were spotted at the last moment. Finally, after nightfall the crew found a frozen lake bed, just west of Kem and let down smoothly, skidding to a safe landing. Of the ninety-seven passengers and twelve crew on board, two passengers were killed from shrapnel when the Soviet air-to-air missile hit the aircraft. No one died during the emergency landing. (20 April)

- Four Imperial Iranian Army CH-47C Chinook helicopters penetrated nine to twelve miles into Soviet airspace in the Turkimenistan Military District. They were first intercepted by Soviet MiG-23 Flogger pilot A. V. Demjanov who mistakenly identified them as Soviet helicopters. The helicopters were intercepted a little later by a MiG-23 pilot. He fired two R-60 (AA-8 Aphid) missiles, shooting down one Chinook, killing eight crew members. He then fired his Gsh-23L 23mm cannon at another Chinook, forcing it to land near Gjaurs. The four-man crew members of this helicopter survived, but were captured by Soviet border guards. The remaining two Chinooks escaped back into Iranian airspace. Shortly thereafter, the Soviets allowed the damaged Chinook to be repaired by Iranians. This helicopter and its four crew members were then allowed to return home. (21 July)

1980

- A Soviet Tu-95 Bear, flying from the Soviet Union to Cuba, entered U.S. airspace and passed very close to Langley Air Force base in Virginia (it could be seen from the control tower). The aircraft was intercepted by F-15s from the USAF 1st TFW and escorted out of U.S. airspace. (1980)
- As many as fifteen Libyan fighters intercepted a USAF RC-135U aircraft of the 55th Strategic Reconnaissance Wing over the Gulf of Sidra. Accounts differ as to whether the Libyan fighters opened fire on the aircraft before being chased away by U.S. Navy fighters. (16 September)

1981

- U.S. Navy F-14A Tomcats of VF-41 flying from the aircraft carrier USS *Nimitz* shot down two Libyan Su-22 Fitter fighters over the Gulf of Sidra. (19 August)

1983

- A Korean Air Lines Boeing 747-230B was shot down over Sakhalin Island by AA-3 Anab missiles fired by a Soviet Su-15 Flagon fighter. The aircraft was off course, likely due to navigation error and had already overflown the Kamchatka Peninsula. All twenty-three crew members and 246 passengers (including U.S. Congressman Lawrence McDonald from Georgia) were killed. (1 September)

1986

- A Corporate Air Services C-123 Provider departed San Salvador-Ilopango airport loaded with seventy Soviet-made AK-47 rifles and one hundred thousand rounds of ammunition, rocket grenades, and other supplies. It flew along the Nicaraguan coastline and entered Nicaraguan airspace near the Costa Rican border. Nearing San Carlos, the plane descended to 2,500 feet while preparing to drop off its cargo. While doing so, it was shot down by a Sandinista soldier using an SA-7 Grail shoulder-mounted missile launcher. CIA pilots Wallace "Buzz" Sawyer and William Cooper were killed in the crash. Loadmaster Eugene Hasenfus parachuted to safety and was taken prisoner. He was later released in December 1986. (5 October)

1987

- West German nineteen-year old private pilot Mathias Rust flew a rented Cessna 172 Skyhawk from Helsinki, Finland, to Moscow, and landed in Red Square. He was not shot down because two Soviet interceptor pilots who were shadowing him were reluctant to open fire on the small plane. After serving eighteen months in a Soviet prison, Rust was released. Soviet Air-Defense Commander Koldunov was removed from his position because of the incident. (28 May)

1989

- A Soviet MiG-23 Flogger took off from an airbase near Kolobzreg on the coast of the Baltic Sea in Poland, on a training flight. After takeoff, the pilot realized he was losing engine power. The pilot ejected and landed safely by parachute. The engine then regained power and the aircraft flew away to the West, guided by the autopilot. The fighter left the airspace of East Germany and entered West German airspace where it was intercepted by a pair of USAF F-15s. The F-15s were denied permission to fire on the MiG and had to let it fly away. Eventually, after flying 560 miles, the MiG-23 ran out of fuel and crashed into a house near Kortrijk, Belgium. An eighteen-year-old man in the house was killed. (4 July)

1990

- PRC MiG-19 Farmer crossed the border into the Soviet Union and landed at Knevichi, a Soviet Naval Air Force base near Vladivostok. The plane and its pilot were returned to China on August 30. (25 August)

U.S. NAVY AIRCRAFT CARRIER INCIDENTS AND CASUALTIES DURING THE COLD WAR

Note: The following was compiled by the Naval Historical Center, Washington, DC. The list is not all inclusive. In fact, the USS Forrestal *survived a number of additional fires, which led to her being dubbed "Zippo" and "Forrest Fire."*

1951

- While at Yokosuka, Japan, aircraft carrier USS *Bairoko* (CVE-115) suffered an explosion and flash fire on flight deck. Five crew members were killed.
- After an F2H Banshee crashed through the safety barrier of USS *Essex* (CV-9), the resulting fire and explosion killed seven sailors.

1952

- While USS *Boxer* (CV-21) conducted flight operations off Korea, an explosion of a Panther jet aircraft (F9F) on the hangar deck caused a fire that ignited gasoline and ammunition. Nine personnel including one officer died of smoke and burns. Helicopters and destroyers of Task Force 77 rescued sixty survivors.
- In an Atlantic collision between the *Wasp* (CV-18) and the *Hobson* (DD-464), 176 were killed. While the *Wasp* turned into the wind to recover aircraft, *Hobson* crossed the carrier's bow from starboard to port and struck amidship, breaking *Hobson* in two.

1953

- Explosion in aircraft carrier USS *Bennington* (CV-20) off Cuba killed eleven, and injured four more.
- A target drone plane accidentally crashed into light carrier USS *Wright* (CVL-49). Three were killed, and four injured.
- Accidental ignition of hydraulic fluid in catapult system started a fire in USS *Leyte* (CV-32) at the Charlestown Naval Shipyard, Boston. Thirty-two sailors and five civilians were killed, and forty were injured.

1954

- While off Narragansett Bay, a catapult hydraulic fluid explosion, followed by secondary explosions, killed 103 crewmen from the aircraft carrier USS *Bennington* (CV-20), and injured 201 others.

1957

- Steam-line explosion killed two and injured five in aircraft carrier USS *Franklin D. Roosevelt* (CVB-42).

1958

- Two were killed and three injured following a steam catapult explosion in USS *Kearsarge* (CV-33), Yokosuka, Japan.
- During predeployment exercises out of San Diego, an attack bomber exploded on the flight deck of aircraft carrier USS *Hancock* (CV-19). Two were killed.
- Flight deck explosion on USS *Ranger* (CVA-61) killed two crewmen during training operations off San Francisco.

1959

- At Norfolk, Virginia, a flash electrical fire in aircraft carrier USS *Randolph* (CVA-15) killed one sailor and severely burned two others.
- During carrier operations, an FJ Fury crashed on the USS *Essex* (CV-9) flight deck, killing two men, injuring twenty-one, and destroying five other planes.
- During a test in the hangar deck of the aircraft carrier USS *Wasp* (CV-18), a runaway helicopter engine exploded, killing two and injuring twenty-one.

1960

- An explosion in aircraft carrier USS *Shangri-La* (CV-38) injured three near Valparaiso, Chile.
- A fire during the building of aircraft carrier USS *Constellation* (CVA-64) at the New York Naval Shipyard, Brooklyn, killed 46 workers and injured 150 (Navy and civilian).

1961

- During operations in the Aegean Sea, a fuel oil fire in USS *Saratoga* (CVA-60) engine room killed seven.
- During a test run from Norfolk to New York, a fire in the machinery room of aircraft carrier USS *Constellation* (CVA-60) killed four men and injured nine others.
- While anchored in Cannes, France, a fire in No. 4 main machinery space of aircraft carrier USS *Independence* (CVA-62) injured four.

1964

- While operating at night off Cape Henry, USS *Randolph* (CVA-15) starboard deck-edge elevator broke loose, dropping five men and one airplane into the Atlantic. Three men were recovered, but two drowned.

1965

- During combat flight operations off Vietnam, USS *Ranger* (CVA-61) suffered a fuel-line fire in her No. 1 main machinery room. One sailor died before the fire could be extinguished.
- A flash fire in USS *Kitty Hawk* (CVA-63) No. 3 machinery room suffocated two sailors.
- While off Norfolk, a catapult launch off *Independence* (CVA-62) ruptured an F-4B Phantom fighter's detachable fuel tank, spilling and igniting 4,000 gallons of jet fuel. Fire destroyed another Phantom and spread into aviation stores before being extinguished. Sixteen sailors were burned and injured.

1966

- USS *Oriskany* (CV-34) fire and explosions in hangar bay during flight operations off Vietnam. During handling in a high-explosives magazine a MK Mod 3 flare was dropped and its safety lanyard inadvertently pulled, starting the fire that ignited more flares, 2.75-inch rockets, and a liquid oxygen cart. Forty-four died of asphyxiation, and one died from burns and injuries.

- USS *Franklin D. Roosevelt* (CV-42) fire in a supply store room asphyxiated eight men, and injured four more.

1967

- USS *Forrestal* (CVA-59) fire and explosions on flight deck during combat operations off Vietnam. After an inadvertent firing of a Zuni rocket that struck an A-4 aircraft, igniting its JP-5 fuel, other aircraft loaded with bombs and missiles were consumed, which led to explosions. Sixty aircraft were damaged or destroyed. Ship damage totaled $72 million. In the incident, 134 men were killed and 161 were injured.
- At Mayport, Florida, a spontaneous-combustion fire in a rag storeroom in aircraft carrier USS *Shangri-La* (CV-38) killed one sailor in the fire party and severely injured another seven.
- During flight operations in the Tonkin Gulf, an accidental Zuni rocket ignition in USS *Coral Sea* (CV-43) injured nine sailors.
- During deck operations in the Tonkin Gulf, a jet blast from a taxiing aircraft knocked an A-4 Skyhawk into the sea, drowning the pilot.
- While at Sasebo, Japan, a fire in USS *Kearsarge* (CV-33) enlisted quarters killed three sailors and injured two more.

1969

- USS *Enterprise* (CVAN-65) suffered an ordnance accident, resulting in fire and explosions while operating off Hawaii. Fifteen aircraft were destroyed and seventeen were damaged. The ship suffered $56.2 million in damages; aircraft losses totaled $70 million. Twenty-eight were killed and 343 were injured.
- An F8H Crusader from VF-24 crashed and went over the side while trying to land on USS *Hancock* (CVA-19). One man was killed.
- An A4E Skyhawk from VA-164 was lost when aircraft nose gear collapsed during catapult from USS *Hancock* (CVA-19), killing one.

1970

- At Jacksonville, Florida, a flash fire in aircraft carrier USS *Shangri-La* (CV-38) killed one sailor and severely burned two others.
- An F-8J Crusader from VF-24 struck the flight deck ramp of USS *Hancock* (CVA-19) and exploded during night carrier qualifications, killing Lt. Darrell N. Eggert.

- An F-8J Crusader from VF-211 crashed into the flight deck of USS *Hancock* (CVA-19), killing Lt. G. J. Carloni.

1972

- USS *Saratoga* (CVA-60) suffered a fire in No. 2 machinery room while at Singapore. Three were killed and twelve were injured.

1973

- No. 1 main machinery room fire in USS *Kitty Hawk* (CVA-63) in South China Sea killed six and injured thirty-eight sailors.
- A jet aircraft crashed into the eastern Indian Ocean after taking off from USS *Enterprise* (CVAN-65). One crew member was killed and another injured.

1981

- EA-6B Prowler crashed into flight deck of USS *Nimitz* (CVAN-68) during night landing. Fourteen sailors and Marines were killed, and forty-five were injured. Twelve aircraft were lost or destroyed at a cost of $73 million.
- A flight deck accident killed one sailor on USS *Kitty Hawk* (CV-63).
- During landing on USS *John F. Kennedy* (CV-67), an A-7E Corsair snapped an arresting cable. Two were killed and three injured.

1982

- A steam accident in USS *Saratoga* (CV-60) during overhaul at Philadelphia injured ten sailors.

1990

- Explosion and fire killed two crewmen and injured sixteen others on board USS *Midway*. The *Midway* was conducting routine flight operations 125 miles off Japan's Pacific coast. The initial explosion was in a fourth deck storeroom; a second explosion occurred in the same storeroom forty-five minutes later.
- Ten sailors were killed when a steam valve ruptured on board USS *Iwo Jima*, which was in the Arabian Sea to take part in amphibious landing exercises.

NOTES

Introduction

1. John Lewis Gaddis, *The Cold War: A New History* (New York: Penguin, 2005).

Chapter 1. First Blood: The USMC in China, 1945–49

1. David Shavit, *The United States in Asia: A Historical Dictionary* (Oxford: Greenwood, 1990).
2. Matthew M. Aid, "The Americans in China; Details of the Recent Conflict of the English and Americans with Imperialist Troops," *New York Times* (27 June 1854).
3. George B. Clark, *Treading Softly: U.S. Marines in China 1819–1949* (Oxford: Greenwood, 2001).
4. Ibid.
5. James A. Warren, *American Spartans: The U.S. Marines. A Combat History from Iwo Jima to Iraq* (New York: Simon & Schuster, 2005).
6. Colin Colbourn, "Caught in the Crossfire: Marines in North China 1945–49," *Leatherneck Magazine* (April 2008).
7. J. Robert Moskin, *The U.S. Marine Corps Story* (New York: Little, Brown, 1992).
8. "Casualties: U.S. Navy and Marine Corps Personnel Killed and Wounded in Wars, Conflicts, Terrorist Acts, and Other Hostile Incidents" (Naval Historical Center: Washington, DC, 2000), http://www.history.navy.mil/faqs/faq56-1. htm
9. Norman Osborn, "Korean War Educator," Korean War Education Foundation (2008), http://www.koreanwareducator.org/memoirs/osborn_norman/index. htm
10. Moskin, *The U.S. Marine Corps Story.*
11. Henry I. Shaw, "The United States Marines in North China 1945–1949" (Historical Branch, Headquarters, U.S. Marine Corps, 29 April 1968).
12. Osborn, "Korean War Educator."

13. Frank Benis and Henry Shaw, *History of U.S. Marine Corps Operations in World War II*, Vol. 5 (Historical Branch, Headquarters, U.S. Marine Corps, 1968).
14. Thomas A. Watson, "Column Ambushed. Marines Strike Back in Fierce Fight on Peking Highway," *North China Marine* (3 August 1946).
15. Benis and Shaw, *History of U.S. Marine Corps Operations.*
16. Ibid.
17. Ibid.
18. Osborn, "Korean War Educator."
19. R. R. Keene, "Shootout at Hsin Ho," *Leatherneck Magazine* (November 1995).
20. Ibid.
21. Ibid.
22. Osborn, "Korean War Educator."
23. 1st Lt. Mildredge Mangum, Sgt. Herbert B. Newman, Sgt. Hobart Walsh, Cpl. Fred Harrington, Cpl. Joseph Perkins, Cpl. Arthur Wedmore, Pfc. Anthol Clark, Pfc. Erie I. Jackson, Pfc. Jacob Jereb, Pfc. John K. Mackenzie, Pfc. John W. Manue, Pfc. Paul M. Orley, Pfc. Athanese, F.20, Parsons, Pfc. Harold E. Pervis, Pfc. Raymond Polman, Pfc. Peter Stankiewicz, Pfc. Dale E. Whiteis, and PM2 Joseph B. Szybillo.
24. Silver Star citation for Pfc. Jacob P. Jereb #575521.
25. Silver Star citation for Pfc. Peter R. Stankiewicz #607299.
26. Silver Star citation for Pfc. Alfred E. Perkey #602381.
27. "Chronology of the United States Marine Corps, 1947–64" (Washington: Historical Branch, G-3 Division Headquarters, U.S. Marine Corps, 1971).

Chapter 2. Elizabeth Bentley: Red Spy Queen, 1945

The following sources were used in writing this chapter. (Authors' note: We have found Kessler's book to be the most complete, accurate, and detailed account of the Elizabeth Bentley story.)

Robert L. Benson, *The Venona Story* (Fort George G. Meade, MD: Center for Cryptologic History, National Security Agency, 2001).

Elizabeth Bentley, *Out of Bondage: The Story of Elizabeth Bentley* (New York: Devon-Adair, 1951).

Michael Farquhard, *A Treasury of Foolishly Forgotten Americans* (New York: Penguin, 2008).

Lauren Kessler, *Clever Girl: Elizabeth Bentley, the Spy Who Ushered in the McCarthy Era* (New York: Harper Collins, 2003).

Elizabeth Kern Mahon, "Scandalous Women: Red Spy Queen: The Story of Elizabeth Bentley," 2008. http://scandalouswoman.blogspot/2008/07/elizabeth-bentley-red-spy-queen.html

Kathryn S. Olmsted, *Red Spy Queen: A Biography of Elizabeth Bentley* (Charlotte: University of North Carolina Press, 2003).

Chapter 3. Lt. Gail Halvorsen and the Berlin Airlift, 1948–49

1. Encyclopedia Britannica Online, http://www.britannica.com/eb/article-9061076/Potsdam-Conference

2. Ibid.

3. "Pas de pagaille!" (Let's not mess around!) *Time* (28 July 1947), http://www.time.com/time/magazine/article/0,9171,887417-2,00.html

4. Robert Daniel Murphy, *Diplomat Among Warriors* (London: Greenwood Press, 1964), 251.

5. "Pas de pagaille!"

6. Robert E. Griffen, and D. M. Giangreco, *Airbridge to Berlin: The Berlin Crisis of 1948, Its Origins and Aftermath* (Novato, CA: Presidio Press, 1988).

7. "The American Experience: The Berlin Airlift Timeline," PBS, www.pbs.org/wgbh/amex/airlift/timeline/timeline2.html (2007).

8. Ibid.

9. William Odell and William Von Sennett, "Berlin Airlift," www.billvons.com/bal/part1.htm

10. Griffin and Giangreco, *Airbridge to Berlin*.

11. Ibid.

12. "The Berlin Airlift," Cold War Museum, http://www.coldwar.org/articles/40s/berlin_airlift.asp

13. "The Berlin Airlift," Berlin Airlift Historical Foundation, http://www.spiritofreedom.org/airlift.html

14. "The Berlin Airlift: U.S. Centennial of Flight Commission," www.centennialofflight.gov/essay/Air_Power/berlin_airlift/AP35.htm

15. Don Vaughn, "Air Dog," *Military Officer Magazine* (May 2005), http://www.moaa.org/Magazine/May2005/f_dog.asp

16. Interview with Gail Halvorsen by telephone, 21 June 2008 (Scott Baron).

17. Ibid.

18. Ibid.

19. Ibid.

20. "Cold War Chat: Retired Col. Gail Halvorsen," CNN Interactive, www.cnn.com/specials/cold.war/guides/debate/chats/halvorsen

21. "Fact Sheet: Lt. Gail S. Halvorsen," National Museum of the USAF, www.nationalmuseum.af.mil/f actsheets/factsheet.asp?id=1106

22. Telephone interview with Gail Halvorsen, 21 June 2008 (Scott Baron).

23. "Cold War Chat."

24. "The American Experience," PBS.

25. Ibid.
26. Interview with Gail Halvorsen, 21 June 2008.
27. "USAF Air Command and Staff College Biography," Maxwell–Gunter Air Force Base (Montgomery, AL).
28. Bethanne Kelly Patrick, "'Candy Bomber' Fed Hopes of Berlin's Children During Airlift," Military.com http://www.military.com/Content/MoreContent?file=ML_halvorsen_bkp

Sidebar: Fatalities of the Berlin Airlift

1. Stewart M. Powell, "The Berlin Airlift," *Air Force Magazine* 81, no. 6 (June 1998).
2. Odell and Von Sennett, "Berlin Airlift."
3. "Two Fliers Hurt in Berlin Airlift Crash," *Stars and Stripes* (European ed., 7 July 1948).
4. Richard Collier, *The Bridge Across the Sky: The Berlin Blockade and Airlift, 1948–1949* (New York: McGraw-Hill, 1978).
5. Edwin Gere, *The Unheralded: Men and Women of the Berlin Blockade and Airlift* (Victoria, BC: Trafford, 2002).
6. Ibid.
7. Ibid.
8. Ibid.
9. Ibid.
10. Ibid.
11. Odell and Von Sennett, "Berlin Airlift" website.

Chapter 4: The First Cold War Shootdown, 1950

1. Tim Dyhouse, "Cold War Memorial Dedicated in Latvia," *VFW Magazine* (May 2000).
2. Tim Dyhouse, "Latvia Erects Memorial to U.S. Airmen," Associated Press (8 April 2000).
3. Tim Dyhouse, "VP-26 Mishap Summary Page" (April 2000), VP Patrol Squadron homepage, http://www.vpnavy.org/vp26_mishap_1950.html
4. Paul F. Crickmore, *Lockheed Blackbird: Beyond the Secret Missions* (Oxford: Osprey Publishing, 2004).
5. Robert Haines, "A Tragedy of Errors," *Naval History Magazine* (April 2003).
6. Tomas Polak and Christopher Shores, *Stalin's Falcons: The Aces of the Red Star Grub Street* (London: Grub Street, 1999).

7. Steven L. Rothert and Daniel B. Wagner, "VP-26 Hosts POW/MIA Ceremony," The Dolphin, Naval Submarine Base, Public Affairs Office, Groton, CT (30 October 2003).

8. "Consolidated PB4Y-2 Privateer," retrieved March 2008 from www.spyflight. co.uk/priv.htm

9. "Shot Down Over the Soviet Union," http://www.zdf-enterprises.de/shot_ down_over_the_soviet_union.4656.htm (2009).

10. Ibid.

11. "VP-26 Mishap Summary Page," VP Patrol Squadron homepage, http://www. vpnavy.org/vp26_mishap_1950.html

12. Haines, "A Tragedy of Errors."

Chapter 5. Actor James Garner in the Korean War, 1950

1. James E. Wise Jr., and Paul W. Wilderson III, *Stars in Khaki* (Annapolis, MD: Naval Institute Press, 2000), 43–47.

Chapter 6. Capt. Eugene S. Karpe, USN: Death on the Orient Express, 1950

1. "U.S. Naval Officer Found Dead in Railway Tunnel near Salzburg," http:// www.arlingtoncemetery.net/eskarpe.htm (2007).

2. Ibid.

3. "Murder Hinted in Tunnel Death of Vogeler Pal," *Washington Times-Herald* (25 February 1950); "Army Presses Hunt for Clues in Capt. Karpe's Strange Death," *Washington Times-Herald* (28 February 1950); Robert A. Vogeler, *I Was Stalin's Prisoner* (New York: Harcourt, Brace, 1951), 17, 64.

4. "U.S. Naval Officer Found Dead in Railway Tunnel near Salzburg"; "Murder Hinted in Tunnel Death"; "Army Presses Hunt for Clues in Capt. Karpe's Strange Death"; "Autopsy on Karpe Is Inconclusive," *Washington Post* (26 February 1950).

5. "Karpe Memorial Rites Held in Bremerhaven," [Washington, DC] *Evening Star* (4 March 1950), A-11; "Arlington Rites Tomorrow for Captain Eugene S. Karpe," *Washington Star* (15 March 1950).

6. Vogeler, *I Was Stalin's Prisoner*, 240–241.

7. Officer Biography Collection, "Capt. Eugene Simon Karpe, USN (deceased)," Operational Archives Branch, Naval Historical Center, Washington, DC.

Chapter 7. CIA Officers John T. Downey & Richard G. Fecteau: Prisoners in China for Two Decades, 1952–73

Authors' note: Upon review of related reference sources, we found the article by Nicholas Dujmovic, Historian, Center for the Study of Intelligence, Central Intelligence Agency, Washington, DC, to be the most accurate and complete account of the Downey/Fecteau capture and imprisonment.

1. Remarks of the Director of Central Intelligence George J. Tenet on Presentation of the Director's Medal to John T. "Jack" Downey and Richard G. Fecteau (Washington, DC: Central Intelligence Agency/DCI Press Release June 25 1998), http://www.fas.org/irp/cia/news/pr062598.html
2. Nicholas Dujmovic, "Studies in Intelligence: Journal of the American Intelligence Professional: Extraordinary Fidelity—Two CIA Prisoners in China, 1952–73" (Washington, DC: Center for the Study of Intelligence, Central Intelligence, 50, no. 4 (2006): 21–26), retrieved 3 June 2008, from https://www.cia.gov/library/center-for-the-study-of-intelligence/csi-publications/csi-studies/; Glenn Rifkin, "My Nineteen Years in a Chinese Prison," *Yankee Magazine* (November 1982), http://www.powernetwork.org/bios/f/f602.htm; Task Force Omega (national POW/MIA information organization), "John T. Downey," http://www.taskforceomegainc/602.html
3. William Leary, "Robert Fulton's Skyhook and Operation Coldfeet," *Studies in Intelligence* 38, no. 1 (Spring 1994), 67–68, retrieved 2 July 2008 from https://www.cia.gov/library/center-for-the-study-of-intelligence/kent-csi/docs/v38a11p.htm
4. Dujmovic, "Studies in Intelligence."
5. Ibid.
6. External Affairs Division, State of Connecticut Juvenile Branch News Release dated September 2002, "Courthouse Named After Judge Downey," http://www.jud.ct.gov/external/news/Press110.html
7. Task Force Omega, Downey.

Chapter 8. No Kum-Sok: Operation Moolah, 1953

1. E. B. Potter, *Sea Power: A Naval History* (Annapolis, MD: Naval Institute Press, 1982), 363–364.
2. Herbert A. Friedman, "Operation Moolah: The Plot to Buy a MiG," retrieved 29 June 2008 from http://www.psywarrior.com/Moolah.html
3. Ibid.
4. Ibid.
5. Ibid.

6. No Kum-Sok with J. Roger Osterholm, *A MiG-15 to Freedom: Memoir of the Wartime North Korean Defector Who First Delivered the Secret Fighter Jet to the Americans in 1953* (Jefferson, NC: McFarland, 1996), 7–10.
7. Friedman, "Operation Moolah."
8. Ibid.
9. Ibid.
10. Kum-Sok with Osterholm, *A MiG-15 to Freedom*, 114–201.

Chapter 9. Mysterious Disappearance of Cdr. Lionel Crabb, RNVR, 1956

1. "How Buster Crabb Died," *Diver Magazine* online (June 1996), retrieved 31 May 2008 from bin/articles.pl?id=3072&sc=1040&ac=d&an=3072:How+B
2. Stephen Dorril, *MI6: Inside the Covert World of Her Majesty's Secret Intelligence Service* (New York: Simon & Shuster, 2000), 620; "How Buster Crabb Died"; John Simkin, "Who Killed Buster Crabb?" *Spartacus Educational* (December 2007), www.spartacus.schoolnet.co.uk/SScrabb.htm
3. Simkin, "Who Killed Buster Crabb?"; "1956: Mystery of Missing Frogman Deepens," BBC ON THIS DAY {9} 1956, retrieved 1 October 2008 from news.bbc.co.uk/onthisday/hi/dates/stories/may/9/newsid_4741000/4741060.stm; "How Buster Crabb Died"; J. Bernard Hutton, *Frogman Spy: The Incredible Case of Commander Crabb* (New York: McDowell, Obolensky, 1960). Author Hutton utilizes extensive resources to prove the theory that Commander Crabb was captured by the Russians and served in the Soviet Navy. However, this opinion is refuted by a rather credible witness at the close of this chapter.
4. "How Buster Crabb Died."
5. Dorril, MI6, 617–618.
6. "How Buster Crabb Died."
7. Dorril, *MI6*, 618.
8. Ibid, 619.
9. "How Buster Crabb Died."
10. Ibid.
11. Ibid.

Chapter 10. Hans Conrad Schumann: Leap to Freedom into West Berlin, 1961

1. David Clay Large, *Berlin* (New York: Basic, 2000), 439.
2. Eric Morris, *Blockade: Berlin and the Cold War* (New York: Stein & Day, 1973), 212–243.
3. Ibid, 442–443.

4. Frederick Taylor, *The Berlin Wall: A World Divided, 1961–1989* (New York: HarperCollins, 2006), 237–239.

5. "The Wall," Episode 9, CNN *Perspective* series, http://www.cnn.com/SPECIAL/cold.war/episodes/09/script.html

6. Taylor, *The Berlin Wall*, 240–241.

7. "The Wall," Episode 9.

8. Taylor, *The Berlin Wall*, 240.

9. Ibid, 241, 265.

10. Ibid, 447.

Chapter 11. Yuri Gagarin: First Man in Space, 1961

1. Jamie Dorman and Piers Bizony, *Starman: The Truth Behind the Legend of Yuri Gagarin* (London: Bloomsbury, 1998), 211–214.

2. Ibid, 12–17; Yuri Gagarin, *Road to the Stars* (Honolulu, HI: University of the Pacific, 2002), 3–19.

3. Dorman and Bizony, *Starman*, 18–19.

4. Ibid, 21–26; David Cullen, *The First Man in Space* (Pleasantville, NY: Gareth Stevens, 2004), 4–13, 16–19.

5. Gagarin, *Road to the Stars*, 75–96; Cullen, *The First Man in Space*, 14–15.

6. Dorman and Bizony, *Starman*, 29–43.

7. Gagarin, *Road to the Stars*, 148–161.

8. Dorman and Bizony, *Starman*, 110–114.

9. Gagarin, *Road to the Stars*, 161–162.

10. Cullen, *The First Man in Space*, 26–27.

11. Dorman and Bizony, *Starman*, 135–154.

12. Ibid, 155–168. Quotation is from the diary of General Nikolai Kamanin, who was responsible for maintaining discipline among the cosmonauts.

13. Ibid, 169–175.

14. Ibid, 177.

15. Ibid, 207–210.

16. David Scott and Alexei Leonov, *Two Sides of the Moon: Our Story of the Cold War Space Race* (New York: St. Martin's, 2004). David Scott commanded the first American mission to the moon and was one of twelve American astronauts who walked on the moon. Alexei Leonov was the first human being to float in open space.

Chapter 12. Maj. Rudolph Anderson Jr.: Cuban Missile Crisis, 1962

1. Michael Dobbs, "Into Thin Air," *Washington Post* (Sunday, 26 October 2003).

2. John T. Correll, "Airpower and the Cuban Missile Crisis," *Air Force Magazine* 88, no. 8 (August 2005).

3. Don Moser, "The Time of the Angel—The U-2, Cuba and the CIA," *American Heritage Magazine* 28, no. 6 (October 1977).

4. Dobbs, "Into Thin Air."

5. Correll, "Airpower and the Cuban Missile Crisis."

6. Dobbs, "Into Thin Air."

7. Ibid.

8. Correll, "Airpower and the Cuban Missile Crisis."

9. Max Holland, "The 'Photo Gap' that Delayed Discovery of Missiles," CIA Archives, Center for the Study of Intelligence, www.cia.gov/library/center-for-the-study-of-Intelligence/csi-publications/csi-studies/studies/vol49no4/photogap

10. Moser, "The Time of the Angel."

11. Robert Kennedy, *Thirteen Days: A Memoir of the Cuban Missile Crisis* (New York: W. W. Norton, 1969).

12. John L. Frisbee, "The First Air Force Cross," *Air Force Magazine* 78, no. 12 (December 1995).

13. Ibid.

14. Bill Sontag, "Laughlin's U-2 Spyplane Pilots to Be Honored at Public Ceremonies," *Southwest Texas Live Magazine* (7 April 2008).

15. Dobbs, "Into Thin Air."

16. Kennedy, *Thirteen Days.*

17. Lawrence Chang and Peter Kornbluh (Eds.), *Cuban Missile Crisis—1962* (New York: National Security Archives, New Press, 1998).

18. Ibid.

19. Dobbs, "Into Thin Air."

20. Ibid.

21. Ibid.

22. Norman Polmar and John D. Gresham, *DEFCON-2* (Hoboken, NJ: John Wiley, 2006).

23. Marion Lloyd, "Soviets Close to Using A-Bomb in 1962, Crisis Forum is Told," *Boston Globe* (13 October 2002).

24. Remarks at Homestead Air Force Base, Florida, Upon Presenting Unit Awards, November 26, 1962, in a speech to members of the 363rd Tactical Reconnaissance Wing, http://www.presidency.ucsb.edu/ws/index.php?pid=9026

25. Frisbee, "The First Air Force Cross."

Sidebar: "Top Gun" Aerial Maneuvers over Cuba That Really Happened, 1962
Note: the following source was used for this chapter.
Charles J. Quilter, *A History of Marine Fighter Attack Squadron 531* (Quantico,
  VA: U.S. Marine Corps History Division, 2001).

Chapter 13. The Palomares Incident, 1966

1. Randall C. Maydew, *America's Lost H-Bomb: Palomares, Spain, 1966*
   (Manhattan, KS: Sunflower University, 1997), 2–14.
2. "This Day in History: H-Bomb Lost in Spain" (17 January 1966), retrieved
   1 June 2008 from http://www.history.com/this-day-in-history.do?action=
   tdihArticleCategory&display
3. Ibid.
4. Maydew, *America's Lost H-Bomb*, 37–50, 82–107.
5. John Pina Craven, *The Silent War: The Cold War Battle Beneath the Sea* (New
   York: Simon & Schuster, 2001), 166–167, 174–175.

Chapter 14. Carl Brashear: An Extraordinary Sailor, 1966

1. Paul Stillwell, "Film Inspiration Dies," *Naval History News* 20, no. 5, 8
   (October 2006).
2. Master Chief Boatswain's Mate Carl M. Brashear, U.S. Navy (Retired), "Man
   of Honor," U.S. Naval Institute *Proceedings*, 126/12/1,174: 79 (December
   2000).
3. Scott Marshall Smith, *Men of Honor* (New York: Penguin, 2000), 265–299.
4. Paul Stillwell, "The Real Carl Brashear," U.S. Naval Institute Naval History,
   Looking Back 15, no. 1, 4 (February 2001).

Chapter 15. Commander Bucher and the Second Korean Conflict, 1966–69

1. "JSA (Panmunjon)," http://www.globalsecurity.org/military/facility/jsa.htm
2. Ibid.
3. Maj. Vandon E. Jenerette, "The Forgotten DMZ Military Review," *U.S. Army
   Command and General Staff College Journal* 68, no. 5 (May 1988).
4. Korea Defense Veterans of America, "Combat Chronology," http://
   kdvamerica.org/CombatChronology.html
5. Richard Kolb, "Fighting Brush Fires on Korea's DMZ," *VFW Magazine*
   (March 1992).
6. Jenerette, "The Forgotten DMZ Military Review."
7. *New York Times*, 4 November 1966, http://www.koreanwar.org/html/dmz_
   war.html

8. "The DMZ War: Operation Paul Bunyan, VFW Post 7591," http://www.vfwpost7591.org/opn-PB.html

9. Lt. Cdr. Daniel Bolger, "Scenes from an Unfinished War: Low Intensity Conflict in Korea 1966–1968," Leavenworth Papers #19, Command and General Staff College, Combat Studies Institute (1991), U.S. ISSN 0196 3451.

10. Andrei Lankov, *The Dawn of Modern Korea* (South Korea: EunHaeng NaMu, December 2007).

11. Bolger, "Scenes from an Unfinished War."

12. Ibid.

13. Ibid.

14. USS *Pueblo* Veterans Assn., "*Pueblo* Incident: AGER Program Background," http://www.usspueblo.org/v2f/background/agerback.html (1999).

15. Ibid.

16. Naval Historical Center, "USN Ships: USS *Pueblo* (AGER-2)," http://www.history.navy.mil/photos/sh-usn/usnsh-p/ager2.htm

17. Lloyd M. Bucher, *Bucher: My Story* (New York: Doubleday, 1970).

18. Ibid.

19. Mitchell B. Lerner, *The Pueblo Incident: A Spy Ship and the Failure of American Foreign Policy* (Lawrence: University Press of Kansas, 2002).

20. Steve Liewer, "Ill-fated Spy Mission Still Haunts Crew of USS *Pueblo*," *Stars and Stripes* (27 January 2002).

21. Ibid.

22. Ibid.

23. Ibid.

24. USS *Pueblo* Veterans Assn., "*Pueblo* Incident."

25. Liewer, "Ill-fated Spy Mission."

26. USS *Pueblo* Veterans Assn., "*Pueblo* Incident."

27. Tony Perry, "Lloyd Bucher, Captain of North Korea–Seized *Pueblo*, dies at 76," *Los Angeles Times* (30 January 2004).

28. USS *Pueblo* Veterans Assn., "*Pueblo* Incident."

29. Ibid.

30. Liewer, "Ill-fated Spy Mission."

31. Bolger, "Scenes from an Unfinished War."

32. USS *Pueblo* Veterans Assn., "*Pueblo* Incident."

33. Perry, "Lloyd Bucher."

34. Bolger, "Scenes from an Unfinished War."

35. Ibid.

36. Jenerette, "The Forgotten DMZ Military Review."

37. Kolb, "Fighting Brush Fires."

38. "North Koreans Down Navy Recon Plane," *Stars and Stripes* (Pacific ed., 17 April 1969).

39. Matthew M. Aid, "1969 EC-121 Shootdown," http://www.korean-war.com/ Archives/2001/04/msg00116.html

40. Col. Karl H. Lowe, "American's Foreign Legion: The 31st Infantry Regiment at War and Peace," Chapter 15, 31st Infantry Regiment website, http://31stinfantry.org/history.htm

41. Ibid.

42. Kolb, "Fighting Brush Fires."

Chapter 16. The USS *Forrestal* Fire, 1967

1. Letter from Naval Aviation Museum to Capt. James E. Wise Jr., granting permission for use of the following article in this chapter: James M. Caiella, "1051 Hell," *Foundation* 24, no. 2 (Fall 2003) (Naval Aviation Museum Foundation, Pensacola, FL, 2003), 48–57.

Chapter 17. The Panmunjon Ax Murders and Operation Paul Bunyan, 1976

1. "Major Incidents in the JSA," 8th Army website, http://8tharmy.korea.army. mil/JSA/JSA%20new/contents/incident.htm

2. John Singlaub and Malcolm MacConell, *Hazardous Duty: An American Soldier in the Twentieth Century* (New York: Summit, 1991).

3. Erik Slavin, "Former Commander Honors Victims of DMZ Ax Murders," *Stars and Stripes* (Pacific ed., 20 August 2007).

4. Rick Atkinson, *The Long Grey Line* (New York: Macmillan, 1999).

5. "The DMZ War: Operation Paul Bunyan," VFW Post 7591, *New York Times* (4 November 1966). www.vfwpost7591.org/opn-PB.html

6. Singlaub and Macconell, *Hazardous Duty.*

7. Ibid.

8. Ibid.

9. Ibid.

10. Jan Wesner Childs, "Military Marks Date of DMZ Incident in Which Two Army Officers Were Slain," *Stars and Stripes* (Pacific ed., 18 August 2001).

Chapter 18. Capt. Bert K. Mizusawa, USA: The Firefight at Panmunjon, 1984

1. Telephone interview with Gen. Bert Mizusawa, 6 August 2008 (Scott Baron).

2. Clyde Haberman, "DMZ Defector Says He Acted Freely," *New York Times* (27 November 1984).

3. Lt. Col. Henry J. Nowak, "Statement Concerning the Firefight in the JSA, Panmunjon, Korea" (23 November 1984).

4. Ibid.

5. Official U.S. Army biography, "BGen. Bert K. Mizusawa."

6. Telephone interview with Gen. Bert Mizusawa.

7. Nowak, "Statement Concerning the Firefight in the JSA."

8. Sgt. Maj. Richard C. Lamb (then SSgt.), 1st Platoon, JSF Company, statement sworn to before Capt. K. C. Deancrane (19 June 2000).

9. Ibid.

10. Telephone interview with Gen. Bert Mizusawa.

11. Lamb, statement.

12. Telephone interview with Gen. Bert Mizusawa.

13. Ibid.

14. Ibid.

15. Ibid.

16. Ibid.

17. Ibid.

18. Nowak, "Statement concerning the firefight in the JSA."

19. "U.S. Awards Bronze Star to Korean Killed in DMZ," Associated Press (1 December 1984).

20. Jimmy Norris, "U.S., South Koreans Honor Soldier Killed in 1984 DMZ Shootout," *Stars and Stripes* (Pacific ed., 23 November 2007).

21. Tim Dyhouse, "Korea GIs receive CIBs Silver Stars," *VFW Magazine* (September 2000).

22. "Col. Bert Mizusawa Promoted to Brigadier General," *Japanese American Veterans Association Newsletter* 2, no. 4 (8 February 2006).

23. Nowak, "Statement Concerning the Firefight in the JSA."

Chapter 19. SSgt. Gregory Fronius and the El Salvador Insurgency, 1987

1. Bradley Graham, "Public Honor for Secret Combat: Medals Granted After Acknowledgement of U.S. Role in El Salvador," *Washington Post* (6 May 1996).

2. Richard W. Stewart (Ed.), *American Military History Volume II—The United States Army in a Global Era, 19172003* (Washington, DC: Center of Military History–Army Historical Series, 2005).

3. Ibid.

4. Graham, "Public Honor for Secret Combat."

5. David K. Shipler, "Slain Adviser the Sole American at Salvador Base," *New York Times* (1 April 1987).

6. Scott W. Carmichael, *True Believer* (Annapolis, MD: Naval Institute Press, 2007).

7. Ibid.

8. John Borrell, "El Salvador Bloody Setback," *Time* (13 April 1987).

9. Carmichael, *True Believer*.

10. Ibid.

11. Silver Star citation for SSgt. Gregory Fronius, http://www.homeofheroes.com/valor/02_awards/silverstar/6_PostRVN/06_elsalvadore.html

12. Stewart, *American Military History Volume II*.

13. Carmichael, *True Believer*.

14. Graham, "Public Honor for Secret Combat."

15. Stewart, *American Military History Volume II*.

Appendix I. Aircraft Downed During the Cold War

Note: The following sources were used for this appendix.

"Aircraft Downed During the Cold War and Thereafter" (8 November 2005), http://www.silent-warriors.com/shootdown_list.html

"Casualties: U.S. Navy and Marine Corps Personnel Killed and Wounded in Wars, Conflicts, Terrorist Acts, and Other Hostile Incidents," Naval Historical Center, Washington, DC, http://www.history.navy.mil/faqs/faq56-1.htm

Robert L. Goldrich, "Cold War Shoot-Down Incidents Involving U.S. Military Aircraft Resulting in U.S. Casualties," *Foreign Affairs and National Defense Division*, Congressional Research Service, U.S. Library of Congress (25 July 2008), http://www.aiipowmia.com/Koreacw/cw1.html

REFERENCES

Aid, Matthew M. 1854. "The Americans in China; Details of the Recent Conflict of the English and Americans with Imperialist Troops." *New York Times*, 27 June.

———. 2001. "1969 EC-121 Shootdown." http://www.korean-war.com/Archives/2001/04/msg00116.html

———. 2005. "Aircraft Downed During the Cold War and Thereafter." 8 November 2005. http://www.silent-warriors.com/shootdown_list.html

"Arlington Rites Tomorrow for Captain Eugene S. Karpe." 1950. *Washington Star*, 15 March.

"Army Presses Hunt for Clues in Capt. Karpe's Strange Death." 1950. *Washington Times-Herald*, 28 February.

Atkinson, Rick. 1999. *The Long Grey Line*. New York: Macmillan.

"Autopsy on Karpe Is Inconclusive." 1950. *Washington Post*, 26 February.

Benis, Frank, and Henry Shaw. 1968. *History of U.S. Marine Corps Operations in World War II*, Vol. 5. Quantico, VA: Historical Branch, Headquarters, U.S. Marine Corps.

Benson, Robert L. 2001. *The Venona Story*. Fort George G. Meade, MD: Center for Cryptologic History, National Security Agency.

Bentley, Elizabeth. 1951. *Out of Bondage: The Story of Elizabeth Bentley*. New York: Devon-Adair.

"The American Experience: The Berlin Airlift Timeline." 2007. PBS. www.pbs.org/wgbh/amex/airlift/timeline/timeline2.html

"The Berlin Airlift Berlin Airlift Historical Foundation." N.d. http://www.spiritof-freedom.org/airlift.html

"The Berlin Airlift: The Cold War Museum." N.d. http://www.coldwar.org/articles/40s/berlin_airlift.asp

"The Berlin Airlift: U.S. Centennial of Flight Commission." N.d. www.centennial-offlight.gov/essay/Air_Power/berlin_airlift/AP35.htm

Bolger, Lt. Cdr. Daniel. 1991. "Scenes from an Unfinished War: Low-Intensity Conflict in Korea 1966–1968." Leavenworth Papers #19, Command and General Staff College, Combat Studies Institute. U.S. ISSN 0196 3451.

Borrell, John. 1987. "El Salvador Bloody Setback." *Time*, 13 April.

Brashear, Master Chief Boatswain's Mate Carl M., USN (Ret.). 2000. "Man of Honor." Annapolis, MD: U.S. Naval Institute *Proceedings*, Vol. 126/12/1,174 (December).

Bucher, Lloyd M. 1970. *Bucher: My Story*. New York: Doubleday Publishing.

Carmichael, Scott W. 2007. *True Believer*. Annapolis, MD: Naval Institute Press.

"Casualties: U.S. Navy and Marine Corps Personnel Killed and Wounded in Wars, Conflicts, Terrorist Acts, and Other Hostile Incidents." Naval Historical Center, Washington, DC. http://www.history.navy.mil/faqs/fag56-1.htm

Childs, Jan Wesner. 2001. "Military Marks Date of DMZ Incident in Which Two Army Officers Were Slain." *Stars and Stripes*, Pacific ed., 18 August.

"Chronology of the United States Marine Corps, 1947–1964." 1971. Washington, DC: Historical Branch, G-3 Division Headquarters, U.S. Marine Corps.

Clark, George B. 2001. *Treading Softly: U.S. Marines in China 1819–1949*. Oxford: Greenwood.

"Col. Bert Mizusawa Promoted to Brigadier General." 2006. *Japanese American Veterans Association Newsletter*, 8 February.

Colbourn, Colin. 2008. "Caught in the Crossfire: Marines in North China 1945–49." *Leatherneck Magazine*, April.

"Cold War Chat: Retired Col. Gail Halvorsen." N.d. CNN Interactive. www.cnn.com/SPECIALS/cold.war/guides/debate/chats/halvorsen

Collier, Richard. 1978. *The Bridge Across the Sky: The Berlin Blockade and Airlift, 1948–1949*. New York: McGraw-Hill.

"Consolidated PB4Y-2 Privateer." www.spyflight.co.uk/priv.htm

Craven, John Pina. 2001. *The Silent War: The Cold War Battle Beneath the Sea*. New York: Simon & Schuster.

Crickmore, Paul F. 2004. *Lockheed Blackbird: Beyond the Secret Missions*. Oxford: Osprey Publishing.

Cullen, David. 2004. *The First Man in Space*. Pleasantville, NY: Gareth Stevens.

"The DMZ War: Operation Paul Bunyan, VFW Post 7591." 1966. *New York Times*, 4 November. http://www.koreanwar.org/html/dmz_war.html

Dorman, Jamie, and Bizony, Piers. 1998. *Starman: The Truth Behind the Legend of Yuri Gagarin*. London: Bloomsbury.

Dorril, Stephen. 2000. *MI6: Inside the Covert World of Her Majesty's Secret Intelligence Service*. New York: Simon & Schuster.

Dujmovic, Nicholas. N.d. "Studies in Intelligence: Journal of the American Intelligence Professional: Extraordinary Fidelity—Two CIA Prisoners in China, 1952–73." Washington, DC: Center for the Study of Intelligence, Central Intelligence, 50(4), 2006. https://www.cia.gov/library/center-for-the-study-of-intelligence/csi-publications/csi-studies/ (accessed 3 June 2008).

Dyhouse, Tim. 2000. "Cold War Memorial Dedicated in Latvia." *VFW Magazine* (May).

———. 2000. "Korea GIs Receive CIBs Silver Stars." *VFW Magazine* (September).

———. 2000. "Latvia Erects Memorial to U.S. Airmen." Associated Press, 8 April.

———. N.d. "VP-26 Mishap Summary Page." VP Patrol Squadron home page, http://www.vpnavy.org/vp26_mishap_1950.html

Encyclopedia Britannica Online. N.d. http://www.britannica.com/eb/article-9061076/Potsdam-Conference.

External Affairs Division, State of Connecticut Juvenile Branch News Release. 2002. "Courthouse Named After Judge Downey." http://www.jud.ct.gov/external/news/Press110.html (September).

"Fact Sheet: Lt. Gail S. Halvorsen." N.d. National Museum of the USAF. www.nationalmuseum.af.mil/f actsheets/factsheet.asp?id=1106

Farquhard, Michael. 2008. *A Treasury of Foolishly Forgotten Americans*. New York: Penguin.

Friedman, Herbert A. N.d. "Operation Moolah: The Plot to Buy a MiG." http://www.psywarrior.com/Moolah.html (accessed 29 June 2008).

Gaddis, John Lewis. 2005. *The Cold War: A New History*. New York: Penguin.

Gagarin, Yuri. 2002. *Road to the Stars*. Honolulu, HI: University of the Pacific.

Gere, Edwin. 2002. *The Unheralded: Men and Women of the Berlin Blockade and Airlift*. Victoria, BC: Trafford.

Goldrich, Robert L. 2008. "Cold War Shoot-Down Incidents Involving U.S. Military Aircraft Resulting in U.S. Casualties." Foreign Affairs and National Defense Division, Congressional Research Service, U.S. Library of Congress (25 July). http://www.aiipowmia.com/Koreacw/cw1.html

Graham, Bradley. 1996. "Public Honor for Secret Combat Medals Granted After Acknowledgement of U.S. Role in El Salvador." *Washington Post*, 6 May.

Griffen, Robert E. and Giangreco, D. M. 1988. *Airbridge to Berlin: The Berlin Crisis of 1948, Its Origins and Aftermath*. Novato, CA: Presidio.

Haberman, Clyde. 1984. "DMZ Defector Says He Acted Freely." Foreign Desk, *New York Times*, 27 November.

Haines, Robert. 2003. "A Tragedy of Errors." *Naval History Magazine* (April).

"How Buster Crabb Died." 1996. *Diver Magazine* online (June). bin/articles.pl?id=3072&sc=1040&ac=d&an=3072:How+B (accessed 31 May 2008).

Hutton, J. Bernard. 1960. *Frogman Spy: The Incredible Case of Commander Crabb*. New York: McDowell, Obolensky.

Jenerette, Major Vandon E. 1988. "The Forgotten DMZ Military Review." *U.S. Army Command and General Staff College Journal* 68, no. 5 (May).

"JSA (Panmunjon)." N.d. http://www.globalsecurity.org/military/facility/jsa.htm

"Karpe Memorial Rites Held in Bremerhaven." 1950. [Washington, DC] *Evening Star*, 4 March.

Keene, R. R. 1995. "Shootout at Hsin Ho." *Leatherneck Magazine*, November.

Kessler, Lauren. 2003. *Clever Girl: Elizabeth Bentley, the Spy Who Ushered in the McCarthy Era*. New York: Harper Collins Publishers.

Kolb, Richard K. 1992. "Fighting Brush Fires on Korea's DMZ." *VFW Magazine*, March.

Korea Defense Veterans of America. N.d. "Combat Chronology." http:// kdvamerica.org/CombatChronology.html

Lamb, Sgt. Maj. Richard C. (then SSgt.), 1st Platoon, Joint Security Force Company. 2000. Statement sworn to before Capt. K. C. Deancrane (19 June).

Lankov, Andrei. 2007. *The Dawn of Modern Korea*. South Korea: EunHaeng NaMu.

Large, David Clay. 2000. *Berlin*. New York: Basic Books.

Leary, William. 1994. "Robert Fulton's Skyhook and Operation Coldfeet." *Studies in Intelligence* 38, no. 1 (Spring). https://www.cia.gov/library/center-for-the-study-of-intelligence/kent-csi/docs/ v38a11p.htm (accessed 2 July 2008).

Lerner, Mitchell B. 2002. *The Pueblo Incident: A Spy Ship and the Failure of American Foreign Policy*. Lawrence: University Press of Kansas.

Liewer, Steve. 2002. "Ill-fated Spy Mission Still Haunts Crew of USS *Pueblo*." *Stars and Stripes*, 27 January.

Lowe, Col. Karl H. N.d. "American's Foreign Legion: The 31st Infantry Regiment at War and Peace." Chapter 15. 31st Infantry Regiment website, http://31stinfantry.org/history.htm

Mahon, Elizabeth Kern. N.d. "Scandalous Women: Red Spy Queen: The Story of Elizabeth Bentley." http://scandalouswoman.blogspot/2008/07/elizabeth-bentley-red-spy-queen.html

"Major Incidents in the JSA." 8th Army website, http://8tharmy.korea.army.mil/ JSA/JSA%20new/contents/incident.htm

Maydew, Randall C. 1997. *America's Lost H-Bomb: Palomares, Spain, 1966*. Manhattan, KS: Sunflower University Press.

Morris, Eric. 1973. *Blockade: Berlin and the Cold War*. New York: Stein & Day.

Moskin, J. Robert. 1992. *The U.S. Marine Corps Story*. New York: Little, Brown.

"Murder Hinted in Tunnel Death of Vogeler Pal." 1950. *Washington Times-Herald*, 25 February.

Murphy, Robert Daniel. 1964. *Diplomat Among Warriors*. London: Greenwood.

Naval Aviation Museum. 2003. Letter to Capt. James E. Wise Jr. granting permission for use of James M. Caiella's article, "1051 Hell." Foundation 24, no. 2 (Fall). Naval Aviation Museum Foundation, Pensacola, FL.

Naval Historical Center. N.d. "USN Ships: USS *Pueblo* (AGER-2)." http://www. history.navy.mil/photos/sh-usn/usnsh-p/ager2.htm

New York Times. 1966. http://www.koreanwar.org/html/dmz_war.html

"1956: Mystery of Missing Frogman Deepens." 1956 BBC ON THIS DAY {9}. news.bbc.co.uk/onthisday/hi/dates/stories/may/9/newsid_4741000/4741060. stm (accessed 1 October 2008).

No Kum-Sok with J. Roger Osterholm. 1996. *A MiG-15 to Freedom: Memoir of the Wartime North Korean Defector Who First Delivered the Secret Fighter Jet to the Americans in 1953*. Jefferson, NC: McFarland.

Norris, Jimmy. 2007. "U.S., South Koreans Honor Soldier Killed in 1984 DMZ Shootout." *Stars and Stripes*, Pacific ed., 23 November.

"North Koreans Down Navy Recon Plane." 1969. *Stars and Stripes*, Pacific ed., 17 April.

Nowak, Lt. Col. Henry J. 1984. Statement concerning the firefight in the JSA, Panmunjon, Korea (23 November).

Odell, William, and William Von Sennett. N.d. "Berlin Airlift" Web site. http:// billvons.com/bal/

Officer Biography Collection. N.d. "Capt. Eugene Simon Karpe, USN (deceased)." Operational Archives Branch, Naval Historical Center, Washington, DC.

Official U.S. Army Biography. Brig. Gen. Bert K. Mizusawa.

Olmsted, Kathryn S. 2003. *Red Spy Queen: A Biography of Elizabeth Bentley*. Charlotte: University of North Carolina Press.

Osborn, Norman. N.d. "Korean War Educator." http://www.koreanwareducator. org/memoirs/osborn_norman/index.htm

"Pas de pagaille!" 1947. (Let's not mess around!) *Time*, 28 July.

Patrick, Bethanne Kelly. N.d. "'Candy Bomber' Fed Hopes of Berlin's Children During Airlift." Military.com, http://www.military.com/Content/ MoreContent?file=ML_halvorsen_bkp

Perry, Tony. 2004. "Lloyd Bucher, Captain of North Korea–Seized *Pueblo*, Dies at 76." *Los Angeles Times*, 30 January.

Polak, Tomas, and Christopher Shores. 1999. *Stalin's Falcons: The Aces of the Red Star Grub Street*. London: Grub Street (June).

Potter, E. B. 1982. *Sea Power: A Naval History*. Annapolis, MD: Naval Institute Press.

Powell, Stewart M. 1998. "The Berlin Airlift." *Air Force Magazine* 81, no. 6 (June).

Quilter, Charles J. 2001. "A History of Marine Fighter Attack Squadron 531." U.S. Marine Corps History Division, Quantico, VA.

Remarks of the Director of Central Intelligence George J. Tenet on Presentation of the Director's Medal to John T. "Jack" Downey and Richard G. Fecteau. 1998. Washington, DC: Central Intelligence Agency/DCI Press Release (25 June). http://www.fas.org/irp/cia/news/pr062598.html

Rifkin, Glenn. 1982. "My Nineteen Years in a Chinese Prison." *Yankee Magazine* (November). http://www.powernetwork.org/bios/f/f602.htm

Rothert, Steven L. and Daniel B. Wagner. 2003. "VP-26 Hosts POW/MIA Ceremony." The Dolphin, Naval Submarine Base, Public Affairs Office Groton, CT (30 October).

Scott, David and Alexei Leonov. 2004. *Two Sides of the Moon: Our Story of the Cold War Space Race*. New York: St. Martin's Press.

Shavit, David. 1990. *The United States in Asia: A Historical Dictionary.* Oxford: Greenwood.

Shaw, Henry I. 1968. "The United States Marines in North China 1945–1949." Historical Branch, Headquarters, U.S. Marine Corps (29 April).

Shipler, David K. 1987. "Slain Adviser the Sole American at Salvador Base." *New York Times*, 1 April.

"Shot Down Over the Soviet Union." 2009. http://www.zdf-enterprises.de/shot_down_over_the_soviet_union.4656.htm

Silver Star citation for Pfc. Alfred E. Perkey # 602381.

Silver Star citation for Pfc. Jacob P. Jereb #575521.

Silver Star citation for Pfc. Peter R. Stankiewicz #607299.

Silver Star citation for SSgt. Gregory Fronius. http://www.homeofheroes.com/valor/02_awards/silverstar/6_PostRVN/06_elsalvadore.html

Simkin, John. 2007. "Who Killed Buster Crabb?" *Spartacus Educational* (December). www.spartacus.schoolnet.co.uk/SScrabb.htm

Singlaub, John, and Malcolm MacConell. 1991. *Hazardous Duty: An American Soldier in the Twentieth Century*. New York: Summit Books.

Slavin, Erik. 2007. "Former Commander Honors Victims of DMZ Ax Murders." *Stars and Stripes*, Pacific ed., 20 August.

Smith, Scott Marshall. 2000. *Men of Honor*. New York: Penguin.

Stewart, Richard W., ed. 2005. *American Military History Volume II—The United States Army in a Global Era, 1917–2003*. Center of Military HistoryArmy Historical Series, Washington, DC.

Stillwell, Paul. 2001. "The Real Carl Brashear." Annapolis, MD: U.S. Naval Institute *Naval History, Looking Back*, 15, no. 1 (February).

2006. "Film Inspiration Dies." Annapolis, MD: U.S. Naval Institute, *Naval History News* 20 (October).

Taylor, Frederick. 2006. *The Berlin Wall: A World Divided, 1961–1989*. New York: HarperCollins.

"Two Fliers Hurt in Berlin Airlift Crash." 1948. *Stars and Stripes*, European ed., 7 July.

"U.S. Awards Bronze Star to Korean Killed in DMZ." 1984. Associated Press, 1 December.

"U.S. Naval Officer Found Dead in Railway Tunnel near Salzburg." 2007. http://www.arlingtoncemetery.net/cskarpe.htm

USAF Air Command and Staff College Biography. N.d. Maxwell–Gunter Air Force Base, Montgomery, AL.

USS *Pueblo* Veterans Assn. 1999. "*Pueblo* Incident: AGER Program Background." http://www.usspueblo.org/v2f/background/agerback.html

Vaughn, Don. 2005. "Air Dog." *Military Officer Magazine* (May). http://www.moaa.org/Magazine/May2005/f_dog.asp

Vogeler, Robert A. 1951. *I Was Stalin's Prisoner*. New York: Harcourt, Brace.

"The Wall: Episode 9." N.d. CNN Perspective Series. http://www.cnn.com/SPECIAL/cold.war/episodes/09/script.html

Warren, James A. 2005. *American Spartans: The U.S. Marines. A Combat History from Iwo Jima to Iraq*. New York: Simon & Schuster.

Watson, Thomas A. 1946. "Column Ambushed. Marines Strike Back in Fierce Fight on Peking Highway." *North China Marine*, 3 August.

Wise, James E., Jr., and Paul W. Wilderson III. 2000. *Stars in Khaki*. Annapolis, MD: Naval Institute Press.

INDEX

ABOUT THE AUTHORS

James E. Wise Jr., a former naval aviator, intelligence officer, and Vietnam veteran, retired from the U.S. Navy in 1975 as a captain. He became a naval aviator in 1953 following graduation from Northwestern University. He served as an intelligence officer aboard the USS *America* and later as the commanding officer of various naval intelligence units. Since his retirement, Captain Wise has held several senior executive posts in private sector companies. His many other books include *The Silver Star, The Navy Cross, Stars in Blue,* and *U-505: The Final Journey.* He is also the author of many historical articles in naval and maritime journals. Captain Wise lives in the Washington, DC, metropolitan area.

Scott Baron, a U.S. Army veteran of the Vietnam War and former law enforcement officer in California, is the author of *They Also Served: Military Biographies of Uncommon Americans* and coauthor, with James Wise, of *Women at War: World War II to Iraqi Freedom, International Stars at War,* and *Soldiers Lost at Sea: A Chronicle of Troopship Disasters in Wartime,* all from the Naval Institute Press.

The Naval Institute Press is the book-publishing arm of the U.S. Naval Institute, a private, nonprofit, membership society for sea service professionals and others who share an interest in naval and maritime affairs. Established in 1873 at the U.S. Naval Academy in Annapolis, Maryland, where its offices remain today, the Naval Institute has members worldwide.

Members of the Naval Institute support the education programs of the society and receive the influential monthly magazine *Proceedings* or the colorful bimonthly magazine *Naval History* and discounts on fine nautical prints and on ship and aircraft photos. They also have access to the transcripts of the Institute's Oral History Program and get discounted admission to any of the Institute-sponsored seminars offered around the country.

The Naval Institute's book-publishing program, begun in 1898 with basic guides to naval practices, has broadened its scope to include books of more general interest. Now the Naval Institute Press publishes about seventy titles each year, ranging from how-to books on boating and navigation to battle histories, biographies, ship and aircraft guides, and novels. Institute members receive significant discounts on the Press's more than eight hundred books in print.

Full-time students are eligible for special half-price membership rates. Life memberships are also available.

For a free catalog describing Naval Institute Press books currently available, and for further information about joining the U.S. Naval Institute, please write to:

Member Services
U.S. Naval Institute
291 Wood Road
Annapolis, MD 21402-5034
Telephone: (800) 233-8764
Fax: (410) 571-1703
Web address: www.usni.org